D1162527

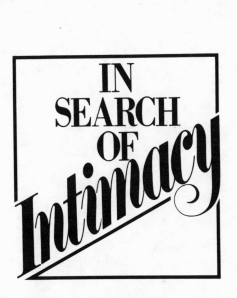

IN SEARCH OF Intimacy

SURPRISING CONCLUSIONS FROM
A NATIONWIDE SURVEY ON
LONELINESS & WHAT TO DO ABOUT IT

IN SEARCH OF Intimacy

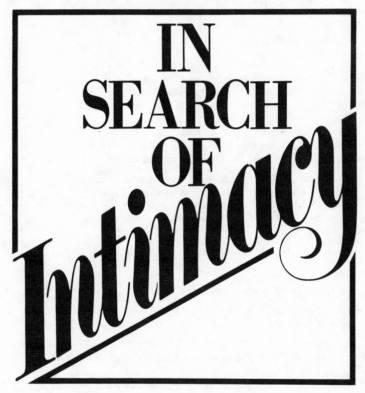

Carin Rubenstein, Ph.D.
& Phillip Shaver, Ph.D.

DELACORTE PRESS / NEW YORK

Published by
Delacorte Press
1 Dag Hammarskjold Plaza
New York, N.Y. 10017

Manufactured in the United States of America

First printing

LIBRARY OF CONGRESS CATALOGING IN PUBLICATION DATA

Rubenstein, Carin.
    In search of intimacy.

    Bibliography: p.
    1. Loneliness.   2. Intimacy (Psychology)   I. Shaver,
Phillip.   II. Title.
BF575.L7R8   158'.2   82-7395
ISBN 0-440-04193-7   AACR2

ACKNOWLEDGMENTS

Psychiatrist Harry Stack Sullivan was on target when he observed that "the problem in Freud's early decades was sexual repression," while today it is "loneliness, isolation, and difficulty in self-esteem." This change first captured our attention a few years ago, when tens of thousands of replies to our surveys in *Psychology Today*, *Esquire*, *Redbook*, and *Ladies' Home Journal* indicated that loneliness bothered more people than almost any other problem. We consulted other national survey researchers and found that they were reaching the same conclusion: Loneliness had become a serious and perplexing problem for millions of Americans.

We decided to probe more deeply into causes and possible cures. When we began, Carin Rubenstein was a Ph.D. student at New York University and Phillip Shaver was coordinator of the doctoral program in social psychology and Rubenstein's advisor. With support from an NYU Challenge Grant, we undertook a series of interview and survey studies that formed the basis of Rubenstein's doctoral dissertation and ultimately led to the creation of this book.

Many people helped us along the way. Staff members of the following newspapers designed, printed, and published our loneliness questionnaire and arranged for us to interview people in their cities: the New York *Daily News*, Worcester (Massachusetts) *Telegram*, Billings (Montana) *Gazette*, Fort Myers (Florida) *News-Press*, Wichita (Kansas) *Eagle and Beacon*, St. Paul (Minnesota) *Dispatch*, and Charlotte (North Carolina) *News*. We benefited enormously from attendance at national conferences and workshops on loneliness, and from reports and manuscripts supplied by researchers and therapists concerned with loneliness, intimacy, and community. We are especially grateful to Claude Fischer, Phillip Fisher, Warren Jones, Peter Monro, Anne Peplau, Daniel Perlman, Harry Reis, Tracey Revenson, Cecilia Solano, and Robert Weiss. Several friends read and commented insightfully on portions of the manuscript: Virginia Adams, Christopher Cory, David Glickhouse, Gail Goodman, Ruth Goodman, Hedwin Naimark, Cathy Pullis, Frances Shaver, Gail Sheehy, Carol Tavris, and Robert Weiss. Betty Kelly, our editor at Delacorte, guided us wisely through several drafts, balancing pointed criticism with optimism and encouragement.

David Glickhouse and Gail Goodman deserve our deepest thanks. They sustained us physically and emotionally while the book was being written, protecting us from loneliness as we struggled to understand it.

CONTENTS

INTRODUCTION
by Gail Sheehy

Loneliness is a by-product of the will toward change. Like pollution and divorce, the loneliness in modern urban society must be seen as more than a mere contaminant. All three, in fact, contribute to the abrasive but animating chemical mix that allows us to define ourselves and direct the enterprises of our lives as no other people have before us. Pollution is the cost of a personal mobility unimaginable even today in bicycle societies such as China. Divorce was the rupture heard around the world when Ibsen's Nora first discovered she could open the tiny doll's house door in the stone wall of male dominance. Loneliness, I submit, may be the natural offspring of twentieth-century American democratization.

The notion that an individual has the right to interpret his or her own life was a revolutionary concept. Such a notion scarcely existed before 1860, and its appearance gave birth to the modern theater. In that theater, as in our daily lives, we became concerned not with kings and queens and unalterable circumstance, not with man as sheep and God as omnipotent, but with the middle-class émigré into the new world of individualism. No concept of truth is unassailable here; no personal identity safe from change.

The wayfarer in such territory must become comfortable with saying, "I am capable of interpreting my own world, my religion, my family life, my morality. I am prepared to accept my differentness from you."

When Picasso shocked Paris in 1907 with *Les demoiselles d'Avignon,* he was predicting the affliction of the second half of the twentieth century—fragmentation. Each man and woman would have to struggle with those many and disparate pieces of the inner universe, trying to fit them together in some form. That inner form might be all they would have to hold on to as they navigated through the broken forms of every code previously known to Western civilization.

The middle class gained a power it would never be fully confident it could exercise. The burden of such independence was daunting, for instance, to no less a wayfarer than T. S. Eliot. Having surveyed The Waste Land, he decided he wanted no part of this democratization. It was more comforting to return to England and a more classified society.

Those who remained gradually developed the willingness to change. And as it turns out in studies of mental health, the willingness to risk change is healthier than a commitment to continuity throughout adult life. Americans who enjoy the greatest sense of well-being are the most likely to describe having undergone a major change in outlook, values, personal affiliations, career, or spiritual beliefs. That's the good news. The bad news is that the process of change produces, along the way, some anxiety, some depression, and of necessity some sense of loneliness.

We are all familiar with the bittersweet loneliness of adolescence, when we make the first painful emigration from home. In recent years we have become more sensitive to the loneliness of the children of divorce, dragging the rags and bones of their divided existence in backpacks between two worlds; the masked loneliness of the frantically busy; the desperate loneliness behind the swizzle sticks on a Caribbean cruise at Christmas; the collapsed loneliness of the compulsive TV watcher whose defense is to eat himself into an aspic and withdraw into a half-doze. We have even begun to confront the resurgent loneliness that washes back over widows and widowers, and to acknowledge the mourning process that can lead them, through acceptance, to a new burst of creativity.

In the early 1970s many Americans became disillusioned with the ability of their government and its leaders to solve their basic problems. If one sees the cycles of history alternating between periods of adventure and periods of retreat, the nation was in retreat from the misadventure in Vietnam and the expensive social experiments of the sixties. People turned against their institutions as the cause of all their problems. Invoking their own physical or economic survival over civil law, people turned their backs on court-ordered busing, armed themselves with guns, dismantled taxes. Each individual began to look to him- or herself as the one form of transport through life that could be trusted. It became imperative that one's physical plant be scrupulously maintained and monitored, not too much baggage was taken on (human or otherwise), and personal radar was not distracted by others' needs or appeals.

But it was lonely.

True, belief in the individual's ability to be the victor over fate or circumstance is the closest thing to a native American religion. Yet beyond the few hours or days of residual results from most contemporary rituals of self-help, they can leave one feeling both alone and lonely. No images of immortality deriving from cultural or religious beliefs exist in these rituals—nothing to counter the unease of suspecting that our lives are meaningless.

The problem with becoming too dependent on private rituals of self-help is this: They shut the individual off from what is out there to be shared—from community, from history, from the greatest comfort of all: to know you are not the only one who fears the freedom to change.

Life on the new social frontier demands a new kind of courage—the courage to commit to uncertain personal relationships. Few social, religious, or moral forms remain as guarantees of the continuity of affections. Yet knowing all the hazards, the hardy will still take the risk of reaching out to others. In fact, the people I have studied who enjoy the greatest sense of well-being are those who are able to be open and intimate with others. Most of them have nurtured a mutual love, where each partner respects the other's differentness. They have more close friends to confide in than the average person. And they enjoy a sense of common purpose within some meaningful community.

If loneliness, then, is a chronic condition, we must learn to capitalize on the individuality it may enhance, even as we resist the emptiness it can produce. The difference between loneliness and solitude, for instance, is crucial. Solitude is not an enemy, though it can be less constructive for those who do not know the skills fully to utilize it.

The great value of this book, I believe, is in making such distinctions clear. Rubenstein and Shaver are familiar with the latest research on love and loneliness, having contributed to it themselves, and present it here in a provocative way. They hold up a mirror that reveals the special kinds of loneliness to which each of us is most susceptible. They also shatter many myths—for example, that men do not need intimacy, that teenagers lead vibrant social lives, that city dwellers are alienated, and that the elderly are isolated.

The book confronts painful issues, but the authors come back to us with confidence and optimism and concrete suggestions for how to build new networks of intimacy. In the end, it is those who take the risks of reaching out toward emotional intimacy who find the joys of companionship.

1

What Is Loneliness?

A few years ago, at a national conference on loneliness, a journalist who wanted to write a book about contemporary hermits gave a talk. The most provocative part of what he had to say was that despite considerable effort he couldn't find a single *real* hermit. Like the legendary Lone Ranger, whose sidekick Tonto was never far away, contemporary "hermits" always turned out to have friends or associates. They all sat around a fire, or in a living room, trading stories from time to time; all eventually came into town to get supplies or sell the products of their labor. Forest rangers proved to have friends down the road, if not lovers on the premises.

A psychiatrist at the conference tried to comfort the journalist by pointing out that many legendary loners hadn't really been isolated either. Thoreau, the famous recluse of Walden Pond, was, said the psychiatrist, "living so close to other people that he could, and did, abandon his cabin when he smelled something good cooking for dinner." Similarly, the religious "hermits" we read about in all periods of history were actually communicating with each other, or baptizing people in the desert, or teaching disciples in mountain caves. Even when literally alone, the hermits were practicing a religion that had been taught to them by other people and that was meaningless except for those teachings. Moreover, most of them were talking to gods, devils, saints, and angels who so resembled people that the hermits were anything but alone in a psychological sense.

Robinson Crusoe lived alone on an island for twenty-four years and remained healthy and sane. But Crusoe, though few people today realize it, was mostly a figment of journalist Daniel Defoe's imagination. The real man who inspired Defoe's story, Alexander Selkirk, lived alone on an island for only four years and he was miserable. According to an eighteenth-century account: "He hated even to close his eyes. Often he cursed the folly that had brought him to this terrible solitude, and sometimes, starting up in agony, he would resolve on suicide. Voices spoke to him both in the howlings of the sea in front and in the murmur of the woods behind. The shore was creatured with phantoms." For the first several months after returning to his home town, he could barely carry on a normal conversation.

If most people, even quasi hermits, have at least some contact with other people, *why are so many of us lonely?* Surveys show that in any given month at least one in four Americans is lonely. Some experts have begun referring to the new "nationwide epidemic of loneliness." But even back in the 1940s, journalist John Gunther, traveling all over the country to research his book on America, called loneliness "one of the supreme American problems."

The epidemic metaphor is misleading. Loneliness is *not* an illness. One of the people we interviewed called loneliness "the new social disease," thus equating loneliness with embarrassing maladies like gonorrhea and syphilis. Actually, loneliness is more like hunger. Just as hunger signals the body's need for nourishment, loneliness warns us that important psychological needs are going unmet. Loneliness is a healthy hunger for *intimacy* and *community*—a natural sign that we are lacking companionship, closeness, and a meaningful place in the world.

Without adequate food, the body languishes and dies; without intimacy, friendship, and community, psychological stability erodes. We need be no more ashamed of loneliness than of hunger. Mild hunger enhances life and makes eating all the more rewarding; mild or occasional loneliness is also life-enhancing. It causes us to acknowledge our separateness and appreciate our deep need for other people. Severe hunger, in famine proportions, is a very different matter; it is a sign of societal failure. And so is widespread loneliness.

If you are lonely, you're not unique. And if thirty-five million Americans are lonely each month, the causes cannot come only from within each person; something must be wrong with society itself. We don't have to look far to see some of the causes: widespread mobility (one in five Americans moves each year); a high divorce rate; impersonal, crime-ridden cities; the substitution of television and home videotape-viewing for face-to-face community life; bureaucratic procedures and letter-writing computers that increasingly take the place of personal business transactions.

Beneath all of these symptoms is a fundamental principle of modern society: People are objects to be used instrumentally in the pursuit of selfish interests and organizational goals. But intimacy and friendship can't be purchased or coerced, nor can they be subordinated, without harm, to other goals. Intimacy for hire is like cheap fast food; one leaves you nauseous or still hungry, the other, lonely and emotionally empty.

Until recently, lonely people felt embarrassed, kept quiet about their pain, and secretly blamed themselves for being unlovable. No one felt comfortable talking about loneliness in public. One of our colleagues, after attending an evening session of the loneliness conference mentioned earlier, boarded a bus in Los Angeles. A friendly stranger asked him why he was so dressed up (wearing a coat and tie), and he explained that he was attending a conference. "On what?" the stranger asked. "Loneliness," he replied. "Oh, I'm sorry," she said, embarrassed. "I didn't mean to get personal!"

Today, loneliness, like sex in the post-Kinsey era, is coming out of the closet. People are beginning to realize that the problem needs to be understood and dealt with, that feeling lonely is nothing to be ashamed of. While we believe that many of the causes of loneliness are societal, it doesn't follow that lonely people can do nothing to help themselves or each other. *Intimacy is attainable.* It is, however, more difficult to sustain than in the past, since we no longer have lifelong guarantees of family and community bonds. It requires more effort and more wisdom on the part of individuals.

Not everyone is lonely, and loneliness, when it does strike, is usually temporary. Understanding the causes of loneliness can help overcome it. For this reason we have put loneliness, and people's varied reactions to it, under our psychological microscope: to see what can be learned about how to cope more effectively with it.

Our Surveys

We began our study of loneliness in 1977. We combed through novels and poems and interviewed students and people we knew to gather clues about loneliness. Our effort resulted in an 84-question survey that could be administered to large groups of people. The questionnaire, which is reprinted at the end of this book, appeared in newspapers all over the country. About 30,000 people returned questionnaires to us. Analyses of their answers, supplemented by interviews of lonely and nonlonely people and insights from a host of other researchers, form the basis of this book.

We will examine what is now known about loneliness, and try to paint a clear picture of it. Our inquiry will lead to a deeply rooted need for intimacy that we believe is innate. Loneliness is somewhat different at different stages of life—during infancy, childhood, adolescence, adulthood, and old age. Each of these periods will be the focus of a separate chapter. Throughout the book, but especially in the final chapter, we will suggest what people can do to avoid, alleviate, and cope with loneliness.

What exactly is loneliness?

It is astonishingly difficult to say. Loneliness is a *feeling* and therefore completely subjective. We can't measure it the way, say, a physician measures a patient's temperature or a physiological psychologist measures a subject's heart rate or galvanic skin response to test for anxiety. Only *you* know if and when you feel lonely. So, in our loneliness questionnaire we measure loneliness by asking people how often they feel lonely and how deeply they feel it. We use eight somewhat repetitive questions to get a total loneliness score. When we refer in later chapters to the results of our surveys and use phrases like "more lonely" or "different levels of loneliness," we will be talking about scores on this scale. (If you would like to answer the questions and calculate your own score, see Appendix B.)

Our Loneliness Scale:

1. When I am completely alone, I feel lonely.
   1. Almost never
   2. Occasionally
   3. About half the time
   4. Often
   5. Most of the time

2. How often do you feel lonely?
   1. Never, or almost never
   2. Rarely
   3. Occasionally
   4. About half the time
   5. Quite often
   6. Most of the time
   7. All the time, or almost all the time

3. When you feel lonely, do you usually feel:
   1. I never feel lonely
   2. Slightly lonely
   3. Somewhat lonely
   4. Fairly lonely
   5. Very lonely
   6. Extremely lonely

4. Compared to people your own age, how lonely do you think you are?
   1. Much less lonely than average
   2. Somewhat less lonely than average
   3. About average
   4. Somewhat lonelier than average
   5. Much lonelier than average

How much do you agree with each of the following?

5. I *am* a lonely person.
   1. Strongly disagree
   2. Disagree
   3. Agree
   4. Strongly agree

6. I always *was* a lonely person.
   1. Strongly disagree
   2. Disagree
   3. Agree
   4. Strongly agree

7. I always *will be* a lonely person.
   1. Strongly disagree
   2. Disagree
   3. Agree
   4. Strongly agree

8. Other people think of me as a lonely person.
   1. Strongly disagree
   2. Disagree
   3. Agree
   4. Strongly agree

You may wonder, as we did, why busy people bothered to fill out our long and taxing loneliness questionnaire. Fortunately, many people took the time to explain. Some, who had never before answered a questionnaire, did so because this particular topic "grabbed" them. Some simply saw the questionnaire as an interesting "puzzle" or intellectual challenge. Others generously wished to help university scholars "in the pursuit of science." A few speculated that "only a lonely person would bother to fill this out." But that wasn't the case.

Many people who weren't lonely tried to compare their answers to those of a real friend or a hypothetical person who was in much worse shape then they. One said, "This questionnaire makes me realize how well off I really am." Some people enjoyed the feeling of accomplishment that comes from careful self-scrutiny: "What an assignment! It was stimulating and helpful in doing a little self-analysis." It also made people feel, correctly, that someone "out there" cares what they think. A young woman from Brooklyn, New York, cheerfully concluded a long handwritten addendum to her questionnaire: "I don't know who you are or if you have read this far, but this questionnaire has helped me. I had the chance, finally, to yell out 'Hey, I'm Carole, the nice Irish/Italian Catholic girl next door. The creative and artistic one. And hey, I'm lonely!' "

Our surveys reveal that almost everyone is lonely from time to time, and that no class of people is immune to loneliness. The lonely include men and women of all ages. They come from every socioeconomic level, race, and religious group, hold every kind of job—from zoo keeper to anesthesiologist—and are almost as likely to live with other people as to live alone. Many married people are desperately lonely, although loneliness is more common, as we would expect, among the single, separated, divorced, and widowed.

How Does Loneliness Feel?

Most people we interviewed had little difficulty describing their feelings of loneliness:

> "It's a desperate longing . . . like a hole or space in the middle of my body, a wound. And I can feel it all the time. Even when I'm with another person, it's there, sort of waiting to grow later on, when I'm alone."

> "A pain in the chest—almost literally a broken heart. The problem is, I need to be needed. That's what I'm missing. . . . Nobody needs me, nobody. I have friends at work and people I can call, but they don't really *need* me."

> "I come home from work feeling empty. I try to tell myself that my projects are going well—and they are. But after a while, that just isn't worth much. I mean, who am I working for? What good is success if there's nobody around to appreciate it?"

When we listened to tapes of our interviews with lonely people, one word recurred frequently: "emptiness."

> "I'm like a shell. Empty inside."
> "It's a coldness or deadness inside, a sinking or empty feeling."

Some people explained their unsuccessful attempts to fill the void: "I get a compulsive need to eat . . . rich, fattening, high-calorie, rewarding foods." "I drink until I fall asleep." "I sit in front of the TV eating chocolates until I feel sick."

Others described feelings akin to anxiety or fear: "a tightness in my throat and chest"; "a dry, gulplike feeling"; "panic, terror." Still others sounded depressed: "sad, hopeless"; "lost, without energy."

None of these feelings is unusual. In fact, since so many people mentioned them to us, we included them on our questionnaire, in a list of the twenty-seven feelings most people associate with loneliness (see question No. 64 in Appendix A). We asked respondents to circle all the feelings that characterized their sense of loneliness. In the end, we found four distinct categories of feelings, two of which are *Desperation* and *Impatient Boredom*. (We will discuss the other two, *Self-blame* and *Depression,* later on.)

TWO CATEGORIES OF LONELY FEELINGS

Desperation	**Impatient Boredom**
Desperate	Impatient
Panicked	Bored
Helpless	Desire to be elsewhere
Afraid	Uneasy
Without hope	Angry
Abandoned	Unable to concentrate
Vulnerable	

Desperation.   These two categories identify two distinct kinds of loneliness. Desperation, or separation distress, is a common response to broken attachments; it typically arises after the death of a loved one, a marital separation or divorce, or any intense form of rejection. Sociologist Robert Weiss called this set of feelings "emotional isolation" and noted its similarity to the panic, fear, helplessness, and vulnerability felt by children when they are unexpectedly separated from their parents. To the surprise and chagrin of many adults, the shattering of intimate ties continues to have this powerful effect throughout life. We always react to separation with loud echoes of the anxiety and desperation we felt as little children.

A young widow, Della Church, speaking about her deceased husband, told us: "I just kept thinking about him, I even got to the point where I could actually see or hear him. I said to myself, 'What's wrong with you? You can't bring him back, you may as well try to forget.' But the more I tried, the more I saw him. I was talking to him. I had vivid dreams of him standing right there. . . . I don't know if I can go on without him."

The first time we interviewed Della she was twenty-three. She had two children but felt so lonely and lost without her husband that she thought she would never recover. This expectation is typical of people who feel desperation as part of loneliness—they mistakenly believe it will never end. But, as Della discovered, they are usually wrong.

We saw Della again, a year after our first interview. During that time, she had changed physically as well as psychologically. She had lost weight, was dressed in a more becoming way, and her face looked lighter, more expressive. She had, we learned, a new boyfriend. Although she still thought about and missed her former husband, Della couldn't live without intimacy. A year after thinking she would never again feel joyful or calm, she was literally unable to remember the depth of her acute loneliness, which we had captured on tape. Her desperation, while obviously very painful, was not permanent.

Impatient Boredom. The second category of lonely feelings, impatient boredom, is different from the deeper, more painful desperation. Impatient boredom is an edgy restlessness, a "nothing to do, nowhere to go" kind of feeling. The friendless homemaker whose husband has been transferred feels it when she finds herself in a new community; so does the lonely traveler sitting idly in a hotel room, or the new retiree suddenly deprived of the eight-hour-a-day companionship of fellow workers. Robert Weiss called this cluster of feelings "social isolation" and likened it to the way children feel when their friends are all away. Suddenly the child's toys and games, so meaningful and engaging in the presence of involved companions, lose their charm and appeal.

A twenty-five-year-old woman from Massachusetts provided a rather extreme example of impatient boredom. "On a typical day? Okay, I get up, wash, dress. Go to work for a few hours. Come home. See my husband. Give him a kiss. Sit down, watch the soapies. Pretty soon he goes to work (on the night shift) and I'm stuck with the kids. Most of the time I watch TV and don't want to have anything to do with the kids. I know that's awful, but I'm so tired of it all! I watch TV every day, probably about 50 hours a week." This woman had no close friends, no personal projects or community involvements, and no clear goals in life; her job, according to her, was "as boring as the rest of my life." She didn't realize that life becomes interesting for most of us only when we invest ourselves in other people.

The two main types of lonely feelings, desperation and impatient boredom, reflect points along an intimacy continuum (see the figure below). For most people, intense intimacy involves a complex combination of psychological and physical closeness. Although not all close relationships need to be physical, and certainly not all sex is psychologically intimate, deep intimacy tends to be physical. Most adults form a stable relationship with a member of the opposite sex that includes sexuality as well as other forms of intimacy. Most other friendships, family ties, and ties to a work group or community fall farther along the intimacy continuum (to the right in the figure). When we break an intimate bond—through death or divorce, for example—we feel desperate. When we are temporarily without familiar friends and community—after moving to a new school, job, or city, for example—we are likely to feel the loneliness of impatient boredom.

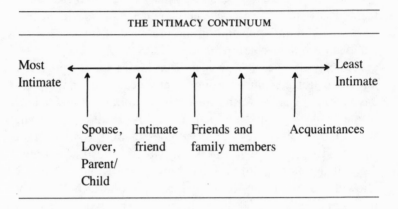

THE INTIMACY CONTINUUM

Most Intimate ← → Least Intimate

Spouse, Lover, Parent/Child — Intimate friend — Friends and family members — Acquaintances

Each of our relationships falls somewhere along the intimacy continuum. The more intimate the relationship, the more intense our loneliness when it is lost or broken.

How Do Lonely People Explain Their Feelings?

Most of the people who replied to our surveys seemed to have no trouble telling us why they were lonely. We had included a list of twenty-one reasons for loneliness mentioned in earlier interviews with lonely people. (See the table below and question No. 65 in Appendix A.)

Statistically analyzing these reasons, we found five distinct categories: *Being Unattached, Needing Friends, Being Alone, Forced Isolation,* and *Dislocation.*

REASONS FOR BEING LONELY

Being Unattached	**Needing Friends**
Having no spouse	Feeling different
Having no sexual partner	Being misunderstood
Breaking up with spouse or	Not being needed
lover	Having no close friends
Being Alone	**Dislocation**
Coming home to an empty	Being far from home
house	In new job or school
Being alone	Moving too often
	Traveling often
Forced Isolation	
Being housebound	
Being hospitalized	
Having no transportation	

For the moment, consider just the two categories in the upper portion of the table: *Being Unattached* and *Needing Friends*. The first concerns separation from, or absence of, a spouse or lover. People who give this kind of reason for loneliness are emotionally isolated and lack both sexual and psychological intimacy.

The second set of reasons—feeling different, being misunderstood, not being needed, having no close friends—corresponds well with what Robert Weiss called social isolation, the need for friendship or community. Again the evidence leads us to believe that there are two fairly distinct kinds of loneliness.

The three sets of reasons in the bottom portion of the table reveal some of the connections between social forces in contemporary America and individual loneliness. *Being Alone,* a common reason for loneliness, is a product of the high divorce rate, the fact that many wives outlive their husbands, and the emphasis in our culture on self-sufficiency and independence. (One fifth of American households are occupied by solitary individuals, a proportion unprecedented in history.) *Forced Isolation* is characteristic of a small minority of older respondents who, in previous eras, would probably have lived with family members. *Dislocation* refers to the nation's high rate of mobility—tens of thousands of us move and travel each year for business, education, and adventure.

All five types of reasons for loneliness remind us that social forces, *not* individual shortcomings, are the ultimate cause of widespread loneliness.

The Paradox of Solitude

Paying so much attention to loneliness risks giving solitude a bad name. It may seem that we think constant togetherness is the answer to all of life's problems. Actually, the capacity for intimacy and the ability to appreciate solitude are two sides of the same coin. As theologian Paul Tillich noted: "Loneliness can be conquered only by those who can bear solitude." Indeed, one of the people we interviewed told us: "Odd as it sounds, I'm more able to be myself when I feel most in tune with my lover. It's easier to concentrate on work, to be creative. I know when we're apart that we'll soon be together, that she's there if I need her. And we're more valuable to ourselves and get along better when we've spent time alone."

Although the words "alone" and "lonely" come from the same middle English root—meaning "all one" (or only one)—they are not psychological synonyms. Many people—for example, those trapped in unhappy marriages or forced to live with relatives who "don't understand"—are much lonelier living with others than are the hundreds of thousands who live alone but have close ties with friends and family. It's clearly possible to be lonely without being alone and alone without being lonely.

To us, *solitude* is a kind of positive aloneness. And, paradoxically, solitude can be a corrective for prolonged loneliness. To the extent that solitude slows our hectic pace, allows us to distinguish genuine from false needs for other people, and encourages personal strengths to emerge, it prepares us emotionally for social responsibility and deeper intimacy.

In extreme forms, solitude has often been used in *rites de passage* to transform boys into men. In many primitive societies, pubertal boys were sent off into the forest, jungle, or plains, and ordered to remain alone for periods ranging from overnight to several months. The boys were thought to die a symbolic death and become transformed: when they returned to the world of the living as men, their boyhood ignorance and dependence were gone forever. If this sounds barbaric, consider that Outward Bound, a popular American recreation group for men and women of all ages, requires its participants to take solo wilderness trips; the experience of solitary survival is assumed to foster independence and self-sufficiency.

Some researchers have tested the idea that solitude can be strengthening. During the sixties and seventies, John Lilly experimented with "restricted environmental stimulation" by placing people in immersion tanks full of warm salt water, asking them to remain inside for hours, even days, at a time. Psychologist Peter Suedfeld claimed more recently that REST, or *Restricted Environmental Stimulation Therapy,* calms mental patients, helps overweight people lose weight, smokers quit smoking, alcoholics reduce their drinking, and stutterers speak more clearly. REST simply places patients in dark, soundproofed rooms for about eight hours without radios, books, or other diversions.

Therapeutic solitude, in order to work, means that participants must not equate being alone with loneliness. But our studies show that people differ greatly in their interpretations of aloneness. We asked, "When you are alone, how often do you feel: afraid, fearful; angry, resentful; anxious, uneasy; calm, quiet; creative, productive; happy, content; relaxed, thoughtful?" We found that chronically lonely people associate solitude with fear, anxiety, and resentment. Infrequently lonely people are markedly different; to them, solitude means calmness, creativity, relaxation, and contentment.

Most people probably don't know how they would react to prolonged solitude. Many do everything in their power to avoid it, fearing they would "crack up" or discover something ugly or unpleasant about themselves. But occasionally, circumstances force people to take the ultimate test. A few years ago we interviewed one such person.

Nicolo de Mora, son of an Italian multimillionaire and at age fifty an irresponsible playboy, was kidnapped, transported far from home in Milan, and locked in a tiny underground cell, his foot chained to the bed. He remained in this dank, windowless pit, completely alone, for seventeen months. At the end of that time, instead of killing him, his captors released him at the bottom of a quarry in southern Italy. His father, the week before, had paid the kidnappers five and a half million dollars in ransom.

Before this enforced *rite de passage,* Nicolo had been a philandering ne'er-do-well, a man who lived in the shadow of his brilliant and successful father; a man who had never done a productive day's work in his life. He detested two things: boredom and solitude. Filling his life with meaningless activity, he surrounded himself with hangers-on, people who took advantage of his generosity but for whom he felt no real love or friendship.

In his dark cell, Nicolo's most precious possession was a

tiny light bulb. Although his captors brought him food and books, they wouldn't let him see their faces, nor did they talk to him. Nicolo passed the time sleeping, dreaming, reading, reflecting, eating, and pacing. His resolution: "I must get out of here alive."

In his dreams, Nicolo replayed past love affairs and revisited Altamura, the childhood home where he had once felt security, warmth, and love. He began to realize what other people meant and could mean to him. At times he was desperate to see a human face and so constructed a "mirror" from a tinfoil chocolate wrapper. He held it up to his face, "just to see two eyes, like having company." Sometimes he imagined he had the company of people who loved him.

After Nicolo's release, he was, at first, euphoric every day. He loved seeing the sun, the sky, and the trees again. Everything he did made him rapturously happy—eating, talking, walking down the street, being with his sons. Having lived through the experience made Nicolo feel strong, for the first time in his life, "like a hero." He was a man who had done something on his own, for himself.

At first we assumed that Nicolo's transformation would be only temporary. After the initial joy wore off, he would surely revert to his old self again. But this didn't happen. Three years after his release, Nicolo has taken over his father's business and is doing an excellent job of running it. His relationships with friends and family have deepened. They are amazed at how much he has changed, and they sometimes joke about his "extraordinarily expensive finishing school."

What Can You Do About Loneliness?

In our surveys we asked people what they do when they feel lonely. Their answers were extremely diverse: Some take tranquilizers, get drunk or stoned, others just sit and think or cry, some go for walks or drives, others visit someone or go shopping. The most common reactions are watching television, reading, listening to music, and calling a friend.

We have concluded from studying lonely people that some of these reactions are much more helpful than others. Solitary television viewing—the most common diversion—seems to be almost as destructive as solitary drinking or pill taking, for example. Other, more active forms of solitude, such as reading and letter or journal writing, contribute to personal strength, self-awareness, and creativity. Establishing intimate ties with others is even more helpful. Since loneliness reflects a need for intimacy, friendship, or community, remedies that don't include these provisions won't work.

Lonely people say they feel "empty." Fearing this emptiness, some surround themselves with people they don't really care about. They would be better off learning the benefits of solitude; but solitude, by itself, is not a solution either. Without intimate relationships and meaningful, shared projects, human existence is hollow indeed. Food, alcohol, and televised soap operas cannot fill the void.

The only lasting remedies for loneliness are mutual affection and participation in a genuine community. Many Americans, it seems, are short on these vital provisions. In subsequent chapters we will explore what can be done about it.

2

Needing Intimacy and Community

To study human sexual intimacy is to witness the rebirth of lavish bodily contact between adults, replacing the lost intimacies of infancy.—DESMOND MORRIS

When I moved to this community, I had neighbors the very next day. The things we did up there, the whole community, we played horseshoes, we went to church together, we would group up when they had holy revivals, and then on Sunday evenings, maybe even on Saturday evenings, we'd come back from service and have our sports. We would play badminton or we'd play horseshoes. Not just one or two of us; we would have the whole bench setting full.—SURVIVOR OF THE BUFFALO CREEK FLOOD, INTERVIEWED BY KAI ERIKSON

When adults are lonely, especially when they long for physical closeness and touching, childhood memories of intimacy float to the surface of consciousness. A thirty-year-old woman, asked to conjure up an image that would represent the perfect solution to her loneliness, described a vague but definitely pleasant vision of herself "burrowing under a male figure who is lying down." Later, we asked her to relax and free-associate to this image—to say whatever came to mind when she focused on it. To her surprise, she suddenly recalled an incident more than twenty years ago when her father, who worked most evenings, was home on a Friday night. While lying on the floor watching television, with an afghan warming him, he let her snuggle up next to him under the afghan. Now, as an adult, when she feels lonely and disconnected, it is this image of warmth and attachment she unconsciously seeks.

Many psychologists claim that relationships with parents are the prototype for all later intimacies. There are good reasons for believing this. As Desmond Morris suggests, sexual intimacy between adults involves a kind of exploratory touching and caressing that is also apparent in mother-infant play. Moreover, adult sexuality incorporates many of the erotic gestures of infancy: mouthing, sucking, kissing, staring into each other's eyes, and cuddling. Adult lovers soften their voices and sometimes talk "baby talk" with each other, as if intimacy were naturally related to being treated like an infant.

Another reason for supposing that adult love is a distant echo of infantile feelings is that adults are so inarticulate about it. When people fall in love, in our culture at least, they seem catapulted beyond the orbit of ordinary social life into an emotional realm that many describe in mystical terms: ineffable, beyond words, out of this world, heavenly. Lovers let down defenses, communicate openly, express feelings they may not have realized they were capable of feeling, and marvel at how well they understand each other. If something is "beyond words," this may be because it was first experienced *before* words—that is, in infancy. And since infants have no defenses and follow no social rules, it makes sense that dropping defenses when in love creates a similar, seemingly mystical state.

We're not saying that adult intimacy is a *regression* to infantile feelings, only that the two are similar (and similarly pleasant), and that a person's intimate history, beginning in infancy, might help explain his or her style of adult love and vulnerability to loneliness.

What Is Intimacy?

The word intimacy comes from the Latin *intimare*, "to make known," and *intimus*, "innermost." The dictionary defines it as "a close personal relationship marked by affection, love, and knowledge of each other's inner character, essential nature, or inmost true self; complete intermixture, compounding, or interweaving." Psychologists have evolved their own list of intimacy's defining features: openness, honesty, mutual self-disclosure; caring, warmth, protecting, helping; being devoted to each other, mutually attentive, mutually committed; surrendering control, dropping defenses; becoming emotionally attached, feeling distressed when separation occurs. Sexual intimacy includes, in addition, physical openness, physical caring, mutual bodily exploration, and physical attachment. The psychological and physical dimensions of intimacy are parallel; one mirrors the other.

Among the people we interviewed were several who said on our loneliness questionnaire that they were not lonely and were happily married. Bob Werner, a forty-five-year-old commercial artist, and his wife of sixteen years, Laura, were among these.

"We still have that original 'in love' feeling. It comes and goes, but it's still very strong at times." (What is the feeling?) "That we are together, beyond normal limits. We have no doubts, no fears . . . in an odd way, we are one unit—two parts fused into one. . . . At those times, I come away from

Laura energized. I have the courage to try things that otherwise might frighten me. It's as if no one can hurt me, no one can bring me down.''

(You said the feeling comes and goes. What does that mean?) ''Well, there are times when I don't like her as much, when we're no longer on the same wavelength. In fact, sometimes I look at her and think 'God, what am I doing with this woman?' It happens much less than it did at first. In the early years of our marriage we called this feeling 'the blahs.' We would admit that, for whatever reason, we just weren't clicking. For me, it would seem that my attraction to her, the excitement of it, had vanished into thin air.''

(What brings you out of that feeling?) ''I'm not sure, really. Sometimes we just leave each other alone for a while, and the blah feeling goes away by itself. Sometimes we do something special—go for a walk, have a long talk, take a weekend away. We get back in touch, and then the fusion and warmth, the pleasure in being together, returns. When that happens again and again over a period of years, you begin to feel sure, even during the blah times, that you'll come back together. And we do.''

(What do you think causes the feeling of togetherness—the oneness, as you call it?) ''Until I met Laura, I hardly ever felt comfortable or unstrained with other people—or with myself. I don't think I understood myself very well; I didn't accept myself and I didn't really care about other people the way I do now. With Laura, almost from the start, I felt accepted. With other women, there was always a voice in the back of my head saying, 'Watch out, protect yourself!' or 'What am I doing here?' With Laura, when the feeling is right, there are no distractions, no reservations. She fills my attention. I am complete and happy.''

In somewhat different words, Laura agreed with Bob but added: ''A relationship has to be conducted, like a piece of music. I think a lot of people fall in love the way we did, but don't know how to keep it going, they don't really try hard enough. Sometimes Bob gets very tired, very depressed. He needs reassurance, someone to lean on. I always try to be there for him. When we aren't getting along or don't see much of each other because we're both working too hard, it takes special effort to wake up our relationship and make it central again."

For Bob and Laura, psychological and sexual intimacy are interwoven. But intimacy need not be sexual, just as sex need not include psychological intimacy. The two forms of communication greatly enhance one another, but they can exist independently. Sheila Donner is a thirty-two-year-old happily married woman. But her most intimate relationship is, she claims, not with her husband but with her older sister. "We've known each other all our lives. We have a million common reference points. For the first twenty years of our lives, we shared everything that was emotionally important."

Until recently Sheila and her sister lived in the same city and saw each other often. Now hundreds of miles apart, they talk by telephone at least once a week. They still have no secrets. "She is my best advisor, and I am hers."

Just as Bob and Laura talk of fusion and oneness in marriage, Sheila says: "Sometimes I wonder whether we are too close, whether our identities are too confused, as if we were almost the same person. It's scary because I can't really imagine life without her."

Why Does Intimacy Sound Feminine?

Relationships like the one between Sheila and her sister, you might guess, are more common, at least in our culture, between women than between men. In fact, to men, our notion of intimacy may sound overly feminine. This is because women are the undisputed intimacy specialists in our society. Men used to be soldiers, breadwinners, and family protectors; women were, instead, warm, nurturant, caring companions and mothers. To the extent that men experienced intimacy at all after early childhood, they did so with the guidance—and usually at the insistence—of women.

To prepare boys to occupy the roles of soldier and breadwinner, parents, coaches, and Scout leaders encouraged them to learn to suppress feelings, withstand pain and injury without crying, and play games involving leaders, followers, and team members. Studies of children's friendships consistently show, even today, that boys tend to play in all male groups, usually rehearsing male roles. Girls more often develop close, loyal friendships and practice being intimate.

The result has been, and to a large extent still is, that when men and women get together and begin thinking about marriage, the men are prepared for the breadwinner role but not at all ready for intimacy. Women, prepared for intimacy, are shocked and disappointed to discover that their potential marital partners know almost nothing about love.

Recent studies show that within the past twenty years psychological differences between men and women have begun to erode. Men are more aware of their need for intimacy, women are more aware of the benefits of assertiveness and independence. Still, women consistently score higher than men on tests of interpersonal communication, empathy, and expression of feelings and affection. Men still score higher than women on tests of initiative, independence, competitiveness, aggressiveness, and dominance.

We don't mean to say that men have a weak *need* for intimacy, only that they tend not to know how to satisfy that need. In a recent study at the University of Rochester, psychologists

asked men and women to keep records of all their social encounters during a two-week period. For each encounter, people in the study recorded the sex of the other person, how
intimate the conversation was, how much they and the other
person had disclosed, and how satisfying the exchange was.
Both men and women were more satisfied by their dealings
with women, and those who spent more time with women had
more intimate experiences, disclosed more, and were less
lonely. The fact that both sexes had more rewarding interactions with women suggests that even among contemporary college students, women are more adept at intimacy.

No one knows for sure whether women are better at intimacy because they learn to be or because they have inherited
a knack for it. To the extent that mothers need special biological proclivities to respond intimately to infants, we can imagine that evolution provided women with a greater sensitivity to
intimacy than men. Also, because a woman can have and rear
only a few children, at most only one every year or so, while
a man can (theoretically) have an almost unlimited number,
women may have been endowed by evolution with a greater
desire for a stable, reliable relationship with a man who could
help assure the children's survival. Anthropologist Ashley
Montagu once wrote that women's natural superiority is "precisely in the capacity to love, in their cooperativeness rather
than aggressiveness."

Beyond whatever biological differences there may be, women
are obviously encouraged by society to practice intimacy more
than men. If a man wants to become skilled at intimate relationships, he will probably have to take lessons from a woman.
Fortunately, it seems likely that both sexes have a biologically
based need for intimacy and a capacity to form lasting emotional attachments. Both men and women are social animals,
after all; both begin life attached to a mother, and all through

history men as well as women have formed long-lasting ties to others.

Recent changes in our society have made the search for intimacy more intense for both sexes. In a probing study, psychologists at Michigan's Institute for Social Research recently documented the "reduced integration of American adults into the social structure." "Social organization, social norms, the adaptation to and successful performance of social roles all seem to have lost some of their power to provide people with meaning, identity elements, satisfaction. . . . Related to this thinning of the social commitment and social investment, we note an increased sensitivity to interpersonal relations—a desire for friendship, warm relationships at work and in the family, a desire for personal impact in everyday encounters."

This turn of events is bewildering to many men, who told the researchers that "lack of warmth and closeness with their children" is what disturbs them most about being a parent. The men apparently want to be intimate with their children, but don't know how. Few women reported this as a problem.

Where, then, do today's men turn for the intimacy they increasingly desire?

To their wives, of course. When asked in the Michigan survey how they handled problems, worries, or periods of unhappiness, married men spoke most often about their wives' support.

Intimacy is "feminine" only in the sense that women are the major intimacy providers. Most likely, men and women need intimacy to the same degree. Ironically, fewer women than men get their needs met, despite women's expertise, because so many men are intimacy-takers rather than givers.

The Origins of Intimacy and Autonomy

If intimacy is vital for human survival—an essential ingredient of infant development and an assurance that adult lovers will stay together long enough to care for their offspring—what might happen if children were raised without intimacy, indeed without any form of social life? The answer, which of course cannot be ethically pursued in experiments on people, is suggested by studies of our distant relatives, rhesus monkeys.

When psychologist Harry Harlow and his colleagues placed infant monkeys in isolation chambers, without a mother or mother substitute, the monkeys were psychologically damaged for life. They behaved like severely disturbed or autistic children—rocking back and forth, mouthing and biting themselves, huddling in a corner, and not playing normally with peers. When they matured, they proved unable to reproduce sexually. When infant monkeys were raised with their mother but then separated from her, they became agitated and distressed, and eventually succumbed to what looked like human depression.

Human infants are even more dependent than monkeys on their parents because, physically speaking, humans are born prematurely: a human infant can't do anything for itself. Because the newborn is neurologically and psychologically underdeveloped, the process of emotional attachment, which in many species occurs immediately after birth, takes several months in humans. During this time, infants get their first lessons in love and loneliness. An infant will, if properly cared for, begin to develop a sense of basic trust, and this feeling will serve as a foundation for all later personal growth. If the infant receives attention and affectionate handling, he or she begins to sense that life is good and the world a friendly place.

If mistreated, abandoned for long periods, or handled tensely and anxiously, the child learns that the world is hostile, painful, unreliable, or cold.

Between five and twelve months of age, infants form an emotional attachment to mother (or any primary caretaker), and secondary attachments to less frequent companions such as father, brothers, and sisters. When infants beyond that age are separated from mother they become extremely upset. If separation is prolonged, they go through three stages, two of which are identical to ones observed in infant monkeys. The first stage is *protest,* a mixture of terror and anger that usually assures mother's reappearance if she is within earshot. The infant cries, wails, and thrashes about. After exhausting itself in protest, the child enters a period of *despair.* It seems listless and uninterested in the world—in a word, depressed. But if mother returns while the infant is despairing, the child will light up and happily cling to her. If she doesn't appear for days or weeks, the human child (unlike a monkey) will no longer seem attached to her. Even if she returns, the child shows little interest and exhibits what psychologists call *detachment.* The child appears not even to remember its mother and seems almost deliberately cool and aloof.

This important sequence, from protest to despair to detachment, characterizes people's reactions to separation all through life. The same feelings reverberate within us whenever we are separated from someone we love.

Infants can tolerate separation better if they are temporarily placed in the care of what psychologists call secondary attachment figures. For infants in families that share child care instead of relying solely on one person, the effects of prolonged separation from that person are probably less severe.

It isn't clear yet what, exactly, makes an infant become emotionally attached to its mother, but the causes seem to be the same as the ones that cement attachments between adults.

One cause is sheer familiarity. Research confirms what we know from experience: Familiarity usually breeds not contempt but greater liking and comfort. Also, mothers and infants share familiar rituals. Babies become accustomed to repeated games, bathing procedures, feeding practices. The caretaker and child are, thanks to daily rehearsals, somewhat like experienced dance partners. Much of what they do together is so intricately intertwined that no substitute caretaker can follow the infant's dance steps comfortably. Another factor is positive reinforcement; both infants and adults become more attached to people who reward them—not only with food, but with smiles, warmth, and gentle handling.

The attachment process serves two purposes in infancy. First, it usually assures that the infant will be protected by parents while it is totally helpless. Second, as the infant becomes capable of moving about on its own, the parents serve as a secure home base, a reference point. Research on both monkeys and humans has documented a nonverbal conversation between infant and parent. "Is this safe to touch?" the toddler's look inquires; and the mother's smile or fearful expression provides the answer.

Young children need intimacy with a reliable caretaker before they can risk confident solitude. Anxious, insecure attachment means anxious, inhibited exploration of the world—and, in some cases, a lifelong fear of being alone.

A college student told us about the following recurrent nightmare. In it, the student is a toddler and overhears his parents arguing about divorce. Suddenly, he is locked in a mailbox outside his house, knowing that his parents have left him forever, and he hears "other children laughing and fireworks and cannons going off." At this point, he always wakes up in a sweat, his heart pounding. He first had the nightmare when, as a young child, his parents actually got divorced. It recurred for several months at around age ten when his mother remarried. And it recurred again for several weeks when he left home and entered college. In recounting his dream, the student linked this feeling to his "irrational fear of being alone." "I try never to be alone under any circumstance. The panic is easier to deal with now—and so is the dream—but it's still my major hang-up."

Moving Toward Separateness and Autonomy

The progression from birth to first attachment, and from first attachment to autonomy, is one of huge psychological significance, and it rarely occurs without hitches. Every person begins life in a womb, symbiotically connected to mother, benefiting from her warmth, nourishment, and protection, without effort. Once out in the world, the newborn (if lovingly cared for) lives with an illusion of harmony and bliss, its every need supplied by parents. But after four to six months of oneness with parents, inexorable physical development of nerves, muscles, and sensory-motor coordination compel the infant to move toward autonomy.

Child psychologists refer to this process as "individuation" or the "second hatching" of the infant. (The first, more literal hatching occurs at birth.) The second year of life is an alternately exhilarating and dangerous time for the child, each venture into the unknown requiring an act of courage. The outcome of such ventures is partly determined by parents' good judgment. Parents are usually torn between the desire to protect and the desire to let go. It is tempting to hold on too tightly, savoring the child's dependency for just a little longer. But to do so risks making the child ambivalent about intimacy, perhaps forever.

The child's wishes at this age are sometimes difficult for adults to understand. The formerly willing cuddler now screams "No!" and wriggles free. The cooperative eater now throws food on the floor, or mouths it playfully before spitting it out. On the other hand, the child is often frightened by the prospect of separateness. Every increase in cognitive sophistication renders the discovery of selfhood more intimidating. From this time on, the growing child will always be vulnerable to fear or anxiety when alone.

The conflict between the desire for oneness with a loving, protective parental figure and the desire for freedom from social restrictions and entanglements lasts a lifetime. What adult hasn't felt like a needy child, wishing to throw off the pretense of autonomy and cling securely to another person? Yet who hasn't also felt burdened by social ties, shackled by marital or family obligations, ready to chuck it all for a life of freedom and adventure?

The potential conflict between the need for autonomy and the need to be dependent is transcended in adult intimacy. Intimate friends or lovers try to satisfy *both needs* for each other. In a good marriage, for example, each partner sometimes needs comforting, warmth, reassurance, and protection. At the same time, each realizes that the other is not really helpless, not always in need of mothering. Like good parents, mature lovers acknowledge each other's rights, privacy, and independence, even though this entails some risk and uncertainty.

Of course, no close friendship, love affair, or marriage lives up to this ideal all the time. But when adults are lonely and in need of intimacy, this is what they long for.

The Need for Community

Mothers and infants and grown-up lovers exemplify the purest forms of intimacy. The corresponding prototypes of ideal community are the family and the small town. Actually, communities involve intimate feelings too—family members care for and support each other and small towns are thought to be like one big family of families, a patchwork of helpful, close, and cooperative relationships.

One of us grew up in such a town, where about ten families had become close friends. All of the children were considered part of the larger family—we even called our neighbors "Aunt Lois and Uncle Bob," "Aunt Molly and Uncle Jack." On an Israeli kibbutz, where one of us has spent some time, the feeling is similar. The kibbutz is a commune, a family of sorts but on a larger and more extreme scale. There, people live together, work together, eat together, and raise their children together. Community members depend on each other completely for their livelihood, their social activities, and perhaps most important, their sense of identity. (Being from a particular kibbutz is like having a particular, well-known family name.)

Although feelings of intimacy and community overlap, they are different in important ways. Intimacy is mainly private; it involves sharing private features of oneself—hidden feelings, hopes, fears, and embarrassments. Community is public; a network of roles and communal obligations. Our public selves are defined partly by these roles and duties. Our private selves— which Americans frequently think of as their "real" selves— may be quite different. Presidents and prime ministers speak an official language in public, for example, but a softer, more intimate one at home.

Community is also more purposeful and practical than intimacy. Two urbanites may begin a heavenly love affair in private and mistakenly believe they don't need anyone or anything else; but if the Teamsters Union goes on strike, the affair and the star-struck lovers may die of starvation. Most communities, like small towns and kibbutzim, constitute economies; they produce and distribute vital goods and services. They also bestow significance, direction, and meaning on the lives of their members—offering jobs, titles, and goals without which no one can feel needed, successful, or heroic. In this sense, any group that assigns roles to members and engages people in activities is a community—businesses, political parties, athletic teams, informal clubs and organizations, bridge partnerships, golf-foursomes, churches, block associations, yoga classes, car pools. The list is endless. To be outside of all such groups is to be lonely indeed.

The two main forms of loneliness—desperation and impatient boredom or emotional and social isolation—are important and healthy signals of unfulfilled needs for intimacy and community. When unattached people long for intimacy, their loneliness is not much reduced by engaging in community activities. When, on the other hand, they feel lost, alienated, identityless, without direction or meaning, intimacy may be soothing and distracting, but it cannot substitute for a valued place in a community.

The need for community, from a psychological viewpoint, is actually a congeries of other needs—for safety, security, recognition, identity, predictability, familiarity, meaning, and direction. We have said that infants would die without intimacy, but they would die just as surely if their families and surrounding communities failed to provide them with food, shelter, and medical care. As we get older, the need for community becomes more psychological—not just physical but deeply internal as well—but it remains just as strong.

Why Friends Are So Important

Most of us are trained for community life during childhood. With our peers we learn how to cooperate, negotiate, and capitulate; we learn how to grow up.

Experiments have shown that having playmates, like having

a mother, is essential for monkeys, too, which suggests that friendship plays an essential role in primate development. Like human children, monkey youngsters learn by playing structured games with peers. In this way, they gradually prepare for adult social roles and adult sexuality. At first, the games seem to be nothing more than physical exercise—running, jumping, climbing, and chasing. Over time, though, playful activities begin to mimic adult social behavior. Males engage in rough and tumble play, a form of wrestling and playful biting that prepares them for real battles in the future. Approach-and-withdrawal, a kind of seductive hide-and-seek, is more common among female monkeys.

From infancy on, monkey play contains mock sexual elements: hugging, mounting, and sexual posturing. As monkeys mature, these acts and postures become more and more genuine, until—at maturity—they are incorporated into sexual intercourse. A monkey raised only with its mother cannot mate successfully as an adult, even though it may try. The inept monkey may attempt to mount sideways, or rub itself on a partner, but these acts obviously won't be very productive.

Human children who grow up without playmates are in similar straits. It would seem, in principle, that parents could raise a child without peers and simply tell the child about social customs and sexual practices. Actually, though, children raised this way would probably be rejected by their peers, just as friendless monkeys are. Most children learn how to behave sexually from their peers; first holding hands, then necking and petting, and finally making love according to the rules of their culture.

Children also learn other important social rules from peers. The ones who seem socially or psychologically or physically different are almost always rejected when they make their first entrance onto the social scene and social rejection is painful for people at any age. But as children grow into adolescents, they become even more highly attuned to the importance of peer acceptance and support. Teen-agers seek reassurance of their worth and acceptability from peers perhaps even more than from parents. What matters is that the right clique approves of them. Even as adults, we never fully outgrow the need to feel that we belong to a group and are part of a community.

The Invisibility of Community

Indian tribal villages, frontier towns, and pioneer wagon trains—these are common, although extreme, examples of communities whose members had survival as their overriding common goal. One can still find such examples on the last American frontier—Alaska.

People who move to Alaska must acclimate not only to a new set of friends and coworkers, but also to a dramatically different environment. In many Alaskan towns, the temperature rarely rises above freezing and the earth never thaws. Residents must perch their homes above the permafrost and use buckets to relieve themselves, since outdoor plumbing isn't feasible. We interviewed a woman who had lived in a small, northern Alaskan town for several years. Patty Worth, at the age of thirty, decided along with her husband that living in Chicago wasn't satisfying. They sensed a lack of purpose and meaning in their lives and felt they had to try harder to find the right niche. Patty and her husband quit their jobs, bought a camper, and traveled all over the country for a year. One of their stops was in a small northern town in Alaska. It was their final stop. They bought a small piece of land with a tiny house, several miles from their nearest neighbor. Patty got a job as a public health nurse. It was a twelve-mile walk or ski over open territory to get to town. Her husband, Jerry, opened his own stained glass workshop and had the only crafts showroom within five hundred miles.

Both Patty and Jerry spoke about their feelings for their new neighbors and friends with a mixture of fascination, pride, and glee. "Up here, you just have to depend on your neighbors for help. It's really a matter of life and death. When we wanted to build an addition onto our house, they chipped in and helped. When one of my friends had a baby, we went over there and helped with the housework and the kids. We're all in the same boat here, and if even one person doesn't help we all sink."

The next time we spoke with Patty she had just had a positive pregnancy test. She was elated. "This is a perfect time for us to start a family. We feel part of a larger family already and we have always wanted to pass that on to children. Now we have something worthwhile to share with our new baby— a first generation Alaskan!"

Unlike Patty and Jerry, most of us take our communities for granted. Like the proverbial fish who doesn't know he's in water, we don't perceive the community around us until it begins to evaporate. If we lose a job or move to a new city or our town suffers a major natural disaster, we are jolted by the loss of community. Suddenly torn from our social and physical moorings, we are frightened, disoriented, lost. At such times it's surprising to find that although we thought we were part of the community, psychologically speaking, it was also "in" and part of us. Those were *our* friends, *our* plans, *our* home, *our* favorite streets and stores, churches and restaurants. If they vanish or we move away, part of ourselves is diminished. This is another meaning of the word "emptiness" used so often by the lonely people we interviewed. It means that a part of oneself that had been invested in a certain community or place is missing.

One man put it this way: "I find it hard to say whether the

emptiness is in me, or in the outside world. When I'm sitting at home feeling lonely, it's like nothing is happening, inside or outside. There's just nothing there, nothing to focus on, nothing to get excited about. I lose track of what I'm supposed to be doing.'' Another said, ''I feel like an empty glass, very fragile, very light. I feel like I have to be careful or the glass will shatter, and I'll be in pieces—maybe not there at all.''

Equating inner and outer emptiness is part of our tendency to confuse inner and outer symbols of the self. ''I'' am both a unique person, with a set of special experiences and feelings, and a social object—a filler of roles, a member of a team. The individual and communal sides of ourselves are, in reality, inseparable. Anything that damages or reduces my public self and its setting also takes something away from the unique me. This is why, each time we move or our outside world changes, we feel diminished, bereft, robbed of something ''inside.'' In the midst of war, urban renewal, or drastic change, we feel empty, lonely.

But the underlying problem is never simply loneliness: it is always the absence of intimacy or community. These two complex needs are important—biologically, psychologically, and socially. With this in mind, we are ready to consider what loneliness, or the need for intimacy and community, looks like at each of life's major stages.

3

Childhood Roots
of Lonelineness

Once, a boy from the area where I lived was telling someone else that he'd skated with absolutely everyone in the class at the rink that afternoon. And I heard him say—quote—*I even* skated with Doris Walsh—unquote—! As though skating with *me* were—were . . . the last thing anyone would do! The pits. . . . I have a memory of trying to tell my mother about that incident, and she just brushing it off.—DORIS WALSH, 52, INTERVIEWED BY MAGGIE SCARF

I remember, when I was about four years old, getting into a fight on Billy Ervin's front porch. I think we were arguing about when the Arthur Godfrey show came on the radio. During the fight, I fell over the side of the porch, hit my head on the sidewalk and had a concussion. My parents were terrified and they hovered over me nervously for days.—PHILLIP SHAVER'S EARLIEST MEMORY

I remember getting lost at a local department store. They had to page my mother. I felt special and proud as I waited for her to come and pick me up.—CARIN RUBENSTEIN'S EARLIEST MEMORY

Psychotherapists sometimes ask patients to describe their earliest memory as a way of tapping central themes in their self-conceptions. It's not assumed that what happened is important, but how a person describes it often is. Is the person invisible or at the center of attention, loved or rejected, happy or sad, isolated or surrounded by friends? The way in which people recount their earliest memory can reveal a great deal about how they feel about themselves and how they live their adult lives. It can also reveal something about their propensity for loneliness.

In this chapter we will examine the ways in which children deal with intimacy, friendship, and solitude. We do this partly to discover what can be done to help children, but also to learn how early feelings and self-images are related to subsequent adult loneliness.

Lonely Adults' Memories of Childhood

We asked adults a series of questions about their relationships with parents. It turns out that the way they respond to each question is connected with their loneliness (or lack of it) as adults. Respondents who say that during childhood they did not have warm, helpful mothers and fathers are more lonely as adults. Moreover, lonely adults more often say that their parents didn't spend enough time with them. They are also more likely than others to feel that they grew up unable to rely on parents as "trusted and secure bases of support." This was the first sign in our surveys that childhood experiences, or memories of them, can be important in thinking about adult loneliness.

In times of need most of us turn to others for help. Psychological studies show that people who are frightened or confused choose to be with others, partly because they desire comfort and reassurance, partly because they want to compare

Which of the following describes your mother (father) and her (his) relationship with you while you were growing up?

1. She (he) and I had a warm, loving relationship; we were very close.
2. She (he) and I had a good relationship; we were fairly close.
3. She (he) and I had almost no relationship; we were not very close.
4. She (he) and I had a very conflicted relationship; we argued often.
5. I didn't live with my mother (father) during most of those years.

How much could you rely on your mother (father) for help when you had any kind of problem?

1. Very much
2. A fair amount
3. Some
4. Not very much
5. Not at all
6. Not applicable

While you were growing up, how much did you consider your parents to be *trusted* and *secure* bases of support? How much could you really count on them?

1. Very much
2. A lot
3. Some
4. Not very much
5. Not at all

When I was growing up, my mother (father) did not spend enough time with me.

1. Strongly agree
2. Agree
3. Disagree
4. Strongly disagree

---

notes, so to speak, to get a handle on their situation. Human beings do this almost as soon as they are born; infants and children cling to parents most insistently when they are frightened, confused, or in pain. Teen-agers spend almost all of their free time with peers. Even adults huddle together in frightening circumstances. During the 1977 New York City blackout, for instance, groups of people spontaneously clustered together at almost every street corner. Quite suddenly, and very unusually, no one was out on the street alone.

Expectations about getting help from other people begin to form very early in childhood, and it seems likely that an adult's ability to deal with stress and anxiety is influenced by how secure he or she felt as a child. Our own earliest memories—described at the beginning of this chapter—show our tendency to believe that people will give us help when we need it. (And in fact, they almost always have.) Doris Walsh's earliest memory, in contrast, is a tale of humiliation and insecurity. She has been depressed for most of her life and has difficulty trusting others and feeling loved. "Mental models," half-conscious beliefs and expectations about oneself and other people, are at the root of most of our adult feelings. And these "models" begin to take shape even before we can talk.

As psychiatrist John Bowlby explains: "[W]hen [one] is confident that an attachment figure will be available . . . [he or she] will be much less prone to either intense or chronic fear than will an individual who for any reason has no such confidence." This confidence (or lack of it) is "built up slowly during the years of immaturity—infancy, childhood, and adolescence." Interpretations developed during those years "tend to persist relatively unchanged throughout the rest of life," unless we actively work on them. In other words, having trustworthy, supportive parents helps us learn to expect (probably unconsciously) that people will be reliable and helpful. This expectation makes it easier for us to open ourselves to others, to take social risks; and this gives us considerable protection against chronic loneliness.

One of the most lonely people we interviewed, a forty-eight-year-old New York woman, didn't show up for our scheduled interview. When we called to make another appointment, she confided: "Well, I really didn't think you'd bother to show up. I mean, I'm not really all that interesting—I don't have anything to say." Later on, we interviewed her and learned that she had grown up feeling about her own parents the way she seemed to feel about us. Not noticing the parallel, she nevertheless revealed: "My parents acted as if I didn't exist. I didn't feel unwanted—I just felt like a cloud, like I could vanish in the night and they wouldn't even notice."

The Lifelong Need for Attachment Figures

Studies of infants show that, for them, an attachment figure must be physically present to reduce anxiety. Infants and toddlers, despite assurances to the contrary, worry when mother is out of sight that she might be gone forever. After the first year or two, though, the need for a parent's actual presence subsides as the child becomes more certain that mom or dad will be available and responsive if called upon. The older child's sense of personal security is based on cognitively complex and flexible assurances: "I'll visit you in the hospital every day." "I'll be next door if you need me." "I'll stay until you fall asleep." Children and adults who accept assurances like these gain the courage to tackle the unknown and to feel comfortable about solitude.

Still, few of us are autonomous at any age, if autonomy means going it completely alone. We can function independently for a while, but do so comfortably only when we are certain that social support will be available if needed. In this sense, adults are similar to children. Even the kidnapped Italian, de Mora, survived only because he knew there were people waiting for him who hoped he would live. Solitary adventurers, traveling sales people, and soldiers may seem more independent, but they too are usually in contact with friends and family by mail, radio, or telephone. Adults can go further and longer than children without social support but no adult can really do without it completely. One of our friends suggested, in jest, that we name this book: "How to Perk Up and Strut Even Though You Know for a Fact That Nobody Gives a Damn Whether You Live or Die." In reality, no one perks up under these conditions, no matter what the stakes. The ultimate solution to the problem of loneliness is intimacy and community. Everyone needs someone to give a damn.

Clingers and Evaders

Children go through three stages when separated from parents: protest, despair, and detachment. Adults do the same whenever they are permanently separated from someone they love. Being a good parent (or a good lover) means being regularly available—physically and emotionally. Inadequate parents raise children who are what Bowlby calls "anxiously attached"—they cling, feel intensely anxious when separated from parents, and lack confidence in themselves and others. If rejection or abandonment goes too far, the child may become permanently detached and aloof, maintaining a self-protective distance from everyone. Both types, the clingy and the detached, suffer from an underlying lack of self-confidence and trust, and both are prone to chronic loneliness.

We believe, in fact, that childhood clinging and detachment—both of which result from fear and insecurity—are reflected in two self-destructive adult behavior patterns, which we call "clinging" and "evading." Laboratory studies of college students show that lonely students act differently from their nonlonely peers. Lonely students, for example, disclose either too much or too little about themselves, causing their partners to withdraw uncomfortably. The overdisclosers or clingers are like clingy children, psychologically speaking. They want social contact so desperately that they can hardly wait to attach themselves, securely and permanently, to somebody. In the process, they overwhelm people with their eagerness for instant intimacy. The clinger's persistent needs and demands, even when accompanied by gifts, favors, and statements of concern, are more than most of us can handle, especially early in a friendship. We back away from the clinger, fearing for our independence and peace of mind. As the philosopher Friedrich Nietzsche observed: "The lonely one offers his hand too quickly to whomever he encounters."

Underdisclosers, or intimacy evaders, in contrast with clingers, defend themselves against the pain of rejection by refusing to open up to other people for fear that their deepest, most "real" self will be rebuffed. They come across as cool, aloof, disinterested, perhaps even snobby. They are actually desperate for contact and can fantasize about it incessantly but are too frightened, too well protected to take a chance on love. Unfortunately, love and friendship are inherently risky—there can never be an advance guarantee of acceptance between strangers. Because evaders rarely express their deepest needs to anyone, they are prone to self-administered anesthesia: solitary drinking or pill-popping, excessive television-viewing or eating.

The price of both self-protective strategies—clinging and evading—is extremely high. Paradoxically, both encourage rejection (just what the person fears most) and guarantee continued loneliness. A defensive pattern established early in childhood—an early method of coping with pain—can persist into adulthood and lock a person into perpetual isolation and loneliness.

Abandonment: Real and Threatened

Being openly rejected, physically abused, or abandoned by parents can have lasting effects on a child's tendency to cling or remain aloof; fortunately, few American children experience this extreme form of rejection. But parents fail to realize that even mild forms of rejection can lead to the formation of self-destructive mental models and behavior patterns. Dangerous parental maneuvers include: punishing children by withdrawing or threatening to withdraw love ("Go to your room and close the door. Mommy doesn't love you anymore"), sulking or turning a cold shoulder when a child needs support, or threatening to abandon the child.

Abandonment threats are alarmingly common. A British study of 700 parents revealed that more than a quarter of them sometimes threatened their children in this way. As one mother said: "I once did—and upset her so much that I've never said it any more." (What did you say?) "Well, she was having an argument with me, and she says to me 'You don't live here. Hop it!' So I says, 'Oh, well, I can do that! Where's my coat? I'm moving!' So I got my coat from the back, and I was gone. I just stood outside the door, and she cried so bitter, she did. As soon as I came in, she got hold of my leg and wouldn't let go."

Another told an even more pathetic story: "Ever since I left her that time I had to go into hospital [two periods, seventeen days each, child aged two years], she doesn't trust me any more. I can't go anywhere—over to the neighbors or in the shops—I've always got to take her. She wouldn't leave me. She went down to the school gates at dinner time today. She ran like mad home. She said, 'Oh, Mum, I thought you was gone!' She can't forget it. She's still round me all the time."

Children can easily interpret parental divorce as abandonment. After all, parental quarreling and screaming, which many young children mistakenly believe is directed at them, and perhaps real parental neglect or intolerance, end with one parent packing and moving out. In our studies of loneliness, adults whose parents had divorced—sometimes decades before our surveys—were especially prone to loneliness as adults. The younger the person had been at the time of the divorce (the youngest less than a year old), the lonelier he or she tended to be as a grownup.

This is extremely troubling, if true; during the next decade almost half of American children will live through a divorce. Many other studies support our findings. In general, parental divorce—but, surprisingly, not the death of a parent—is associated with children's subsequent (adult) anxiety-proneness, low self-esteem, low trust in other people, loneliness, poor health, and doubts about the viability of marriage.

Divorce, by itself, isn't the main culprit, however. Most studies show that the *quality* of home life—how often parents argue, whether children perceive their parents' marriage as happy—is more important than whether the parents stay together. Fighting, intimidation, and hostility between parents, which may be present either in unhappy intact or in divorcing families, are more traumatic for the child than divorce itself. This probably explains why parental death seldom leaves the same negative traces that divorce does. Thus, intense, long-term parental conflict predisposes children, especially young children, to later loneliness.

The key word is "predisposes," since by no means do all children with conflicted parents display these problems. One woman without such problems wrote to us after reading a newspaper story about our research: "There is no doubt in my mind that divorce has a lasting psychological impact on children which will manifest itself differently depending on the individual circumstances. But happily I have not turned out to be a 'basket case.' In fact I don't think I differ significantly from people raised in intact families."

She went on: "My circumstances are somewhat unusual in that although my parents divorced when I was approximately four years old, I was raised by my father while my mother had visitation rights. Without question, the support I received from my father's brothers and sister, and my grandparents, played a major part in promoting my stability. There were rough times (hating my mother's new husband, parents sometimes pulling both ways) but there were pluses also—double Christmases and birthdays, and knowing that both parents cared very much and wanted me with them."

The important issue, as this woman observed, is not divorce per se, but how *wanted* the child feels. The negative effects of divorce can be ameliorated by such sturdy social supports as the ones she received from her father's family.

Why Self-Blame?

A sad fact about divorce is that because of children's cognitive immaturity—their inability to understand complex emotions and social relationships—they are likely to view themselves as the cause of parents' disagreements. A young child finds it very difficult to distinguish between "He left because of his own problems" and "He left me because I did something wrong." Once this belief becomes ingrained, it can be quite difficult to eradicate.

In *Kramer vs. Kramer,* a film about divorce, six-year-old Billy Kramer revealed his thoughts to his father, Ted:

TED: Now I want you to go to sleep 'cause it's really late.

BILLY: Daddy. . .

TED: Now what is it?

BILLY: Are you going away?

TED: No, I'm staying right here with you, you're not going to get rid of me that easy.

BILLY: That's why mommy left, isn't it. 'Cause I was bad.

TED: Is that what you think? (*Billy nods.*)

No, that's not it, Billy. Your mom loves you very much. And the reason she left doesn't have anything to do with you. I don't know whether this is going to make any sense, but I'll try to explain to you. OK? (*Continues.*) I think the reason why mommy left was because for a long time now, I kept trying to make her be a certain kind of person, Billy. . . . And now that I think about it, I think that she tried for so long to make me happy, and when she couldn't, she tried to talk to me about it, see, but I wasn't listening, 'cause I was too busy. . . .

It's obvious, when you think about it, that despite Ted's care and sensitivity, Billy won't be able to make much sense of his father's explanation. In fact, Billy is incapable of understanding any truthful explanation, since he can't yet comprehend the intricacies of adult relationships.

Recent studies of children of divorce find that most young children think just like Billy, that is, they tend to blame themselves. Older children are less likely to do this and more likely to become angry rather than guilty, because they understand that the divorce was the parents' doing. Still, the experience of divorce can contribute to a child's loneliness. In fact, nine-

and ten-year-old children of divorce, more than children of any other age, explicitly mention their intense loneliness in interviews with psychologists. The older children's ability to understand their parents' feelings actually augments their loneliness in some cases, because they notice that their parents are so involved in their own conflicts that they have little time for children.

What, exactly, does parental divorce do to children? We believe it influences their "mental models" of themselves and their social relations. Over the years, these models, which include unconscious images, assumptions, and explanations of how others react to oneself, become more elaborate and more difficult to change. Just as adults find it difficult to alter a golf swing or a regional accent once it has been practiced for decades, they find it difficult to alter assumptions about their personal flaws and the probability that they will be rejected by new acquaintances.

A man, fifty-three years old, from north Kansas City wrote to us that reading our comments about divorce "really hit home." It allowed him to make a connection between his "terrible sense of loneliness and frustration" and his parents' divorce when he was twelve. "My father left us for another woman," he wrote. (Notice, he still thinks in terms of his father leaving him.) "I sought friends as a solace. . . . I keep having this feeling of male rejection that should have been worked out many years ago." He noted, correctly, that perceiving the connection between his current "clinginess" and earlier hurts was a step toward better, more lasting friendships.

Feeling confident about the kindness and helpfulness of other people is a crucial feature of our mental models of social life. To be self-assured we must believe that loved ones have responded to our calls for support and protection in the past and will continue to do so in the future. We should also feel that we *deserve* their support. These two beliefs might, in principle, be completely independent. After all, if parents once failed to respond supportively to us, this probably had nothing to do with our actual worthiness, but indicated their inadequacy as parents or their preoccupation with other pressing problems. In fact, though, young children (and even some adults) are unable to distinguish between "These particular people don't love me" and "I am inherently unlovable." For this reason, early experiences with rejection, abuse, neglect, and lack of support can make a person both distrust others and dislike himself; it can make him simultaneously hostile and destructively self-critical. Lonely respondents in our surveys were both more likely than other people to have low self-esteem *and* more likely to be dissatisfied with the people they meet. Self-blame and hostility toward others appear to go hand in hand, then, and both are related to loneliness.

Siblings: Do They Help?

Of course, our mental models aren't based solely on interactions with parents. In families with more than one child, the children play together constantly, and they influence each other's self-images and social skills. Until recently, psychologists focused mostly on the rivalry and jealousy siblings feel for each other. There is no doubt that such rivalry exists—recent research shows it can last a lifetime—but it is only one part of the strong bond between siblings.

Most studies indicate that firstborn children are different from laterborns, with the differences probably being due to social experience. Firstborns, who monopolize their parents' attention for at least a year, tend forever after to try to please authority figures. They also score higher than younger brothers and sisters on measures of intelligence: frequent early dealings with adults seem to sharpen their intellectual skills. Firstborns who have grown up with younger siblings tend to be leaders;

they know how to manage subordinates effectively, though some seem a bit too bossy. More of them are famous; there are substantially more firstborns than laterborns included in *Who's Who in America.* Unfortunately, they are also likely to be less comfortable than their younger siblings when it comes to socializing.

Laterborns are less dependent and more relaxed in groups; they tend to be more jovial, more popular, and more courageous—more of them engage in contact sports such as football and wrestling. (Firstborns favor golf and tennis.)

The number of brothers and sisters in a family may influence children's social skills. One psychologist videotaped casual conversations between male and female college students while they were sitting in a waiting room. They had been scheduled, unbeknownst to them, so that a firstborn and a laterborn showed up together, one a man and one a woman. Analysis of the videotapes revealed that the smoothest, most successful discussions occurred when one of the participants was a man who had grown up with an older sister. The outcome was best of all when the woman had grown up with an older brother. Evidently, both men and women may pick up socially useful skills by growing up with an older sibling of the opposite sex.

Studies of college students and adults find that most Americans feel closer to a brother or a sister than to their fathers, and about as close to their closest sibling as to their mother. Clearly, when thinking about family influences on loneliness, we need to include ties to brothers and sisters.

Early Steps Toward Friendship

Although siblings may have been our first and even closest friends, most of us made other friends early in life. And most of us went through some early rejections. Even if most adults can't or don't want to remember, social rejection or lack of friends is just as painful in childhood as it is later on. In fact, people like Doris Walsh, the woman with whom no one would skate, sometimes retain their sense of social failure that began with early failures of friendship.

In recent years, psychologists have filmed thousands of scenes of children at play, to find out what determines whether their peers accept or reject them. Elementary school classrooms, they find, are divided along popularity lines as early as fourth grade. Some children are popular, and they form an interlocking clique at the top of the social pyramid. Other, less popular children are not as well integrated into such groups and spend most of their free time alone. Sometimes the unpopular children try to form friendships with each other, but these attempts usually fail.

What makes some children more socially successful than others? Researchers asked fourth-grade boys to name the three classmates they liked most and the three they liked least. On the basis of this information, the psychologists classified some as *popular* (most often liked), some as *average,* some as *rejected* (least liked), and some as *neglected* (not named at all).

They then assigned one boy of each type to each of several play groups, which met for 40 minutes a week for six weeks. Some groups contained only boys from the same school who knew each other; others contained only strangers (from different schools). Observing the boys playing together, the psychologists noticed that by the third week even the boys in groups composed of strangers seemed to have stepped into their former social roles (popular, rejected, etc.). Apparently, the children consistently behaved in ways that caused their peers to accept or reject them.

Popular boys, even in groups of unfamiliar peers, came to be viewed as leaders. They asserted rules in a positive way, avoided giving offense, and were not possessive. They seemed to be normsetters in every situation. *Rejected* boys got into fights, made more aversive comments, and were more possessive. When not talking inappropriately, they left the group to play by themselves. The other boys viewed them as disruptive, said they talked too much, and actively avoided them.

Neglected children made fewer comments and seemed reluctant to lead or stand out. They were perceived as shy and were pretty much ignored by the boys who already knew them, but *not* by the strangers. They seem to have been adversely labeled and stereotyped by their familiar peers but were capable of changing to some degree in the presence of new playmates.

Another experiment showed that withdrawn or neglected children can benefit from social skills training. Here, the researchers tried peer therapy with four- and five-year-old children. Socially withdrawn children played regularly with a younger child "therapist." Weeks later, they were observed to spend twice as much time playing with classmates and had become the same as normal children. Unsociable children who played with same-age peers also became more gregarious, but the gain wasn't as great as for the younger "therapist" group. The researchers decided, on the basis of detailed observations made during the "therapy" sessions, that by getting withdrawn children to play with a younger child, they could make formerly withdrawn preschoolers show kindness and leadership, two characteristics they hadn't displayed before.

Popular and unpopular elementary school children behave in very different ways. When joining a play group, unpopular children tend to ask questions, say something irrelevant about themselves, or state their feelings. Says one researcher, they "seem to try to exert control and divert the group's attention to themselves, rather than attempt to integrate themselves into the ongoing conversation of the group. They introduce new conversational topics abruptly and direct the conversation to themselves. . . ." When unpopular children use these strategies, they almost always get rejected.

Here is an example of an unpopular child, four-year-old Carl, trying unsuccessfully to join a game. (Not only is he inept, but he further alienates the boys he wants to befriend by threatening to call the teacher.)

> ALLEN: We're policemen. We're rounding up muggers and puttin' 'em in here (a jail made of large blocks).
>
> BRIAN: Yeah, we have the keys. We lock up the muggers so they can't get in trouble.
>
> CARL: (Just arriving.) I've got a new shirt . . . Look at my new shirt. Can I play? I can be a policeman, too.
>
> BRIAN: No! Get out! You're not our friend today.
>
> CARL: Let me play. I wanna play! I'm going to tell the teacher.
>
> ALLEN: Come on, Brian. Let's get in our car and look for muggers. (They make motor noises and ignore Carl; eventually he wanders away.)

There are remarkable similarities between unpopular children's self-focus and lack of tact (à la Carl) and the social ineptitude of lonely adults. One researcher videotaped conversations between lonely and nonlonely college students, and then compared the conversations with those between nonlonely students. The tapes revealed that the lonely students were more self-preoccupied; they seemed to focus on their own thoughts and feelings and missed conversational leads offered by their partners. In the end, the lonely people felt awkward and were convinced that their partners disliked them.

The researcher wondered whether the lonely students' poor attentional and conversational patterns could be altered by a social skills training program. Perhaps, he reasoned, lonely adults (like lonely children) don't realize they are self-focused and unresponsive. They may need advice about how to pay attention to other people's comments, how to ask follow-up questions, how to ignore their own self-consciousness.

The researcher trained several lonely male students to be more socially sensitive by explaining conversational skills, especially attentive listening, and by playing tape-recorded examples to them. The students then practiced the skills with a female partner, listened to tapes of the practice sessions, and received further advice.

Two weeks later, the researcher observed the students' behavior in a get-acquainted situation, and asked them how lonely, self-conscious, and shy they felt. The trained students were now no different from nonlonely people in their conversational style, and they felt less lonely, self-conscious, and shy. Apparently, the simple training program had worked—a promising result for lonely people of all ages.

Why Aren't All Children Popular?

Unfair as it seems, children have very different degrees of social skill. But why? One reason is that poor relations with parents or siblings set the stage for insecure or troubled relations with friends. A second possibility is that some children are just temperamentally less sociable and extroverted than others. Researchers believe that the tendency to be sociable is, to some extent, inherited. Certain infants are sociable almost from birth, smiling frequently and obviously enjoying cuddles and caresses, which encourages family members to respond warmly to them. In contrast, some infants seem uncomfortable with physical closeness. Being cuddly with them is less rewarding for family members, who learn not to be too affectionate; with experience, these children become even less socially oriented. For both kinds of children, temperament and experience reinforce each other, unless family members deliberately encourage the unsociable child to be sociable. Later in life, both types will have friends, but the unsociables probably won't have as many friends and won't enjoy large social gatherings.

Children sharpen their social skills by being with siblings and other children. It seems likely that they benefit from variety among their friends—some older, some younger, some same-sex and some opposite sex, some who share their tastes and others who don't. This raises a fourth reason why some children lack confidence. They, like adults, discriminate against each other on the basis of physical attractiveness, handicaps, race, and so on. If this tendency isn't moderated by parents and teachers, rejected children suffer. Perhaps you are one of many adults who were, for example, overweight when young. If so, you probably know how difficult it is to alter a mental model of yourself that was strongly affected by cries of "Hey, fatso!" and by always being the last one chosen for the softball team.

Just as young children learn to blame themselves when they feel ignored, abandoned, or rejected by *parents,* they are vulnerable to self-doubt when ignored or rejected by peers. Psychologist Zick Rubin noticed this while observing preschool children for a year. "Even for a five-year-old, questions of 'Why doesn't he like me?' and its common sequel, 'What's wrong with me?' are likely to arise." In one particular episode observed by Rubin, a boy named Erik became visibly upset after being rejected by his best friend. Said Rubin, "Erik's displays of sadness, hostility, and attention-seeking can be understood as reactions both to his sense of loss and to his newly aroused feelings of doubt about his own self-worth."

As rough as the childhood friendship business seems to be (at least when viewed from an adult perspective), there are reasons for believing that children's bluntness can sometimes serve a useful purpose. Rubin witnessed the following interchange:

(David and Tony are sitting together at the drawing table.)

DAVID: Do you like my drawing?
TONY: No.
DAVID: You have to like it.
TONY: I don't have to like it if I don't want to.
DAVID: Why?
TONY: I don't like it, that's why.

Rubin comments: "David is [an] overly indulged child. During the first three years of his life, he learned from his parents to expect praise for whatever he did. Tony, although he is David's closest friend, does not feel the need to indulge him to such an extent." Rubin expresses his hope that "from a series of such encounters with his friend, David will obtain a more accurate picture not only of his public appeal as an artist but also of the degree of approval he can expect from others."

Although peer rejection is rarely as potent a force as rejection by parents, since parents come first and are relied upon by young children more than friends, the child who has trouble making friends will be a lonely child, and may be more vulnerable to loneliness later in life.

Children and Solitude

Though we would obviously like to eradicate childhood loneliness and promote friendship, it doesn't follow that constant togetherness is the proper goal for children, any more than it is for adults. In Chapter 1 we distinguished between loneliness and solitude, the latter being a positive form of aloneness. We mentioned that chronically lonely adults tend to view aloneness as frightening, while nonlonely adults view it as an opportunity for relaxation and creativity. We also suggested that some forms of solitary activity—reading, writing, painting, playing a musical instrument, for example—are more beneficial than others, such as overeating, taking drugs, and passively watching television.

Most children can and should play alone creatively at times. When they do, they tend to act out, rehearse, and try to understand issues that bother them, express feelings freely, and come to terms with uncertainties and fears. As they grow older they can enjoy music and art and write stories and letters. In other words, they can learn to enjoy solitude in ways that will serve them well both in the present and later in life. They will learn to do this partly by observing parents and siblings, partly by being encouraged to pursue their own interests. If parents and siblings seem bored or anxious when they spend time alone, observant children will learn to react the same way. If other family members flip on the television set as soon as they anticipate being alone, young children will probably do the same. In this way, they learn to devalue solitude, accept televised fantasies instead of creating their own, and lean toward boredom and sad passivity when other people aren't around.

In short, "solitude skills" are just as important and just as educable as social skills, and both are buffers against loneliness all through life.

Alleviating Childhood Loneliness and Its Aftermath

On the basis of studies of childhood attachment and friendship, we can offer a few suggestions. Since almost every child loses friends, changes schools, and feels rejected from time to time, the goal cannot be to prevent loneliness entirely but to reduce its frequency, intensity, and negative side effects.

Parents should never, even in jest, threaten to abandon their children; almost always, young children will take these threats literally. When a loss occurs in your child's life, be honest about it. Don't say, "He's gone on a long trip," if in fact he will never be back. Don't say, "She's just sleeping under the ground,'' when in fact she's dead. Such deceptions, though well-intentioned, prolong the child's uncertainty and add to his or her confusion at a time when uncertainty is pure torture. Eventually, the child's hopes must be shattered, and the loneliness and disappointment will be immense.

From adults we've spoken to about childhood, we've compiled a list of horror stories—children barred from funerals so they wouldn't see a dead body, or children led to believe that father wasn't dead, just "away." Said one young man, several years after such treatment, "I kept wondering why he'd gone, why he didn't love me." Some of these people, as adults, have unusually intense and "irrational" fears of people leaving them, even when the people are merely going to work or flying to another city on business. Some have a strange fear of *others* flying, in contrast to the more common fear of flying themselves. This is one way of feeling fear of abandonment. If you have such fears, it may help to trace their roots—especially if you know they are connected with earlier losses. One loss doesn't necessarily imply another.

When children yearn and grieve for a lost loved one, don't say, "Big boys don't cry" (or the female equivalent). Actually, boys and girls who experience painful losses should cry, for the same reasons that healthy adults and infants do. Grieving is an important natural healing process for the bereaved of any age. Don't tell a child not to talk about a departed person (like a deceased or divorced parent); this merely forces the child to think the issues through in confused silence. No admonition will stop the child from thinking about lost attachments. (If as a child you were taught to suppress tears, you ought to do yourself a favor and relearn how to cry.)

Since we know that young children are likely to blame themselves when someone rejects or leaves them, we should do everything in our power to counter this tendency. Also, since a child will fear, when one parent departs, that the other is also about to leave, tell the child that the inference is mistaken. Many young children, after the death of a parent, fear that they, too, are destined to die soon. This fear can be intensified by theological discussions of how "We're all going to join Daddy in Heaven." If possible, after a divorce, both parents should assure the child of their continuing love; and the assurances should be backed up in action. Missed visitations and broken promises are much more damaging than most parents realize.

Don't hesitate to seek professional help for yourself or your children. In difficult times we can all use help; getting it is a sign of good sense, not something to be ashamed of. Many counselors and therapists specialize in divorce or widowhood, and they can be extremely helpful to you if you are a single parent. Many schools are developing support programs and discussion groups for children from divorced families. Look for such programs in your area. Mental health professionals are increasingly interested in *preventive* care; they want to help before the damage or pain gets worse. They can help make difficult transitions easier. Nonprofessional support groups, such as Parents Without Partners, can also be very helpful to you and your children. If there's no good group in your area, help start one.

What about friendship and community among children? Much of the effort has to be made by the children themselves, since many social skills are learned directly from peers in a school of hard knocks. Still, parents can encourage siblings to play together and can organize play groups and instigate cooperative play among young children. They can also model useful social skills. They can respect their older children's friendships and realize that moves from one neighborhood or city to another disrupt children's social networks just as much as adults'. Sometimes this disruption can be eased by telephone calls and visits.

If your child is handicapped or a member of a minority group and is socially isolated because of this, you may be able to help by organizing discussion or play groups among similar or sympathetic children. For example, groups have been formed all over the country for children with scoliosis (curvature of the spine). At group meetings, children air their common fears and problems and help each other emotionally while becoming more confident and self-accepting. (This is good for them for the same reasons that groups like Parents Without Partners are helpful for recently divorced adults.)

During rough periods in a child's life—developmental transitions, moves, prolonged illnesses—offer the child extra social and emotional support. You can honestly assure the child that loneliness is natural at such times, a sign that each of us has a deep need for other people; the loneliness will subside once the child recovers from the immediate problem. Meanwhile, encourage the child's own creative activities; teach him or her to appreciate periods of solitude; don't allow television to become a substitute for social life; encourage the child to rely on brothers, sisters, and friends.

If you were isolated or rejected as a child, or remember being the unaccepted new kid on the block, you might try to discover what these experiences have contributed to the way you feel in social situations today. Which uncomfortable situations bring to mind earlier parallels? Having made these connections, you can be more careful to view your own social life from an adult perspective, not through the eyes of a once-rejected child. Destructive mental models are surprisingly persistent, but fortunately, they *can* be changed.

4

Lonely Adolescence: Does It Ever End?

"I had a boyfriend during those years but I didn't like him much."—18-YEAR-OLD GIRL

"Miss Watson she kept pecking at me, and it got tiresome and lonesome. . . . I went up to my room with a piece of candle, and put it on the table. . . . I felt so lonesome I most wished I was dead. The stars were shining, and the leaves rustled in the woods ever so mournful; and I heard an owl, away off, who-whooing about somebody that was dead, and a whippowill and a dog crying about somebody that was going to die; and the wind was trying to whisper something to me, and I couldn't make out what it was, and so it made the cold shivers run over me."—HUCKLEBERRY FINN

Ours is a youth-oriented culture. Adults hide gray hair, oil away wrinkles, and wear tight jeans; teen-agers are presented in advertisements as ideals of vitality and sociability. Yet our surveys show that *adolescents and young adults are lonelier than any other age group*. In city after city, we found they were not only more lonely, but also more frequently bored, had lower self-esteem, were more dissatisfied with life, and less gratified by friendship, love, and sex.

Other studies agree. A nationally representative survey of Americans eighteen and over found that younger people were least happy, least positive about their lives, and most likely to describe life as hard. They experienced some positive feelings, most notably "excitement," but negative feelings predominated: loneliness, boredom, depression, and emotional upset. In a study of Americans at four different stages of life—high school graduation, first marriage, middle age, and preretirement—another team of psychologists found that high school seniors were the loneliest, and also the most depressed, bored, and restless. Still another study of a large group of ten- to eighteen-year-olds found that over half were lonely—a much greater proportion than in similar surveys of adults. The conclusion seems unanimous: *Adolescents and young adults are exceptionally vulnerable to loneliness.*

Adolescent feelings reverberate throughout adulthood whenever circumstances resurrect adolescent challenges: establishing a firm identity and forming new intimate attachments. If at any age we change careers, get a divorce, have a first child, move to a different community, watch children grow up and leave home, our sense of identity and security is threatened, and painful adolescent feelings may recur. In this sense, adolescence never really ends.

Separation: Second Chorus

When an infant "separates" from its parents, the distance traveled is physically minuscule but psychologically earth shattering. Being able to crawl and then walk makes the child more independent than before, although he or she frequently returns to parents for safety and emotional refueling. During the second year of life, mental maturation allows the child to distinguish between self and parents, the first small step toward becoming an individual.

Adolescent separation is a much bigger step—in fact, a quantum leap. The youth realizes that he or she has a one-way ticket to adulthood, which will probably include marriage and becoming a parent. The transition is a little like emigrating to a foreign country that you've only vaguely heard about, knowing you can never return home. The adolescent must eventually abandon a child's body, childish modes of thought, and childhood roles, including total dependence on parents. Saying good-bye to all that while learning to understand and control a new self—with new feelings, capacities, and responsibilities—requires courage and strength and gives a young person a great deal to mourn. Loss at any age triggers loneliness. Since the adolescent's psychological losses are enormous, it's no wonder teen-agers frequently feel lonely.

Just as an immigrant is likely to feel both exhilaration at the prospect of a new life and homesickness for his old country, the adolescent vacillates wildly between positive and negative emotions. According to psychoanalyst Anna Freud: "It is normal for an adolescent to behave for a considerable length of time in an inconsistent and unpredictable manner; to fight his impulses and to accept them; to ward them off successfully and to be overrun by them; to love his parents and to hate them; to revolt against them and to be dependent on them; to be deeply ashamed to acknowledge his mother before others and, unexpectedly, to desire heart-to-heart talks with her; to thrive on imitation and identification with others while searching unceasingly for his own identity."

Adolescents depend on their parents and other adult authorities even when they seem to resist their influence. Many forms of rebellion fit a pattern that psychologists call "negative dependence." Especially between the ages of twelve and fourteen, youngsters may simply do the reverse of whatever their parents tell them—an adolescent version of the two-year-old's "No!" Many try to separate by literally running away; hundreds of thousands of teen-agers do so each year, most of them between thirteen and sixteen years of age. Older adolescents are free to "run away" in a less obvious manner by going to college far from home or taking a job in a distant location. Physical distance is no guarantee of psychological independence, though; the runaway's thoughts, feelings, dreams, and activities are still likely to be focused directly or indirectly on parents.

As a lonely twenty-one-year-old divorced woman from Worcester told us: "I ran away for the first time when I was fifteen. All I could think of, really, was *getting out!!* I mean I wanted to get as far away from *them* [her parents] as $53 would take me. And I really concentrated all my energy on this. On getting away from *them*. I even did stuff I *knew* would drive them crazy if they ever found out; I hitchhiked, went home with strangers for the night, smoked pot, once I didn't wash my hair for almost three weeks. It was like at the end of every road, they were there, sort of egging me on, to do all kinds of things I actually got tired of doing after a while. It took me a couple of years to get out of it. I mean trying to get at them all the time."

Prolonged for years and involving extended economic dependence on parents, adolescence may be more difficult now than ever before. In other cultures and at earlier points in our own history, adolescence hardly existed as a stage of life. Young people moved quickly from childhood to adult responsibility—to marriage and support of a family. As late as 1890, only about five percent of fourteen- to seventeen-year olds even attended high school. By 1920, the figure was over 30 percent; in the 1950s, 80 percent; and by 1980, not only was the figure still higher, but about half went on to college, effectively postponing the onset of adulthood from thirteen to at least twenty-two.

As our culture has become more complex, adolescence has been stretched to make time for learning new skills, with the result that adolescents aren't sure whether they are children or adults, and many find that in their twenties (or even thirties) they are *still* struggling primarily with issues of identity and independence.

Adolescent Bodies and Minds

Separating from parents would be difficult enough even if nothing else were changing in the adolescent's life. But in fact, both body and mind are undergoing revolutionary changes.

A high school senior at boarding school, interviewed by journalist Maggie Scarf, said, looking back on puberty: "I was feeling pretty lousy about myself. . . . Scared, I guess. I was scared—a lot. Feeling kind of helpless about things. . . . Everybody else, the kids I knew, seemed so 'with it' . . . and I really wasn't. I can remember feeling *gross*. Like my body was gross and I was gross and I was a fat slob. Yeah, 'gross' and 'slob' are good words because that's how I really felt the whole time. And there was this *frightened* feeling, you know— because I was changing. Obviously, I was changing. I was, um, getting breasts, y'know, and I'd already gotten my period—but I guess that at home they didn't *realize* I was changing. . . . It was as if, to them, I was still a little girl."

Adolescent friendships are often disrupted by puberty. Little boys with soft skin and high-pitched voices suddenly find themselves out of sync with former chums who now have whiskered faces and hardened muscles. Girls of the same age can look either like children or young women, and the more developed ones may feel like a child in the wrong body.

In examining the results of a study that followed a group of adolescents well into adulthood, psychologist John Clausen found that the timing of physical maturity has profound social and psychological consequences. During adolescence, early-maturing boys are more poised, relaxed, good-natured, and unaffected, while late maturers are more attention-seeking and tense, and especially immature when in the presence of their parents. The early-maturing boys have high status among their junior high and high school classmates. Clausen attributes this to strong social stereotypes associated with different body types. So-called mesomorphs—those of medium weight with muscular bodies—are seen by both adults and children as athletic, aggressive, friendly, and as having leadership qualities. Endomorphs (the chubby type) and ectomorphs (the skinny type) are disdained. Having a mesomorphic build, according to Clausen, is especially important for working-class boys in the junior high years, when athletic prowess becomes publicly important. Physique and sexual maturation contribute to adolescents' emotional and social development, and thus indirectly to loneliness.

Other studies indicate that junior high students judge their late-maturing peers as less popular, more restless and bossy, less self-assured, less attractive, and less likely to be leaders. And these judgments seem to stick. A study of college students showed that those who had matured late felt more guilty, inferior, and depressed and needed more sympathy and encouragement than those who had matured early.

Another study of men in their thirties documented that early maturers (a designation made more than fifteen years before the study) were more socially and personally successful than late maturers; they had higher occupational status and were more successful in formal and informal social activities and in business-related social life. It's quite possible, then, that the prestige, self-confidence, and social skills handed to the early-maturing boys render them less vulnerable to adolescent and adult loneliness.

For girls the research findings aren't as clear: it seems that early-maturing girls may be more anxious and embarrassed than their less developed peers because of their newfound sexuality, but they also enjoy greater prestige. In Clausen's study, peers judged early-maturing girls to be more popular, friendly, and self-assured, even though subjectively, as indicated by other studies, the girls may have felt awkward and uncertain about how to handle their new appearance.

A well-endowed friend of ours recalls: "All of a sudden, in seventh grade, older boys, and even grown men driving through the neighborhood, would slow down their cars and creep along beside me when I was walking home from school. They would just stare and it really scared the hell out of me."

Some studies suggest that the girls who feel best are the ones who develop in synchrony with most of their classmates. Since various studies disagree about the effects of early and late maturation in girls, we can't be sure about the psychological effects. In any case, the psychological differences between early- and late-maturing girls diminish by late adolescence—much sooner than for boys—and so seem to have less impact on loneliness in the long run.

Several studies show that the most popular teen-agers, of both sexes, are those rated by peers as most physically attractive. This jibes with scores of studies of college students that demonstrate that more attractive students are also presumed to be nicer, more intelligent, more trustworthy, and more deserving of help. It's not farfetched to guess that good-looking adolescents have an easier time making and keeping friends. If this experience bolsters their self-image and encourages them to develop social skills, the benefits could last a lifetime. Later in life, if attractive people are less lonely than the unattractive, this could be due as much to genuine self-confidence and social know-how as to appearance.

Adolescent experiences are important partly because of their long-term effects on self-concept. We have interviewed formerly fat and once unattractive people whose social relations are still influenced by long-standing negative self-perceptions, even though today these people seem quite attractive. Many ugly-duckling teen-agers are delighted to be perceived as attractive in college or at work, but they may remain deeply uncertain about which self, the new or the old, is real. Many fear that at any moment they may return to their former (and as they see it, unlovable) selves. This is a common theme in people's dreams and fantasies. One thirty-five-year-old college teacher, now a very thin and muscular jogger, told us about a recurring dream. "I am sitting in a class—thin, as I am now— and the teacher is my old fat self. I am frightened and disgusted by him. I wake up horrified."

Adolescents' self-perceptions are powerfully affected by the attitudes and comments of their parents. We interviewed a very attractive nineteen-year-old woman in New York whose father had always led her to believe that she was ugly. She still complained of being awkward, unable to make friends, and painfully lonely. In Chapter 3 we mentioned that youngsters create mental models of self, which are expectations about future relationships. These models evolve gradually, as later experiences elaborate on earlier ones. By the time we reach adulthood, our mental models are so fortified by habit that they easily become self-fulfilling prophecies. Since loneliness is often associated with self-deprecatory mental models, reworking them is a major part of freeing oneself from loneliness.

During adolescence, childhood self-concepts (positive or negative) may receive either reinforcement ("I'll always be a reject") or disconfirmation ("All of a sudden, people really like me"). These new assumptions, whatever they are, will be incorporated into teen-agers' mental models and influence later adult relationships. If the models are negative, depicting the person as isolated or unlovable, he or she will be especially vulnerable to loneliness. If the models are positive, the person will be more adept at handling periods of transition and solitude.

Not only do mental models change subtly due to new experiences and new information, but basic thought processes themselves—the architects of the mental models—undergo a drastic transformation during adolescence. Jean Piaget, the Swiss developmental psychologist, was the first to characterize what he called the shift from "concrete operational" to "formal operational" thought. In their early years, children tend to think concretely rather than abstractly, conceiving of themselves in terms of hair color, size, favorite possessions, and the location of their house. They can't think very clearly or complexly about personality and motivation or about their own thought processes. Neither can they, Piaget discovered, think about thinking. Finally, they have trouble imagining hypothetical transformations of reality—for example, what the world would be like if everybody were honest or if everyone made the same amount of money.

In adolescence, all of this changes. For the first time, youngsters can reflect on their own thoughts and feelings and imagine how others think and feel about them. This is probably the origin of adolescents' extreme self-consciousness and conformity. They tend to believe, because their internal life has suddenly become evident to them, that everyone else can (and wants to) see through them. "He's going to know!" they say, about something that he has no way of knowing. (An adolescent girl, having worn a bra for the first time, told a psychologist friend of ours: "It was so embarrassing. Everyone *knew* I was wearing it!") By granting their imaginary audiences so much power, teen-agers feel compelled to conform to group standards: "What if they don't accept me?" It's hard for someone with fears like this to relax, trust, and have satisfying intimate relationships, especially with those mysterious aliens, the opposite sex.

This doesn't keep adolescents from trying, of course—or from claiming success. Because adolescents haven't been able to discuss adult feelings with parents, they have no way of knowing that in their earlier years most adults have had all the experiences that suddenly occupy them. "What do *you* know about love?" cries the outraged teen-ager to her mother, who twenty years before confronted her mother with the same question.

Cognitive changes are also partly responsible for teen-agers' interminable telephone conversations. "Well, how did you feel about that?" "Why did you do it?" "He thought that you thought that I thought. . . ." This kind of discussion, full of comparisons of thoughts and feelings, is beyond the mental capacity of children, but can be absolutely riveting for adolescents.

The outlandish in-group mannerisms of each new generation of teen-agers are made possible by their new-found cognitive abilities. Adolescents need to distinguish themselves from parents, just as two-year-olds distinguish, in a simpler way, between self and mother. At the same time, teens have to garner acceptance from each other, fearing that failure to conform will mean total isolation. The easiest way to accomplish both goals, separation from parents and peer acceptance, is to invent a new in-group language, a special mode of dress, and group self-conceptions. "We" are beatniks, hot rodders, hippies, punk rockers; "you" are conservative and outmoded.

We both remember observing rigid dress codes during junior high school. In Iowa during the fifties, boys who wanted approval had to slick down their hair, turn up their collars, and slide their jeans so far down that the crotch seam waggled back

and forth just above the knees. In Pennsylvania during the sixties, "conservs" were forbidden to wear white socks or bright
colors. Acceptable girls wore only black, brown, or navy blue.
Each new cohort of teen-agers inevitably invents its own set of
absurd rules.

Adolescent Self-Esteem

It's worth thinking about why loneliness is so intimately tied
to low or shaky self-esteem. For infants, self-esteem is related
to feelings of competence ("Look, I can jump high!") and
being loved by parents. As children grow older and spend more
time in school with peers, their self-esteem is more and more
dependent on peer acceptance and academic or athletic prowess. During elementary school, the tasks and activities that lead
to self-esteem are fairly continuous. School is pretty much the
same from year to year; sex and driving cars are issues for the
distant future; "playing" is still the child's main vocation.
Children's self-esteem is, therefore, fairly stable; kids generally know who they are, what they should and shouldn't do,
and how other people are likely to react to them from day to
day.

But as they enter their teens, children's self-concept and self-
esteem are vigorously shaken. The first challenge for many
twelve- and thirteen-year-olds is the transition from sixth to
seventh grade, usually entailing a move from one school to
another, exposure to many different classmates, and changes
in classroom procedures. Asking children of this age to explain
their academic, athletic, and social successes and failures, psychologists find that the teen-agers say they became terribly
confused and anxious when advancing from sixth to seventh
grade. Once-secure children suddenly feel helpless and bewildered by overwhelming changes.

Research also shows that self-esteem plummets during puberty, followed by a gradual increase over subsequent years. In a classic study of the adolescent self-image, sociologist Morris Rosenberg found that 12- to 14-year-olds had lower self-esteem than 8- to 11-year-olds. Other researchers studied a group of boys from age 15 to 23 and found that self-esteem increased significantly across that age period. Our own studies document a continued increase in self-esteem from age 18 to old age. When it comes to self-esteem, older is clearly better.

In Rosenberg's study, adolescents with low self-esteem were more emotionally vulnerable—more sensitive to criticism (becoming more deeply disturbed if laughed at, scolded, or blamed), more bothered by others' opinion of their failures, and more touchy and easily hurt. Socially, they tended to be shy, awkward, and unable to make conversation. They believed they were unlikable, lacking such desired qualities as respect, pleasantness, and popularity. The teens with low self-esteem also trusted people less than their peers with higher self-esteem did and were more detached, docile, and submissive. Not surprisingly, teen-agers who thought well of themselves participated in more clubs and organizations, were more active in student activities, and were more likely to be informal opinion leaders. (Twice as many highs as lows had been president or chairman of a group.) Adolescents with low self-esteem daydreamed more and were more concerned with personal problems, a pattern many will carry into adulthood.

According to Rosenberg, teen-agers with very low self-esteem put up a false front to convince others of their worthiness or retreat into a world of fantasy where they can imagine themselves as worthy. Both tactics interfere with friendship and intimacy, both lead to feelings of isolation and to what Rosenberg called a "fundamental feeling of loneliness." This helps explain why so many adolescents believe that no one understands them. In our surveys, more than a third of 18- to 25-year-olds, the largest proportion of any age group, said that one of their major reasons for feeling lonely was "being misunderstood."

Many of the lonely young adults we've studied seem not to have overcome their low adolescent self-esteem. In commenting on their uneasiness with people—while admitting a desperate need for them—these self-disparagers invariably make statements like this one, from a twenty-year-old woman living in Billings, Montana: "People just make me nervous. Usually when I'm with a bunch of people I'll just sit there and listen and I'll examine every one of them and what they have to say. . . . And the reason I don't like it is nobody knows I'm there. If I said a word, everybody would turn around and say, 'Who are you? Where did you come from?' They would never have known I was there all the time."

Young Love and Friendship

If adolescent relationships can lastingly affect self-image and self-esteem for some people, it's important to consider what these relationships are like.

We asked about forty college freshmen to look back on their high school romances. A few seemed to have had satisfying mutual attachments, but among the rest, two clear patterns stood out: "pining" and "pseudoattachment." Those who pined felt madly attracted to someone but were unwilling or unable to tell the person. Either they were afraid to make advances lest they be rejected, or they went out with the person but weren't able to talk openly. One eighteen-year-old boy, Ken, said "I really loved her. I thought about her all the time and imagined what we'd say to each other. But when I was with her, I couldn't be myself. She never really knew what I thought or who I was." Of course the reason she didn't really know these things is that Ken had no idea how to communicate them. Intimacy involves sharing core beliefs and feelings, revealing deep commitments, fears, and uncertainties. Ken, like most young American men, had neither the courage nor the training to communicate intimately. What he and his girl friend hadn't realized, and what takes most young adults years to discover, is that men like Ken usually need guidance in intimacy from a woman more experienced with close relationships.

The college freshmen whom we called pseudoattached were or had been "going with" someone but didn't really know or care much about the person. One eighteen-year-old, Donna (quoted at the beginning of this chapter), typifies pseudoattachment: "I had a boyfriend during those years, but I didn't like him much. . . . I needed someone to take me places, and he seemed willing, but we never really talked much about anything. I felt a lot closer to my dog than I did to him."

Other young women explicitly told us they had rejected Donna's solution to the problem of high school dating and had decided not to date at all. Said nineteen-year-old Sharon: "The guys I went out with just wanted to bed down with me and then talk to their friends about it. That wasn't what interested me, so I decided the hell with it. I'm hoping that older college men will be different."

Not all teen-age love affairs are unfulfilling, but enough are to make psychologists wonder why. Psychoanalyst Erik Erikson, writing about stages of personality development, offered one important reason. The major task of adolescence is identity formation, creating "a sense of sameness, a unity of personality . . . felt by the individual and recognized by others as having consistency over time." This involves experimentation, posturing, frequent changes in goals and imagined selves. According to Erikson, a person can't really experience mature love or sex until he or she has an identity to share intimately with another person. Also, mature intimacy requires a certain degree of commitment, and commitment isn't possible prior to identity. If a person changes drastically from week to week, there is nothing to "commit." Thus, in Erikson's theory of personality development, establishing intimacy is the task of young adults (in their twenties) who have already acquired a sense of themselves. Until then, says Erikson, all sexual relations are "of the identity-searching kind"—not a bad description of the adolescent dates Sharon and other college freshmen told us about.

Of course, lacking a firm identity and being incapable of committed intimacy doesn't prevent adolescents from experimenting with "love" and sexuality. In 1979, over half of all teen-agers in the United States—70 percent of the young men (ages 17 to 21) and 50 percent of the young women (15 to 19)—had had sexual intercourse. The risk was not only that many of the women would become pregnant (there were about one million teen-age pregnancies that year), but that even more would come away from early sexual experience confused or disappointed.

Sex without intimacy can be terribly lonely. It is also likely to be poor training for mature sexuality. Many of the adults we interviewed told us about unfortunate sexual habits they had learned early: female passivity, male premature ejaculation, quick sex rarely leading to female orgasm. Thirty-five-year-old Jack Radloff was typical: "I'm embarrassed when I look back on it. I tried to make it with every girl I dated. Most of them resisted, but I badgered some of them into it. I knew nothing about their feelings—and nothing about female sexuality. The idea was to put another notch on my gun, get another story to tell my buddies. We used to trade tales about nipple size, girls' oohs and ahs, our irresistible powers, and all that. After I got married it took my wife a long time to turn me into a human being sexually. At first, I used to think, 'Who does she think she's talking to? I'm a lot more experienced than she is.' But she turned out to be the pro after all.''

Relations between young men and women are hampered by rigid stereotypes about the way each sex is supposed to behave. In childhood, most boys and girls associate mainly with members of the same sex, a tendency that liberated parents and teachers have been helpless to change. When the two sexes begin to date during adolescence, they are like alien creatures to each other—members of previously hostile and distinct tribes. Moreover, sex-role stereotypes dictate that girls be open with their feelings and seek stable relationships, while boys are supposed to be tough, closed, and out for sexual conquest. Establishing genuine intimacy between these polar opposite roles is a challenge even for the most patient adults and is clearly beyond the reach of most adolescents.

Teen-age boys and girls also place different emphases on same-sex friendships. Girls are more anxious than boys about friendship, and their friendships are characterized by more tension, jealousy, and conflict. In a classic study of teen-agers, psychologists Elizabeth Douvan and Joseph Adelson interviewed 3,500 American boys and girls. They found that for 11- to 13-year-old girls, friendship was based on mutual activity rather than intimacy—they wanted to keep busy and cooperate but not necessarily to be close. For older, 14- to 16-year-old girls, friendships were emotional and intimate. At this age, girls spent more time with friends than with family. They demanded loyalty, trust, security, and support from friends and were desperate if they failed to get them. The 17- and 18-year-old girls were calmer about their relationships with girl friends and more secure about their boyfriends. During these years, then, girls' capacity for intimacy increases and so does their independence and self-esteem.

Boys were generally more relaxed about and distant from their friends. They wanted friends mostly for cooperation, amiability, and assistance in times of trouble. They were less interested than girls in emotional intimacy. For them, intimacy was postponed, to be learned later, if at all, in relationships with women. As anthropologist Ashley Montagu said: "It is the function of women to teach men how to be human." Women today have many other functions, of course, but teaching intimacy to men is still a major one.

Traditional sex roles, which are changing only gradually, assign task-oriented activities to men and social and emotional activities to women. This division is projected downward onto children and adolescents; boys are encouraged to compete in athletics and girls to care about feelings and friendship. As a result, studies of high school students repeatedly find that the boys with the highest self-esteem are athletes while the girls with the highest self-esteem are those who are socially popular.

Having a positive self-image, for most teen-agers, means having friends and feeling accepted, not getting straight A's. A massive study of Illinois high school students proved this point and also revealed that a majority of teen-agers felt left out of the "leading crowd." Perhaps this is one reason for most adults' memory of adolescence as an unpleasant time; studies of life satisfaction agree that adolescence is a lifetime emotional nadir. Since most adolescents don't quite know how to maintain intimate friendships, they value popularity. This is unfortunate, because popularity is, by definition, in short supply, while friendship, mutual self-disclosure, and emotional support are potentially available to everyone.

Our surveys show that loneliness is related more to intimacy than to popularity. Although young respondents (18 to 25) socialized more than people in any other age group—13 hours a week—they reported having the fewest *close* friends, and almost half considered themselves slightly, moderately, or very unhappy. A frantically busy social life is no guarantee against loneliness.

Young Adult Transitions

When Erikson's concept of "identity crisis" first became popular, it was oversimplified and taken to mean that identity crystallizes during adolescence and rarely presents a problem later on. Recent research on adult development paints a more complicated picture. Adult life, in the United States at least, entails one difficult transition after another. Surveys reveal that the major accomplishment of each decade between eighteen and fifty, at least according to what people say, is "feeling a new, firm sense of identity." It's not just that identity keeps getting clearer and stronger, but that new changes and challenges demand new aspects of identity. Young adults who have weathered the shifts from sixth to seventh grade and from junior high to high school are frequently called upon to endure the transition to college and from there to graduate school or a job. Once on the job, they may well be transferred from one city to another, move to a new job, or be fired. In each of these transition periods, the person's previous identity and security are shaken, friendships are dissolved, and new ones are needed.

In the late 1970s, two thirds of all Americans between twenty and twenty-nine years of age moved, a process which, according to our research, left them lonely for about a year after each move. Many moved in connection with getting an education, which for young adults can be a lonely process.

In a study of undergraduates at the University of Pennsylvania, psychologists found that 78 percent of the students suffered from at least one symptom of depression each year; in addition, almost half became intensely depressed. The psychologists explained that after establishing a relatively secure life by the end of high school, college students became depressed at the loss of all their close ties. Disconnected from hometown social supports, they "almost inevitably" felt lonely.

The psychologists pointed to four specific causes of "college blues": feeling excluded, feeling unloved, having no one to discuss problems with, and feeling alienated.

Psychologist Carolyn Cutrona followed the incoming freshman class at UCLA through the 1979–1980 school year. During the first few weeks of class, a large majority of freshmen felt lonely. Later in the year, Cutrona reinterviewed the now veteran freshmen and found only about one fifth of them still lonely, the rest having found new groups of friends. In trying to figure out why this minority remained lonely, Cutrona discovered that these students tended to blame their loneliness on themselves (a dangerous ploy which we will discuss later on), thus increasing their self-doubts and sad feelings. She also found that they placed their wholehearted attention on establishing a stable love relationship, to the exclusion of friendship. Apparently, they defined themselves as emotionally rather than socially isolated—as looking for love rather than friendship—but love proved more difficult to find on schedule.

When students graduate from college, the traumatic transition process repeats itself—with added pressure to make lasting commitments to a mate and a career path. Having constructed a college identity, the bewildered graduate watches a good part of it dissolve in a simple June ceremony. Many of the lonely young adults turned up by our surveys fell into this category. One single man we interviewed had gone to graduate school simply for lack of anything better to do: "I really feel lonely now, more than ever. And I feel dumb, too. I mean, I'm supposed to be grown up finally, and independent, and know what I want from life. But I feel like everybody my age except me must know what they are doing and where they are going. Sometimes I don't see the point of anything." Several told us of drifting into marriages because "it seemed like the right time to do it."

Not all dislocated young people can or wish to enter graduate school or get married. Some are prime targets for religious cults and similar groups. A psychologist interviewed over one hundred members of nine such groups, ranging in age from seventeen to thirty. The largest number, he found, had been attracted during or soon after college. Almost half of the members of such groups as Hare Krishna, Divine Light, 3HO, and Jesus People said their reasons for joining were feeling lonely, rejected, or sad; not belonging anywhere; feeling that life had no meaning and that they were drifting. Almost all of them said the psychic pluses of such organizations included a newfound sense of security and confidence, being calmer, healthier, and happier; and being able to form more rewarding friendships.

We interviewed a former cult member, Jon Schwartz, a son of a liberal Jewish couple from suburban Long Island, who had drifted out to California after graduating from college. While wandering the streets of Berkeley, Jon was asked by "a couple of nice, friendly guys" to a communal dinner. Later, he was invited to a "weekend in the country," which turned out to be a full-blown indoctrination session. "They never left me alone. They were instructed to 'love-bomb' me twenty-four hours a day, and I guess they did a pretty good job. I felt great at the time and ended up becoming a member for three years. For a while, they really seemed to have the cure for loneliness."

Solitude: Healing Splits in the Self

Solitude can be a healing experience for lonely adolescents because their central concern is to sort out new and conflicting feelings, ideas, and commitments. It seems paradoxical that aloneness is sometimes a cure for loneliness, but when loneliness stems from an insecure sense of self, relaxation, private fantasy, and reflection can be very helpful. Adolescents sometimes realize that loneliness can be mainly within themselves; it isn't always an interpersonal problem. People can be out of touch with parts of themselves. Loneliness is a subjective warning signal, telling us that we are missing something—but what we miss is not always another person; it can be lost portions of ourselves. One twenty-year-old we interviewed kept mentioning that she didn't feel "real." "I haven't felt real for the past six months," she claimed. "And I can't stand to be alone. I just can't." Another sixteen-year-old described her feelings awkwardly but characteristically: "I went through a phase of, you know, my body was here but my mind wasn't and I felt distant from everybody, but now I'm sort of back on the ground slightly, you know. I still wander off now and again, but you know, [when I was] about thirteen or fourteen, fifteen, it was really, for about three months, I just wasn't really here."

Clark Moustakas, a psychologist who has written extensively about the potential benefits of loneliness, captures well the adolescent's discovery: "To be lonely means to experience the agony of living, of being, of dying as an isolated individual or to know the beauty and joy and wonder of being alive in solitude." To an adolescent, the self in all its depth and complexity is a new, bewildering discovery; to be alone with it is both frightening and exhilarating. If the fear of loneliness (which for an adolescent may feel at times like the threat of total disintegration) is allowed to subside, as it will if one waits it out in relaxed solitude, the result can be liberating. (This is as true for adults as it is for teen-agers; see Chapter 8.) As Moustakas says, "In real solitude," which is distinct from desperate loneliness, "we are expansive, limitless, free. We do not disguise our feelings from ourselves but rather we renew contact with ourselves and discover who we are."

We asked several young adults about their teens, and learned of many forms of adolescent solitude. One man told about sitting "in a treehouse left over from childhood. I could go up there, out of sight, and listen to the breeze move through the leaves. That was my safe spot, the place where I could get my head straight. I think it had some special significance for me *because* it was my childhood hideout. When I sat in it as a teen-ager, I sort of knew I would never be a kid again. And that was part of the specialness.'' Other people said they found healing solitude in art museums, walks through a park, or even "driving aimlessly around the L.A. freeways.''

The wear and tear of social life is especially hard on teen-agers, who are, as we have seen, conflicted, confused, painfully self-conscious, and eager to conform. Being alone in a relaxed, thoughtful, or creative way can be a comfort for adolescents who have been lucky enough to learn how to do it.

Pitfalls of Adolescence and Young Adulthood

The most dangerous consequence of adolescent and young adult loneliness is suicide. In the late 1970s, suicide attempts were more common among people in their early twenties than in any other age group, and suicides among 15- to 24-year-olds rose at an unprecedented rate. Psychiatrists who treat troubled adolescents report that their most common problems are depression, conflict with parents, and feelings of inadequacy, isolation, and loneliness. All of these have something to do with the absence of adequate social bonds. In our studies, one third of people under twenty-five said they were lonely both because they had "no close friends, no one to talk to" and felt "different from everyone else, alienated.''

A 1981 press release from the American Psychological Association warned: "Parents, guardians, teachers, and others who observe teen-agers should be aware of an adolescent's unspoken cry for help. For example, parents should be concerned if their child craves social isolation and communicates infrequently. Teachers should be aware of changes in students, such as decreased motivation, declining grades, sleeping in class, and nervous habits.'' The difference between healthy solitude, on the one hand, and social isolation and infrequent communication, on the other, may be difficult to detect. The important distinction is between using solitude for renewal of vitality and using it to deepen and intensify depression and discontent.

Short of suicide, there are many ways to dull the pain of separateness and isolation. One is to use drugs or alcohol. It's difficult to know how much of adolescent drug and alcohol use is due to the drugs' emotional pain-killing properties and how much to their role in promoting feelings of oneness with a group. Studies of adolescent drug use show that drugs are used most often at social gatherings. Sociologists who studied 800 fifth- to twelfth-graders in Illinois schools found that over half of the high school students had used marijuana, most often at parties and dances or concerts and movies. When asked why they had tried grass, the students usually said ''because friends do it'' or to find out ''what drugs are like.'' Even more had tried alcohol (92 percent by the eighth grade). The sociologist attributed the growing use of drugs to a ''snowball effect,'' younger children being persuaded to smoke and drink in hopes of gaining approval and respect from older peers.

More evidence for a snowball or conformity effect was provided by an ingenious study of seventh and eighth grade students in a 2–2–2 school system (which has only two grades in each school; 7 and 8, 9 and 10, 11 and 12). They grew up more slowly (drinking, smoking, and dating less often) than similar students in a traditional 3–3 school, where ninth graders could influence them. The ninth graders, when in school only with tenth graders, actually grew up faster—smoking, drinking, dating, having sexual intercourse, and using drugs more than ninth graders did in the 3–3 school.

Although teen-age drug use shouldn't be taken lightly, we are more concerned about *solitary* drug use, which contributes to social isolation and deepens loneliness, than about occasional light drug use in groups, which simply may be a ritual element of today's adolescent communities.

Perhaps the most dangerous substitute for intimacy and community is a drug only by analogy. Television, which writer Marie Winn called the "plug-in drug," is a common palliative for loneliness. In our studies, young adults (18 to 25) were more likely than any other age group to react to loneliness by watching television. Sixty-one percent did this, compared with only 22 percent who "drink or get stoned." Peter Blos, a psychoanalyst who specializes in problems of adolescence, has concluded that many middle class youths become habituated to constant sensory stimulation—from television, loud music, and drugs—and this reduces their capacity to be alone and be introspective. In a study of Illinois high school students, the ones classified as "social failures"—those who had low social status and low self-esteem—watched television most often. In our own studies, too, young adults who thought of themselves as unattractive watched television more often than those who felt attractive. In another study of college students, psychologists found that those who had few dates watched more television, as did those who were dissatisfied with their relationships.

To us, extensive, solitary television viewing seems potentially more harmful than occasional, social marijuana smoking. Watching television is generally a substitute for social life, not a route into it. Television may take your mind off problems for a while, but in most cases the problems will be waiting when the set is turned off. Watching with a group of people— family or friends—isn't much better if no one talks about the programs or about each other's reactions to them. Silently watching television with family members isn't much different from riding a bus with a group of strangers.

The images of love, beauty, and adventure presented on television raise expectations and aggravate needs while encouraging facile or passive "solutions" to social problems, such as buying new cosmetics or riding on the Love Boat. They fit all too well into the adolescent daydreams psychoanalyst Peter Blos calls "rescue fantasies:" "If only I had a boyfriend, if only I were more confident and attractive, if only I were someone else," or "If only I had a car, more money, the powers of Superman or O. J. Simpson." Such fantasies contribute little to genuinely rewarding social relations. Becoming dependent on television as a loneliness reducer is a lot like becoming addicted to any other tranquilizing drug. Used in small doses for relaxation, it's harmless enough; used as an anesthetic for loneliness, it becomes part of a downward spiral toward greater loneliness and depression. In Chapter 8 we will talk about breaking out of this spiral.

Staving Off Youthful Loneliness

Loneliness is a natural part of adolescence and young adulthood and few young people avoid it entirely. Their goal should be not to blot it out entirely, but to cope with it effectively and learn social and solitude skills that will enhance life for years to come.

If you are the parent of a teen-ager or young adult, you can help your child in several ways. One is by being a good example of noncoercive intimacy. Be available to talk openly about problems and feelings, but don't pry, intrude, or command. Gently encourage friendship, participation in school and community activities, and keep in mind that lengthy telephone conversations, unorthodox mannerisms and clothing styles, and the need to fit in with a group of peers are all part of establishing an identity. Most adolescents, despite obvious attempts to become independent, share many values with their parents. Most side with the same political party, for example, and adopt similar religious beliefs. Notice how much you and your child have in common, not just how much you disagree.

Research shows that adolescents benefit from mature, relaxed contacts with adults. One of the best settings for this is the workplace. Teen-agers can perform valuable part-time work, be recognized for it, and learn to carry on conversations with adult customers and coworkers.

Adolescents, just like adults, want to be treated as individuals, not as members of a stereotyped group. Each one is unique and deserves unique treatment.

Don't worry too much about drug use. The vast majority of today's teen-agers experiment with alcohol and drugs but don't become addicted to or troubled by them. We both tried a range of drugs at that age, and no longer have much interest in them. Most of our friends fit the same pattern. Parental panic attacks and rash pronouncements about the hazards of drugs merely drive a child away. If a young person uses drugs or gets drunk often, or does it alone, concern is warranted.

The biggest danger in adolescence is severe depression. While some unhappiness and alienation is normal, intense and prolonged loneliness and depression are not. If your child, or a young friend, seems isolated and dejected for weeks and is losing weight and sleeping poorly, seek professional help. Long-term depression is a serious illness for which, today, we are fortunate to have cures.

If you are an adolescent or young adult, the best thing you can do for yourself is to refuse to be overcome by problems. Contrary to what some nostalgic adults may tell you, these are probably *not* the best years of your life. (This claim is usually made by adults who wish they could carry their hard-earned wisdom back in time and reinhabit a youthful body.) But it need not be a miserable time, either. We focus here on the negative side of youth because we want to understand why young people are especially lonely. But adolescents are more like adults than they are different; few are delinquents, few are full-time rebels, few fall into serious depression—contrary to stereotypes which are sometimes inadvertently strengthened by psychologists writing chapters like this one. When you do have bad days and painful experiences, maybe it will help to realize that the future will be better. Somewhere in the expanse of time before you lie the happiest days of your life. For now, accept the challenge of learning what love and friendship are about.

5

Adult Loneliness: Broken Connections

Love is something far more than desire for sexual intercourse; it is the principal means of escape from the loneliness which afflicts most men and women throughout the greater part of their lives. . . . Nature did not construct human beings to stand alone, since they cannot fulfill their biological purpose except with the help of another; and civilized people cannot fully satisfy their sexual instinct without love. Those who have never known the deep intimacy and the intense companionship of happy mutual love have missed the best thing that life has to give.—BERTRAND RUSSELL

The loneliest time in my life was in the few months right before I decided to file for divorce. Almost every night, I cried in bed next to my husband, after he fell asleep. I was so miserable! We couldn't talk at all, and he had no idea what I felt. . . . I needed someone very badly, but he just wasn't the right someone.—30 YEAR-OLD WOMAN, ONE YEAR AFTER HER DIVORCE

Americans believe that "love and marriage go together like a horse and carriage," even though no one travels that slowly anymore. Most expect marriage to banish loneliness, to meet virtually all needs for intimacy and friendship. This is just as true today as it was when almost all marriages lasted a lifetime. Today, more than a third of marriages end in divorce. Divorce is not a rejection of marriage, however, but, as historian Carl Degler put it, an excuse for the "endless pursuit of the *perfect* marriage."

Most of us are hot on the trail, but is marriage really worth all the trouble?

Benefits of Marriage

In a word, yes, at least for a while. Americans usually satisfy their strong need for intimacy within marriage. Research shows that married men and women are, in general, better off psychologically than single men and women. Among our survey respondents, married people were less lonely than the unmarried and described themselves as generally happier and healthier. Other national surveys find that married Americans are more satisfied with most aspects of their lives, happier, and more optimistic than single Americans. Among our respondents, the ones who were married and in love at the time of our survey were much less lonely than those who were married but no longer in love. Loneliest of all were people who were married but had never been in love with anyone. The issue, then, is love or intimacy, not marriage per se, but for most Americans marriage is the preferred route to intimacy.

In studying men from the Harvard classes of 1939 to 1944, now middle-aged, psychiatrist George Vaillant identified thirty men as "best outcomes" and found that all had been happily married for at least ten years. They also had close friends. Only 3 percent were in poor health, and almost none had seen a psychiatrist during the previous year. The thirty worst outcomes, on the other hand, tended to be divorced and friendless. They had made an average of 150 trips to the psychiatrist within a year, and 50 percent suffered from poor health. More than half were heavy users of alcohol or tranquilizers. Marriage and friendship, not income or profession, were the keys to health and happiness.

Other researchers asked 2,300 randomly selected adults from the Chicago area how often, if at all, they felt each of the following symptoms of depression: lack of enthusiasm, poor appetite, feeling bored or uninterested, loss of interest in sex, trouble falling or staying asleep, crying easily, feeling downhearted or blue, feeling low in energy or slowed down, feeling hopeless about the future, thinking of suicide, and feeling lonely. By this definition, married people were least depressed and the formerly married were most depressed (especially the newly separated).

Of course, simply being married doesn't automatically guarantee mental health or freedom from loneliness. A British study showed, for example, that wives who receive emotional support from their husbands are less likely to be depressed than wives who don't. Support involves appreciation of the spouse's value—what the researchers called affirmation—and affection and closeness, or intimacy. A study focusing on these two dimensions revealed that husbands who receive affirmation and intimacy from their wives are least depressed, and that affirmation is especially important for nonworking wives (probably because they can't attain it outside of marriage as easily as working husbands and wives can). The researchers measured affirmation and intimacy by asking:

> How strongly do you agree or disagree with the following statements?
>
> —My (husband/wife) appreciates me just as I am.
>
> —My (husband/wife) seems to bring out the best qualities in me.

—My marriage gives me enough opportunity to become the sort of person I'd like to be.

—I can really talk with my (husband/wife) about things that are important to me.

—My (husband/wife) is a good sexual partner.

—My (husband/wife) is affectionate toward me.

(These might be good questions to ask yourself about your own marriage or relationship.)

While the need for intimacy is universal and perhaps even innate, surprisingly it is sometimes worse to have loved and lost than never to have loved at all. Just as the loss of a family fortune can devastate a wealthy person, even if he or she then lives at what other people consider a comfortable level, so can the loss of intimacy overwhelm a newly separated or widowed person. We know that the formerly married are more likely than the married to be psychiatric patients and to commit suicide. The married also seem to be healthier and have a lower death rate than comparable unmarried people.

James Lynch, a psychologist who specializes in psychosomatic medicine, looked at statistics on premature death due to heart disease and noticed that unmarried men and women, of all races and ages, had higher death rates—in some demographic categories five times higher—than the married. He concluded that above and beyond diet, exercise, and preventive medicine, a crucial element influencing physical health and ultimate mortality is "the ability to live together" and to "maintain human relationships."

Still, we can't be sure whether disturbed or unhealthy people simply never marry or that there is a psychologically protective effect in having an intimate tie. Probably both factors influenced the findings.

Why Husbands Get More from Marriage

Although marriage usually benefits both sexes, it is slightly more rewarding for men than women. In our surveys, husbands were less lonely than wives, and single and divorced men were more lonely than single or divorced women. Women, who are more satisfied with their friendships than men, seem better able to find helpful social support after a marriage fails. They are also better equipped to live alone, having mastered more of the required skills—shopping, cooking, cleaning, and daily planning. (Most men have relied first on a mother and then on a wife to do these things for them.)

In our studies, women who lived alone were less lonely than men in the same situation. Although single men and women spend equal amounts of time alone and socializing each week, the women participate in more groups, have more close friends, and attend social, church, and civic meetings more often than men. Women were more satisfied than men with living alone and also felt better about the number and kinds of friends they had. Finally, the women were more sexually satisfied than the men, even though their level of sexual activity was actually lower than the men's.

In our society, most men find intimacy only in marriage. "I didn't really realize how high the payoff was until our separation," a New York banker, thirty-six, told us. "She had made a warm little cocoon for me to come home to and hide in, but I had never noticed it. She talked to me when I needed company, soothed me when I needed comfort, and made my life *easy*. Now, I come home to a cold, empty apartment and feel so neglected, really full of self-pity. I seem to have no life left—just work and sleep. That's it, period."

Sociologist Jessie Bernard drew an enlightening distinction between "his and her marriages." "There are two marriages," she said, "in every marital union. His and hers. And his . . . is better than hers.'' Married men are mentally healthier, have fewer stress symptoms, are less often convicted of crimes, earn more, and die later than unmarried men, Bernard noted. They are also happier than single men, contrary to the stereotype of the carefree bachelor and the henpecked husband. More wives than husbands report marital frustration and dissatisfaction. They also report more marital problems, and more wives than husbands consider their marriages unhappy, regret them, and consider separation or divorce. Up-to-date studies indicate that wives still express more resentment and irritation with husbands than vice versa. Part of the reason may be that wives see themselves as shouldering most of the household and family burdens, even if they work full-time. But perhaps more important, husbands don't meet their wives' needs for intimacy as well as wives meet their husbands' needs.

Men benefit from marriage in two ways that reduce loneliness. They gain intimacy, and some valuable lessons on its importance and how to achieve it, from their wives, the intimacy experts. They also gain friendship and community, because their wives maintain ties with friends and relatives (by arranging dinner parties and family get-togethers, sending Christmas cards, and calling sick relatives). Thus, a wife provides a man with a whole range of supportive relationships, protecting him from loneliness, stress, and stress-related diseases.

Men don't provide the same benefits for their wives, at least not during the first decade or two of most marriages. Less well-trained for and attuned to intimacy, men are more likely to allow their wives to suffer from emotional isolation (perhaps without knowing it). Ill-prepared to be social directors, they also contribute less to the couple's friendships. This is why, when a marriage ends, the husband is usually less able than the wife to bounce back—unless he already has another social director in the wings. (Divorced and widowed men, on the average, remarry sooner than their female counterparts.) On the other hand, two to five times as many women as men are depressed, in part because men aren't adequate emotional companions for them.

What If You're Unmarried or Newly Single?

Being single, by itself, doesn't have to mean being lonely.

Single people who have intimate ties with others are usually no lonelier than the married. The key is learning how to obtain intimacy and friendship without a spouse. From what we've said already, it's not surprising that men have more trouble with this than women do.

Living Alone. Solitude isn't synonymous with loneliness. Most adults do some of their best thinking and relaxing when alone. Most artistic masterpieces have been created by people working in solitude. Nevertheless, living alone is associated in our surveys with loneliness, and "being alone" is the most frequently mentioned reason for feeling lonely. Why?

First of all, reactions to solitude depend on a person's *interpretation* of being alone. We know from our research that chronically lonely people interpret being alone in a negative way; for them, solitude automatically means fear, anxiety, or anger. Nonlonely people are quite different; when alone, they typically feel calm, creative, happy, and relaxed. Our studies also establish a link between fear when alone and problematic childhood attachments. People who couldn't trust or rely on their parents, or who suffered major losses during childhood are more likely, years later, to feel anxious when alone.

Second, if we exclude the newly widowed or divorced (who are usually quite lonely) from the ranks of those living alone, living alone doesn't look so bad. "Aloners" have no more stress symptoms, for example, than "togethers." "Loners" are reportedly happier than "togethers" and actually have more

friends, even though they spend more time alone. These findings are similar to sociologist Claude Fischer's. In 1977, he
and his colleagues interviewed 1,050 residents of a northern
California community to learn about their social ties. He discovered that people who live alone are *not* socially isolated. In
fact, they have more ties with friends than other people do,
although they have fewer contacts with relatives.

It's reassuring to learn that living alone isn't necessarily
harmful, because more Americans are living alone now than
ever before. In 1940, the first time the Census Bureau bothered
to check, only about 8 percent of American households contained just one person. The number rose slowly to 9 percent
in 1950; then faster, to 13 percent in 1960; to 17 percent in
1970; and to an all-time high, 22 percent, in 1980.

Historians tell us that Americans traditionally lived in large
households, not so much because several generations of the
same family lived together (few actually survived long enough
to become grandparents), but because most homes contained
boarders, servants, apprentices, and all sorts of unrelated people. Although they may not have lived harmoniously, our predecessors rarely lived alone. Now, many young people live
alone while postponing marriage, older women outlive their
spouses and live alone, and nearly half of the newly separated
and divorced split off into new, one-person households. These
days we probably have to work a little harder than Americans
did in the past to establish solid friendships, but there is no
evidence that we're failing to do this.

One reason why people who live alone may not be lonely is
simply that intimacy can be found outside of marriage. Although we often read about swinging singles and one-night
stands, research shows that sexual promiscuity is relatively rare.
Instead, most single adults (like teen-agers, as mentioned in the
previous chapter) form a series of intimate ties, or serial at-

tachments. Such relationships, as extended in time as many marriages, usually provide adequate intimacy and desired independence. If singles have close friends (and Fischer's research shows that most do), loneliness shouldn't be a major problem for them. Unlike the newly divorced people we surveyed, for example, "coming home to an empty house" doesn't seem lonely and sad to them.

One man we interviewed, Roger Solman, forty-one, is a New Yorker and a confirmed "bachelor." He is, however, on his third live-in roommate, having lived with three different women for periods ranging from two to five years. "I really feel as if I'm married now, and I did before, too. We are sexually faithful, we share income and decide on major expenses jointly. I don't see much difference between this and marriage, except that we aren't quite sure it will last forever. I think we're not sure we'll be the same people, with the same needs, forever. Since we don't want children, this situation suits us fine. But let me tell you, breaking up a relationship like this is just as painful and scary as getting a divorce."

Although perhaps based somewhat on fear of commitment, Roger's relationship seems to fulfill his and his partner's needs for intimacy. He is also involved in his community, in a number of ways, as a member of a block association and a volunteer in a recreation program for neighborhood children. In this way, as well as his work, he is "generative," in Erik Erikson's terms; he is contributing something to others and to the next generation. Having children is the most common way to do this, but not the only way by any means.

What if you're single and temporarily without a partner? People who ask us about this admit to becoming more and more distressed and anxious about their lack of intimacy as time goes by. One lonely single man asked us, on a radio call-in show, if we thought dyeing his hair would make him more attractive to women. (Obviously, we couldn't answer.) Perhaps the best advice one can offer the unattached is not to be a clinger, consciously and unremittingly on the prowl for love and romance. Concentrate instead on friendship. Making close friends requires exactly what falling in love does—trust, affection, revealing yourself, and caring very much about someone else's welfare. Having friends will cure one form of loneliness (social isolation), making you feel more secure and better about yourself, and more able to face the difficulties of finding sexual intimacy. Rarely can satisfying intimacy be attained by someone who is desperate and anxious.

Loneliness in Marriage

Just as being single doesn't preclude intimacy, being married doesn't guarantee it. One woman, married for fifteen years to a cruel and abusive alcoholic, told us of her delight at breaking out of her marriage. "I feel like a real person for the first time in my life. I'm not afraid. I do what I want! And I know exactly what that is. I never, never knew being alone could be so good."

Many people get married believing that never being alone means never having to say you're lonely. But marriage is far from lonely-proof. It doesn't insure intimacy, and an affectionless marriage can actually be lonelier than affectionless singlehood. In most troubled marriages, psychological intimacy is first to go, while daily routine—and sometimes uninspired sex—lingers on. Studies of divorced couples show that many remain together long after they have suffered an almost complete breakdown in communication and caring.

In examining relationships without intimacy, we found that people who were dissatisfied with their marriages and sex lives were particularly lonely. Almost a third of all lonely married people (about 13 percent of the married) said they were not in love. One woman wrote on our survey questionnaire: "I have spent twenty years in a loveless marriage. That was lonely! Only in the last three months have I been able to recognize and try to deal with the problem.'' She went on to say that fear—''the fear of spending the rest of my life alone''—prevented her from taking action.

Another woman solved the problem of a lonely marriage by falling in love with someone else. ''I am in a dissatisfying marriage,'' she wrote from Montana, ''but health and money make change impossible. . . . Yes, I am in love, but not with my husband. I loved him with no return for six years and finally gave up on him. My present lover and I love equally but are not in a position to do anything to change.''

Over a year later, we received another letter from this woman. She had thought for months about her answers to our survey and had been saddened by the futility and hypocrisy of her life. She had decided to leave her husband. ''I have absolutely no money now, and may even be jeopardizing my health by doing this. But I wanted to let you know that your survey really made me think about my loneliness in marriage. It was horrible! I don't know if I will marry my lover; I'm afraid that it might not work out. Still, I have been relieved of my tired old worn-out marriage. Hallelujah!''

The divorced woman we quoted at the beginning of this chapter, like many other people we interviewed, told us she had been much lonelier while married than after she was divorced, although it took some time to feel completely comfortable about her decision to leave her husband. More women probably feel this way, since they are quicker than men to notice a lack of intimacy. In our studies, twice as many married women as married men—15 percent versus 9 percent—were very lonely.

In general, then, marriage confers the benefits of intimacy on most of its participants. But when it fails, it is more like prison than paradise.

Single Again: Divorce and Widowhood

Divorce is the most important cause of adult loneliness in America. And right now the United States has the highest divorce rate in the world. Census Bureau demographers have estimated that of all marriages that women in their twenties will make, between 40 and 50 percent will end in divorce. (For those married in their thirties, the rate will be even higher.)

If half of all married Americans will go through a divorce at some time during their lives, it is important to consider how people react to marital separation and divorce, how they cope with being single parents, and how the successful ones deal with loneliness and form new attachments.

Although more and more couples are divorcing, and divorce has become almost expected (indeed, in some circles it is rare to meet anyone who hasn't been divorced), its psychological repercussions can be severe. Surprising as it may seem, people's response to divorce is often very similar to reactions after the death of a spouse. Divorce, like the death of a spouse, disrupts familiar life patterns. As sociologist Peter Marris has written, both require that the "essential thread of continuity" be repaired. People grieve when they divorce although they may feel it is inappropriate or embarrassing, and their grief has to be worked through just as if they were mourning a death. Even when the recently divorced begin to reformulate their goals and evolve new meanings for their lives, the feelings they have for their former partners—usually a mixture of affection, fear, and anger—are unlikely to disappear. A newly divorced woman confessed to Robert Weiss in one of his "Seminars for the Separated": "Wednesday afternoon I had the second of two conferences with my husband and his lawyer and my lawyer and myself. At the end of the second one I told my lawyer that I was not going to do any more. In preparation for seeing him I had gotten myself as beautiful as I could. And

I felt that as long as my husband was in the room, I felt protected, and that it was just the two of us, not the lawyers. And, at midnight, I was sitting in bed, eating vegetable soup, my first meal of the day, and I wanted to call him and say, 'What a colossal mistake we've made. I only feel together when I'm with you.' "

Separated partners are likely to think about and feel impelled to make contact with their "ex." Like the newly widowed, they suffer from hyperalertness, restlessness, and feelings of fear or panic. Insomnia and loss of appetite are common. As one divorced man in his forties told Robert Weiss: "My hands are shaky. I want to call her again but I know it is no good. She'll only yell and scream. It makes me feel lousy. I have work to do but I can't do it. I can't concentrate. I want to call people up, go see them, but I'm afraid they'll see that I'm shaky. I just want to talk. I can't think about anything besides this trouble with Nina. I think I want to cry."

Many recently divorced people scan their surroundings for signs of the former spouse and some drive by the person's house "just to see if he (or she) is home." These are signs of the amazing persistence of emotional attachment. Weiss found that even men and women in deeply unhappy marriages felt anxious, even terrified, at the thought of divorce. They were sometimes moved by overwhelming anxiety to call or visit an estranged spouse for whom they consciously had felt nothing but hatred.

Simply stated, emotional attachment is stronger than romantic love. It doesn't fade quickly and can't be instantly transferred to a new person or willed away. Only time and effort, along with the establishment of a new attachment, can ease the pain of separation from someone to whom you have become emotionally attached. Robert Weiss analyzes the erosion of romantic love and the stubbornness of attachment as follows: "Even when marriages turn bad and the other components of love fade or turn into their opposites, attachment is likely to remain. . . . [It] seems, at least in many individuals, to have an imprinted quality; once a certain other has been accepted as an attachment figure, that person [continues to] elicit attachment feelings."

A woman whose divorce was recently granted put it this way: "I don't understand myself. I don't love him. I don't even like him. I want no part of him, really. But sometimes I get so lonely for him. Even when we were making each other miserable, it mattered to him that I was there in the morning. Now I get an empty, scared feeling that nobody cares whether I live or die."

Only during the past ten years, while the divorce rate has skyrocketed, have psychologists devoted much attention to victims of divorce. They find that divorce involves losses of several kinds: emotional, social, economic, and familial. The immediate emotional impact of divorce is due to the loss of intimacy and the frustrating search for a replacement. The social consequences include the loss of a major social role—husband or wife—and, most likely, the loss of several friends. Both partners usually suffer an economic loss—usually the wife more than the husband. Finally, most fathers lose the sense of being part of a family when they give up daily contact with their children; mothers feel overburdened by having too many family chores. Taken together, these losses pack a powerful wallop and temporarily stretch many newly divorced people to their emotional limits.

In an attempt to determine the most traumatic period in the divorce process, psychologists have asked people who file for divorce if and when the following events occurred: their health was poor; they had the greatest difficulty sleeping and working; they felt the most lonely, depressed, worried, and pessimistic; they had an unwanted weight gain or loss; memory difficulty; they stopped caring about themselves, increased smoking and drinking, and felt angriest with their spouse. The most traumatic time turned out to be when couples made the final decision to divorce; next was the point of final separation. Women were particularly troubled during the predecision period—perhaps because more of them initiated divorce proceedings. Men were more troubled once the proceedings had begun.

Loneliness is one of the most pressing and excruciating problems connected with divorce. Psychologists Judith Wallerstein and Joan Kelly spent five years studying divorcing families in the San Francisco area. They interviewed parents weekly for a month and a half, when they first came for divorce counseling in 1971; then again eighteen months later; and finally, five years after the divorce. Loneliness and emotional isolation were evident from the start: "Husbands and wives had lived together as strangers for many years. . . . Communication was poor or almost nonexistent. . . . There were many cases of infidelity and an astonishing degree of sexual deprivation and loneliness." The women felt "belittled and unloved"; the men described an "incompatibility of interests, goals, and values" between them and their wives.

At the time of the first follow-up, eighteen months later, "The pervasiveness of profound loneliness among (both) men and women was striking." About 40 percent of the men and two thirds of the women described themselves as lonely; about half of them said they were "painfully so." (The relatively low proportion of lonely men may be because more men than women in this particular sample had begun extramarital love affairs before the divorce.) Eighteen months after the divorce, a substantial minority of both men and women were seriously depressed. Many were also still hurt and angry. About half were having reservations about the divorce—wondering if it had been such a good idea.

Through all phases of the study, including the period before the marriage ended officially, men dated more than women, although a quarter of the men didn't date at all during the first six months after the breakup. (Some were still closely attached to their families and friendly with their wives; others were too depressed to initiate new sexual or social relationships.) About a third of the women began active social lives right away.

Wallerstein and Kelly were surprised by the length of time most people needed to recover from divorce. After five years, only two fifths of the men and one third of the women felt the divorce was a dead issue. In fact, it was unusual to find both ex-spouses with the same sense of "psychological closure" on the divorce. One fifth still had mixed feelings about it; another fifth viewed the divorce as deplorable. In this study, women took about three years to restabilize while most men did so after about two years. (Remember, most of these women re-tained custody of the children, and many of the men already had a new partner at the time of the divorce.)

Although most psychologists believe there is no such thing as a "victimless divorce," many studies suggest women may have an advantage over their former husbands in psychological recovery. Research shows that the more social ties—with rel-atives, friends, and community—the newly divorced have, the fewer adjustment problems they suffer. And divorced women, more often than divorced men, have strong social networks— in line with their differential expertise in the field of intimacy. Asking divorced men and women if they had sought help or advice from a spouse, parent, child, relative, friend, neighbor, coworker, doctor, clergyman, counselor, lawyer, or self-help group, a psychologist found that people turned most often to friends and former spouses. Women, however, were more likely than men to speak to someone other than their spouse about their problems and more likely to speak to more than just one person. When asked who would ideally be most helpful, more men than women said their former spouse would be. Men's reticence to confide in friends may contribute to their relatively poor mental health after divorce, since for them divorce is doubly difficult. Not only have they suffered the loss of the person closest to them (as have most women), but they have also lost the person best able to help them cope with it.

In our loneliness studies, too, divorced women had more close friends than divorced men and were more satisfied with their friendships. While divorced men spent more time in singles bars than divorced women, the women participated more often in social groups, church, and cultural activities—presumably more emotionally rewarding involvements. Divorced women earned significantly less than their male counterparts and were more likely to have children living with them. Finally, divorced men were significantly more lonely than divorced women.

The conclusion from research seems unanimous: Women get along without men better than men get along without women. Surely, we all need intimate and social ties, but most women seem to have greater social resources outside of marriage than men do and are therefore better able to cope with the temporary loss of intimacy.

Although marriage usually begins with a *feeling,* "being in love," after a husband and wife have lived together for some time the two become *cognitively* and *behaviorally* intertwined in a very complex way. In a psychological sense, each makes up a large part of the other's world; their expressions and movements and joint daily routines are part of each other's "mental models" (discussed in Chapter 3). Like mother and infant, they often behave as if engaged in an intricate dance, each taking cues from the other. If one partner suddenly disappears, the other's carefully constructed mental models and dance steps—their expectations, assumptions, concerns, and rituals—are rendered obsolete.

Nevertheless, desolation due to death of a spouse is easier for most of us to comprehend than the similar postdivorce state. Since a spouse's death is usually unexpected and uncontrollable, it makes sense for the survivor to be crushed and disoriented. Couples who are divorcing, we might think, should be delighted to get rid of each other. They have typically been quarreling and hurting each other's feelings in the worst possible way. Not infrequently, both partners are exhausted and unable to argue or compromise further. Nevertheless, after a divorce, most people miss their former partner and can think of no one better to turn to, even when their difficulties are due indirectly to the divorce.

The Psychology of Mourning

Peter Marris argues that we all have an inherent psychological "conservatism," which explains the universal response to loss, whether the loss involves a person or a place. The tendency to expect the familiar and resist change is due to the stability of our mental models of social life, which contribute to social order and personal survival. We need continuity, if not complete stability, in order to cope with the demands of daily life. When a familiar model is violated, as it is with any change of home, job, or marital status, we feel stressed. Loss of an intimate attachment, the most extreme form of change, is the most stressful.

The death of a spouse is one of the most dramatic changes imaginable. John Bowlby claims that, upon suffering a loss, all psychologically healthy individuals go through four identifiable stages of mourning. The first is *numbness,* with occasional outbursts of distress and anger. This is usually short-lived, lasting several hours to a few weeks. People who have incurred a sudden, inexplicable loss are at first unable to incorporate it into their thinking. It is too discrepant from their expectations and assumptions, in addition to being emotionally painful. Gradually, however, their belief in the reality of the loss sets in, and they begin *yearning and searching* for the loved one, which can go on for months or years. This second stage of mourning includes distress, anger, restlessness, insomnia, and a preoccupation with thoughts of the loved one. Many people report having vivid dreams of the dead husband or wife; some even say they have a continuing sense of the person's presence.

In one study, done in Wales, over 200 widowers were asked to report any postbereavement hallucinations or ''sense of the presence of the dead person.'' Almost half of the bereaved had experienced hallucinations, many occurring years after the death of the spouse. Some felt only a sense of the spouse's presence, others ''heard'' the person's voice, and a few thought they had felt the person's touch. Twelve percent claimed to have spoken with the departed spouse. The survivors of the happiest and longest marriages (those with stronger and cognitively more elaborate attachments) were more likely to have these kinds of experiences. In other studies, 50 to 90 percent of widows in various cities around the world reported hallucinations of their lost husbands. Evidently, such experiences are perfectly normal.

Attachment early in life keeps infants close to their mother, and part of early attachment behavior includes searching for her in times of trouble or need. At first this means crying out, or crawling to places where she can usually be found. According to Bowlby, this response, in somewhat altered form, also occurs when adults mourn. The bereaved person cries, yearns for the return of the lost spouse, obsessively thinks about the person, hallucinates the person's presence in places where he or she was usually available, and may even cry out for the deceased like a needy child. These responses are so deeply rooted that they may occur even when we try to maintain self-control by suppressing them.

The third stage of mourning, after yearning and searching, is *disorganization and despair*. A year after their husbands' deaths, research shows, two out of three widows still think about and dream of them and their health almost always suffers. Insomnia is widespread, as are headaches, tension, anxiety, and fatigue. The widow's task, overwhelming for many, is to redefine and reorganize her life. This *reorganization* process, the fourth and final stage of mourning, may require years.

Loneliness is a regular part of normal mourning. All widows experience intense loneliness, especially at night, and it can't be completely alleviated by friends or children. Attachment to a spouse is specific, and specifically meets the need for intimacy; it cannot be replaced by more general social supports although support is very beneficial during the grieving process.

During the grieving period, even signs of depression are normal. Two British researchers convincingly demonstrated a link between loss and depression by comparing depressed female outpatients with comparable but nondepressed women living in the same borough of London. Records of the recent experiences of the depressed women revealed that most had suffered what the researchers called a "severe life event." Almost all of the "events" involved the loss of either a close friend or spouse. About two thirds of the depressed women had experienced a recent loss due to death or illness of a child or spouse, divorce or separation, or the loss of a job or home. In contrast, only 20 percent of the nondepressed women had experienced a loss. The depressed women also lacked intimate confidants, had three or more children living at home, were not employed outside the home, and were more likely than the nondepressed women to have lost a mother before the age of twelve.

People who realize that symptoms of depression are a natural consequence of loss can express their sadness openly and begin slowly to rebuild their social and emotional lives. They should expect this to take some time and be as patient with their feelings as they would be with a severe physical injury that needed to heal. This doesn't mean that mourners should do nothing but feel sorry for themselves. Going out with friends, returning to work, staying involved in the community—all are parts of recovery, too. Ultimately, only social connections bring a person out of loneliness.

Life-Sustaining Friendships

So far we have been discussing the loss or absence of intimacy, including the ways in which friends and relatives can help people recover from such losses. But friends are essential in their own right. For example, married men who rely solely on their wives get shortchanged, missing the intimacy, affection, and life-giving support of friends.

Although many have tried to define friendship precisely, few have been successful. A *Psychology Today* survey on friendship found that people value the following qualities of their friends: the ability to keep confidences, loyalty, warmth and affection, supportiveness, and frankness. In the few weeks prior to the survey, each of the respondents had had an intimate talk with a friend, asked for a favor or were asked to do one, and had shared a meal with a friend. Almost everyone believed that friendship is a form of love—three quarters said they would declare their love to a friend.

Sociologist Claude Fischer defined friendship in greater detail for his study of social networks. He asked people to name people who did any of the following:

—cared for their home when they went out of town

—talked to them about work decisions

—helped with household tasks

   —engaged in joint social activities

   —discussed spare-time activities

   —served as the respondent's fiancé(e) or best friend

   —discussed personal worries

   —gave advice which they considered when making
     important decisions

   —would loan them a large sum of money

The interviewees named an average of ten or eleven people who lived within an hour's drive.

Fischer also asked his respondents to name someone they considered a confidant, someone who provided critical emotional support and guidance, with whom they could talk about personal matters, and whose opinion they would seriously consider in making an important decision. As other studies have shown, men were more likely than women to have no confidants other than their spouses. "Wives substitute for a range of social contacts in men's lives, although husbands do not do the same for women," Fischer concluded.

Throughout life, men seem to have difficulty forming close friendships, although they often report having many "friends." Their self-deception is evident when they say this but go on to reveal dissatisfaction with both the number and quality of their friends. Part of the problem may be in men's tendency to confuse instrumental business associates with close friends. Work relationships are often based on goal orientation, self-control, and cool competitiveness—not on self-disclosure, affection, or trust, the essential building blocks of friendship. Women have traditionally learned to seek intimacy and be trusting and may therefore be better able to form mutual friendships. On the whole, men and women seem to have very different friendship-making capacities, a handicap for men that may contribute to early mortality.

These differences are obviously not a recent development. They were evident at the end of the eighteenth century, when poet Samuel Taylor Coleridge wrote: "A woman's friendship borders more closely on love than man's. Men affect each other in the reflection of noble or friendly acts, whilst women ask fewer proofs and more signs and expressions of attachments."

In his study of Harvard graduates, George Vaillant linked men's capacity for friendship to their mental health. The healthier and happier "friendly" men, he said, had lasting marriages and several close friends with whom they enjoyed regular recreation. "Lonely" men were socially and emotionally isolated and afraid of "the imagined dangers of human intimacy." One such man, when Vaillant asked him to describe his closest friend, named a war buddy he hadn't seen for fourteen years!

We've noticed two very different kinds of intimacy avoidance in men. The most common is exemplified by the popular high school athlete turned professional who enters a conventional marriage without ever learning about tenderness, deep communication of feelings, or emotional reliance on another person in times of stress. To him, this kind of intimacy is a sign of weakness. He seems happy and successful to outsiders and may have a regular set of friends with whom he plays tennis and goes fishing. As long as life is going smoothly, this kind of person functions well enough, but under severe stress—when deeper social and emotional support is needed—he begins to drink and refuses to confide in anyone. This is one route to alcoholism and, in extreme cases, to the kind of suicide that shocks neighbors and coworkers. "He was feeling so well," they say. "We just played golf with him yesterday."

The second kind of evader is more complex and less common. He badly needs affection and loyal support, and at some level he knows it. But he has been so painfully rejected in the past, often by a parent, that he doesn't trust anyone enough simply to ask for their love. Instead, he erects a formidable barrier—of vulgar language or sloppy dress and unkempt hair or cigar-smoking and drunkenness—and dares potential friends and lovers to cross it. His game, not always evident, is "If you reject me because of my rudeness or demeanor, I'll know you aren't a good bet to give me the affection I need, and I'll shrug you off as a fool with superficial standards. If you decide to brave my smokescreen and befriend me anyway, maybe I'll let you love me." Behind their self-sabotaging screens, these people can be quite lovable, but few of us are patient enough to find that out.

We've been talking primarily about men, because we believe that more men than women fear intimacy, but there are intimacy evaders among women, too, and of the same types.

Surviving and Repairing Broken Connections

If your marriage is unsatisfying, ask yourself what is wrong. Is it lack of time together? Have the two of you grown apart psychologically? Do you or your partner have trouble being intimate? Some difficulties respond well to vacations or other simple changes that discourage deadening routines and encourage relaxed discussions. Marriage workshops, encounter weekends, and various forms of counseling for couples can be very helpful, when they are led by competent professionals.

If your partner is abusive or alcoholic, or emotionally disturbed enough to require professional therapy, there are many treatment programs across the country that you can attend together. If patient, repeated efforts fail, you should ask yourself whether it might not be better to abandon this particular ship. You deserve to have your needs met, and some people simply can't meet them.

Marital disruption is stressful for everyone, and loneliness is among the most common distresses. The loss of security and love, for anyone at any age, is painful. Fortunately, it is rarely permanent. In due time, people recover and find new love.

If you are recently separated, divorced, or widowed, grief is a *natural* and *necessary* reaction. In fact, you *must* grieve. Normal mourning consists of yearning, searching, obsessively thinking about and perhaps even hallucinating the presence of your former partner. Only by living through the despair can you recover a sense of purpose and meaning and make room within yourself for new intimacy. Don't attempt to suppress lingering feelings of attachment toward your former partner. Just as you still have mixed and powerful feelings about your parents, you will always react in a special way to the presence or memory of your ex-husband or wife.

Divorced people we interviewed sometimes seemed troubled by this, thinking it meant they were disloyal to a current lover. Others just seemed puzzled by it. A woman from New York wrote on her questionnaire: "It is possible to be alone and never be lonely. It is also possible to be lonely and never be alone. Since the death of my first husband, there has been a core of loneliness within me, a void that is never filled, despite the fact that I remarried less than a year after his death." If this kind of loneliness is mild and tinged with affection as well as sorrow, it is natural. Only if it indicates incomplete mourning (as it may in this example) is it dangerous.

Divorced men seem especially vulnerable to incomplete mourning. They, more often than their ex-wives, either latch on to a new partner too quickly or race through a series of impersonal sexual encounters. What's more, because of their sex-role training, men are often poorly prepared to confide in friends and fend for themselves at home. This makes premature remarriage all too tempting. If you are in this situation, try relying more on close friends and admit that you are sometimes frightened, confused, and lonely. If discussion groups for divorced people are available in your area, consider joining one to help you through this rough period.

For some newly divorced people, living alone is the most distressing aspect of being single. If you've never lived alone before, or have a long-term fear of solitude, coming home to an empty house can be horrible. If possible, resist the temptation to tranquilize yourself with pills, alcohol, or television. Most of us, even solitary adventurers, feel frightened and uneasy when first alone, but soon the agitation subsides and leaves us feeling calm and strong.

This isn't to say you should spend all of your spare time alone. Relying on other people eases the pain of separation.

When thinking about how your marriage got off the track—and everyone who's been divorced does—don't be too hard on yourself. Like a young child, you may be prone to place too much blame on yourself. No doubt, as an adult you know that you contributed to whatever problems existed in your marriage, but you should also realize that self-castigation only adds to your pain. Self-analysis and self-improvement are fine, and you should look forward to improving yourself in the future. But there is a major difference between self-reproach and self-improvement. Give yourself the benefit of the doubt.

If you are divorced, you will probably remarry (most Americans do). There is no need to rush into it; in fact, you need time to figure out what kind of partner really suits you. If you do find yourself ready for marriage, try to hang on to realistic standards. Don't get caught up in the endless pursuit of the perfect marriage. Nothing is perfect, least of all a relationship between two mere mortals.

6

Making Contact in Old Age: The Best Years of Our Lives?

The main thing is not to let yourself get depressed in old age. After I lost my husband and my daughter, I remained for a whole year in the house. One night I sat down and took inventory. My dead loved ones wouldn't want me to live a life like that. I wasn't being true to them. So I got up and got dressed. I said, I must go out into the fold again between my people.—79-YEAR-OLD WOMAN INTERVIEWED BY BARBARA MYERHOFF

"Simpatico" is one of my favorite words. You don't need to know Spanish to understand it. If you have a simpatico friend, you know it and she knows it, and you're both happier. She shares your joys and forgives your failings. I feel very rich with so many simpatico friends. Some I seldom see, but we write and the letters are cherished. Still young at heart, but outside, 87 and counting.—ADELE ADAMS, AN 87-YEAR-OLD RESPONDENT TO OUR SURVEY

Most people assume that loneliness and old age are necessary partners. They couldn't be more mistaken.

A few years ago, in a survey study of adult psychological development, we asked people of all ages how happy they were and how happy they expected to be at each of several age periods in the future. The younger the respondents, the sooner they expected their happiness to decline (also, the earlier they thought their sexual satisfaction would decline). Many seemed to believe that life ends at forty, if not before. But older respondents were actually happier than younger ones, and they didn't expect their happiness to decline until very late in life.

Indeed, many older Americans not only "rage, rage, against the dying of the light," following poet Dylan Thomas's advice, but find themselves in one of life's most rewarding seasons. Our loneliness surveys contradict pessimistic portrayals of old age in America. In every city we studied, *loneliness declined with age,* and the same conclusion has been reached in other recent studies. People over sixty have higher self-esteem than young adults and a firmer sense of identity. They are less often bored than the young, get drunk less often, and despite the onset of chronic illnesses such as arthritis, have fewer acute health problems (colds, flu, stomach problems, headaches). In one interview after another, elderly people told us: "I'm busier now than ever before and freer to do what I like. I do repair jobs for my neighbors and relatives, go down to the beach with my friends, attend church on Sundays and Wednesday nights, and read whatever I please. I get tired quicker, and I'm a little stiff sometimes, but in most ways I'm at least the same as I was twenty to thirty years ago."

Another man, eighty-three years old, told us: "Except for high blood pressure, I couldn't be better. We were fortunate enough to have invested in land years ago when it was cheap. Now we have the money to visit our children, go with friends to Phoenix for a month in the winter, and play golf here all summer. Some of my close friends have moved or died, and I miss them terribly—I wish that I could share with them what

I'm experiencing now. But overall, I feel very grateful and happy to be here. I have a lot to do before I move on to the next life.''

An older woman wrote on her questionnaire: "I see my grandchildren every weekend, help my daughter at her store during the busy periods, and play bridge as often as I can. A gentleman friend of mine owns a boat, and we take trips around the lake when it's sunny. My church group does volunteer work at Mercy Hospital. It's a full life.''

A sixty-nine-year-old New Yorker told us: "I'm writing a family history—something my kids asked me to do. Until they were thirty, they didn't give a damn about who they were or where their family'd come from, but now, all of a sudden, they're interested. While working on this, I go down to the library and look through old newspapers and magazines, and I find out many interesting facts. Some people probably think I'm obsessed with the past; I keep bringing it up with my friends and my kids. But it's so vivid for me now, and I feel like I have a special perspective on it.''

What about all those heartrending stories of lonely, isolated older Americans living in terror? Unfortunately, such people do exist, but they constitute only a small minority of America's elderly. In one of the most extensive studies to date, psychologists interviewed 2,500 people sixty-five and older in Denmark, Great Britain, and the United States. They hoped to discover the "exact life conditions" of the elderly in industrial societies. They found, in all three countries, that "relatively few old people feel lonely often." Only 9 percent of elderly Americans said they were often lonely (7 percent of the British; 4 percent of the Danish). Fewer than 4 percent (in all three countries) lived alone and had seen no one for over a week. The researchers concluded that "much of the pessimistic and misleading speculation about the loneliness of the elderly in industrialized countries" has been quite "wide of the mark."

In studying representative samples of Americans, pollster Louis Harris found that most people dramatically overestimate the problems of the elderly. While only 12 percent of people over sixty-five complain that loneliness is a serious problem for them, a full 60 percent of younger Americans *think* it is. Over half believe that oldsters suffer a great deal from not being needed—while only 7 percent of those over sixty-five complain of this. Over a quarter of the young think the elderly don't have enough friends, but only 5 percent of the elderly agree. Ironically, most people over sixty-five believe that they are the happy exception to the sad rule of aging; 56 percent of *older* Americans feel loneliness is a serious problem for "most people over sixty-five." Thus, the elderly themselves share the widespread negative stereotype of the elderly, each happy old person believing that he or she is a rare case. Sixty-four percent of the elderly agree that "as I grow older, things seem better than I thought they would be." As one elderly man told us: "I am still the same person, but more myself. More relaxed and more grateful for the beautiful things in life."

A consequence of the popular stereotypes that old people are wrinkled, infirm, and "not all there" is that most of us expect all old people to be fairly similar. Nothing could be further from the truth. The elderly are at least as diverse as people of any other age, and probably more so. They are vastly different in education, wealth, health and physical fitness, interests, and personality. Some are married, some not. Some work until the end of life, many retire, at a variety of ages. Some depend on children for assistance, but many have children who still depend on them. Pollster Louis Harris concluded: ". . . there appears to be no such thing as the typical experience of old age, nor the typical older person. At no point in one's life does a person stop being himself and suddenly turn into an 'old person.'"

The only thing old people have in common is their age.

Why Aren't They Lonely?

The older people who replied to our surveys have more close friends than young adults do and belong to more clubs and organizations. Harris found, too, that 94 percent of those over sixty-five have close friends, and almost all of them had seen their friends in the days just before they were interviewed. He also found that one fifth of the elderly do volunteer work (church and civic activities), bringing them even more social contact. Other studies reveal that most elderly widows (about half of women over 65 are widows) know five or more of their neighbors well enough to visit frequently. In short, elderly Americans are *not* socially isolated, even though more than a third live alone. Among the older people we interviewed who lived alone, most were gracious and relaxed hosts. In their homes we were happily inundated with tea and cakes, sage advice, and fond reminiscences.

The elderly have more contact with family members than most people realize. Four of five elderly Americans have living children, and two large-scale studies recently showed that over three quarters of the elderly had seen at least one of their children during the previous week. Although the number of older people living with children has declined since the 1950s (mainly because the elderly can now afford to be independent), the proportion who live near a child has actually increased. About half live a few minutes away from a child, and a full 80 percent live within an hour's drive. Despite high mobility, then, most older Americans are not cut off from their families.

Unless or until an older person becomes ill and dependent, he or she is likely to give more help to children than they give in return. The elderly help with home repairs, housework, and childcare. Of the 75 percent of the elderly in Harris's study who had grandchildren, almost half had seen them in the past day or so; another quarter had seen their grandchildren within the past two weeks. This frequent contact suggests that the elderly are doing a lot of baby-sitting. Almost all were still giving gifts to family members, two thirds were helping out when someone was ill, and 45 percent were helping financially. Considering the increasing divorce rate, it's likely that now, more than ever before, single parents are turning to their own parents for help. In fact, divorce is creating a new kind of extended family, which provides young children with as many as four sets of grandparents.

Only 3 percent of Americans over sixty-five are childless, unmarried, and without brothers and sisters. About three quarters have at least one living brother or sister, and according to the Harris study, almost half see each other every week or so. In addition, there are cousins, nieces, nephews, and other relatives. Once again, the elderly appear to be anything but socially isolated.

Even though contact with family members is important to the elderly, when they feel lonely it is most likely because they are isolated from friends and neighbors. In a recent study of older widows, for example, those with close friends were more likely than those without to take walks, go shopping and attend meetings, religious services, and church social events. The elderly, like Americans of any age, prefer the companionship of similar-age friends to that of relatives or kinfolk. We all know that family ties are valuable, but they are given, not fully chosen; friends, on the other hand, are there because we choose them and they choose us. As one seventy-two-year-old grandmother explained it: "I know my children mean well, and I love seeing them and my grandchildren, but their visits leave me pooped out! It takes a whole day to recover! My friends live more at my pace, they like doing the things I like. All in all, and I'm a little embarrassed admitting this, I'd say I prefer talking *about* my family but talking *with* my friends." Perhaps this is why Leisure World and other such communities for the elderly are so popular and successful, despite critics' claims that age segregation is deplorable. Old people in such communities can visit or be visited by younger friends and relatives whenever they please, but most of the time they remain comfortably and safely ensconced among same-aged, likeminded peers.

Intimacy in Old Age

Many of the married elderly find themselves enjoying the deepest, most satisfying period in their marriage. Those who once feared intimacy or were too busy to explore it may now relax, let down barriers, and enjoy each other. A seventy-year-old woman told us: "In the beginning, we thought love was sex. Then, it was raising a family. Now we realize that it's always been about sharing things, helping each other, just *being there* for each other. His loyalty and support have been extremely important to me. I feel that most of our job is finished now, and we have done it pretty well. Now we can bask in success the way people do at any age when an important job is over. We feel very comfortable with each other, and very grateful. We rely on each other." A seventy-four-year-old man said: "I look at her affectionately and think, 'This is the girl I knew in 1930, the woman of 1950, now gray-haired, but still a delightful old lady!' You know, I can look at her and still see her as twenty-five, just the way I do with myself sometimes in front of the mirror. It's odd, but I feel like I'm still the same guy I was fifty years ago, except that someone has put me in this aging body. I think of Clara the same way. She used to be the belle of the ball, and no young person looking at her now realizes that. So my love for her, and my acceptance of myself, are tinged with wonder and compassion. We've been through so much together."

* * *

A group of sociologists in California interviewed over a thousand married couples from three generations of families—grandparents, parents, and grandchildren. They asked couples how often they: calmly discussed something together, were sarcastic, worked together, refused to talk, laughed together, had a stimulating exchange of ideas, disagreed about something important, became critical and belittling, had a good time together, and got angry. The young marrieds had the greatest number of positive interactions and the middle-agers the fewest; the elderly were in-between. But the young couples also had the most negative interactions while the elderly had the fewest. The researchers concluded that because honeymooners are striving for intimacy (a goal which, as we've stressed, can take years to achieve), their early married years are intense and unstable. The grandparents, on the other hand, are happy to have achieved a comfortable state of intimate companionship.

Surprising as it may seem, given the common belief that sex and lust wither with age, sexual feelings and habits don't change very much between middle and old age for married Americans. (The "married" qualifier is important since most older people, at least in this generation, confine sex to marriage.) William Masters and Virginia Johnson, the sex researchers, interviewed 157 women between the ages of fifty and eighty and found *no decline* in female sexual responsiveness. From interviews with 245 men, however, they concluded that men's responsiveness wanes somewhat with age. The most important factor in keeping sexuality alive, said Masters and Johnson, is continuing to engage in sexual intercourse. As with any other physical activity, the rule is "use it or lose it." Other studies confirm that elderly people who enjoyed sex in the past are more likely to enjoy it later in life, to be more interested in it, and to engage in it more often. As for the decline in male potency, much of it is probably due to fear, embarrassment, and unwillingness to experiment with alternatives to sexual intercourse.

Intimacy isn't limited to marriage, of course, and doesn't require sex. The elderly have a unique opportunity, because of their decreased work and family obligations, to explore close friendship in depth. They may, if they choose, be less defensive than younger adults, less worried about others' superficial opinions and rules for relationships. They have proved themselves many times over and can now relax and reflect on the meaning of it all.

We interviewed one adventurous woman who, at the age of eighty-six, formed an intimate friendship with a forty-year-old woman she had hired as a secretary. A former missionary in China, the older woman began a teaching career in India at seventy-two and remained there, at work, until her retirement at ninety-five. The woman had scores of friends—almost four hundred people attended her hundredth birthday party—but her secretary-friend was her dearest companion and closest confidant until her death at a hundred and one.

Maintaining this close friendship may have contributed to her long life. A team of psychologists interviewed elderly San Franciscans several times over a three-year period, asking: "Is there anyone in particular you confide in or talk to about yourself and your problems?" Over half (57 percent of the men and 69 percent of the women) said they had such a confidant. Those who did also felt "young" and satisfied with life, and were judged healthier by a psychiatrist working on the project.

Men's and women's confidants differed in the same way that (in Chapter 5) we said younger adults' do: Men most often confided in their wives, while women frequently chose a friend, relative, a grown child, or some combination of these. Again, we see that many husbands are not complete companions to their wives, although wives are, in their husband's opinion, sufficient. It also turns out that widowed women live just as long as their unmarried age-mates, but widowed men die much sooner than their unmarried peers. Widowers die at a normal rate only if they remarry. Having a confidant, then, may be not only psychologically important, but necessary to sustain life.

Alternatives to Marriage

Most older people who are still married, especially women (because women typically live longer than men), will eventually face widowhood. The never-married have one advantage over the married; at least they never have to suffer this terrible loss. But are older people who have never married lonely for other reasons?

A sociologist interviewed single old people in Detroit and found that although they tended to be lifelong isolates, the singles weren't especially lonely in old age, they were just as positive about their lives as the married, and even more positive than the divorced and widowed. They valued their independence and were glad not to be responsible for others.

We also interviewed several older respondents to our loneliness surveys who had never married and came to a somewhat similar conclusion: The lifelong singles were *not* lonely. We didn't find, however, that our never-marrieds were isolated. Sixty-six-year-old Flo Mack is a good example. She never married, and instead devoted most of her life to caring for her sick and elderly parents. "I concentrated all my time, money, effort, love, and tenderness on my parents," she says, without bitterness. Since the death of her father (at ninety-three), she has taken on a variety of volunteer activities. Her warmth and vitality are directed outward, and she rarely worries about herself, avoiding what she believes is the main cause of loneliness. "If you are always thinking of yourself and your interests and what you want your own way, then you'll never get out of it.''

Seventy-five-year-old Susan Poole also never married. She has been living alone for the past twenty-two years, working until her retirement eleven years ago. Deeply religious, she attends Mass every day and has been active for twenty-five years in the Legion of Mary, volunteering at hospitals and visiting old people in nursing homes. Although financially poor, she claims to have a "wealth of friends." An adamant New Yorker, she told us she often thought about returning to her native Ireland, but realized she loved New York so much "I could never be happy in any other country or any other city. It's a grand and glorious feeling to see the Statue of Liberty in the harbor.''

William Davis, a gaunt, distinguished New England gentleman, is also a lifelong single. Now retired, he has lived alone for thirty-five years but reports that he is never lonely. He is on the board of at least half a dozen commissions and historical societies and feels that "through lots of sweat and thought and labor" he has made a lasting contribution to his favorite community, Worcester, Massachusetts.

In various ways, these happy elderly people who never married have satisfied their need for intimate attachments outside of marriage. All have someone or something to care for and be committed to: parents, a faith, a community.

Imaginary Intimacy

While interviewing people for this book, especially older people, we noticed that some seem to have intimate relationships with, and care very deeply about, someone or something other than a real flesh-and-blood person. Not knowing exactly what to call this, we have chosen the controversial term "imaginary intimacy" since—different as the examples are—

they all involve mentally projecting intimate responsiveness onto some one or some thing else.

One example is a woman we've seen regularly and talked with in New York's Washington Square Park. Every day, early in the morning and late at night, she painstakingly walks her dog Sarah to the Square. She suffers from tremors and has bad feet, so it takes her a long time to get to her special bench, even though she lives only a block from the park. The trip is mainly for the dog's benefit, "so Sarah can have a change of scene."

For this woman without a family, the dog is a comfort and a source of delight. "She's the only living relative I have. . . . I'd be lost without her. She's good company. She looks you in the eye and barks. She's especially responsive and darling. It's a great experience to live with someone so sweet. How many married people can say that of their mates?"

The woman is, as she refers to herself, a "dog person." She has many friends and acquaintances, but her most intimate attachment is to her almost human-sized dog.

She understands the role the dog plays in her life. "There is an emotional gap that the dog fills. Dogs are not critical. They accept you for what you are."

Sarah is the woman's fourth poodle, probably her last. (She wouldn't reveal her age, but she is well beyond eighty and has written a will providing for the dog.) Sarah is the first female poodle the woman has had. The other three were also large black poodles, but they were males. Each lived until exactly the age of twelve and a half years, she says. For over forty years, then, her constant companion has been a large black poodle. All of her dogs have had family names; Sarah was the name of her mother.

Another example of imaginary intimacy is familiar to anyone who knows several widows or widowers. For some of them, the intimate relationship they had with their spouse never really ends. Their need for intimacy seems to be met, most of the time at any rate, by a continuing closeness to their dead spouse.

A good example appears in the following excerpt from our interview with a sixty-four-year-old, rarely lonely widow from Worcester: "He's been gone for years, but I still think about him. When I'm rearranging furniture or redecorating, I know just what he would say . . . what he would like, and I usually try to do it that way. . . . When I'm making a tough decision, I sort of . . . think for him; I imagine what he would want me to do. . . . Sometimes I have the strongest sense that he's watching me, making sure I'm all right." For many elderly people, this kind of imagined intimacy is bolstered by religious beliefs—for example, that the husband is looking down from heaven and able to intercede on his loved one's behalf.

An infant's willingness to risk separation from parents is based partly on the ability to form mental representations of them. The *image* of mother can sustain a toddler during her brief absence. Watching preschool children play, one frequently hears them whisper: "Mommy says don't do it. Mommy says be careful." The absent mom isn't really absent psychologically.

Later on, many children create imaginary playmates. One of us has a four-year-old niece who said recently, "I have a sister." (Not true.) "Her name is Sherry." (The name of a little girl who lives down the street.) For weeks after this announcement, the niece and her playmate reportedly had all kinds of exciting adventures, none of them visible to the adult observer.

Both kinds of images, the infant's of mother and the child's of an imaginary friend, are psychologically healthy. They sustain the child's feelings of security and affection when no one is present to offer the real thing. And psychologically speaking, the imagined relationship is not necessarily a pale reflection of reality nor a poor substitute for it. At a deep level, the mind knows what it lacks, and in dreams and waking fantasies it attempts to provide what is missing.

Like young children, the elderly may be especially capable of using imaginary replacements of real human attachments. They are closer to the end of life and more willing than young adults to remain single if their spouse dies. Few, at least among the contemporary elderly, are willing to have sex outside the framework of marriage, so there is no real or psychological competition for the image of the dead spouse. Also, the elderly have more time alone in which to feel the full power of imagination. Like an only child, or any of us when alone for an extended period, an elderly person has the time and absence of distraction necessary to create vivid fantasies. Finally, it is possible that the elderly are more in touch with their deep feelings and fantasies. Carl Jung claimed that only after age forty can most people allow themselves to experience all that is within them. Perhaps this is especially true for people past sixty.

The elderly's broadened capacity for intimacy—with pets, with images of deceased loved ones, and perhaps with God—may be one clue to their ability to resist loneliness.

Why Some Succumb . . .

Although we found, generally speaking, that older people were not particularly lonely, about 10 percent of our older respondents were.

Regardless of whether these lonely older people were emotionally or socially isolated, their loneliness was usually due to some kind of *loss:* recent death of a spouse, recent retirement, declining health (loss of health and vitality), or lowered standard of living (lost freedom and financial independence).

Elderly widows and widowers, just like their younger counterparts, feel lonely, anxious, and depressed for more than a year after the death of their spouse. This by itself probably explains the loneliness of most old people who are lonely. For a few, retirement may be just as devastating as widowhood, since it involves the simultaneous loss of friends, recognition, and purpose. Perhaps worst of all is the combination of poor health and low income, a circumstance which leaves many older people with few resources—especially for making friends.

Except that these problems (poor health and limited income) tend to gang up on people late in life, loneliness in old age isn't very different from loneliness at any other time. In our studies, lonely old people (as compared with their less lonely age-mates) had fewer friends, belonged to fewer groups, socialized less frequently, and spent more time watching television. They were dissatisfied with their friends and their living situations, felt they had little control over their lives, and when alone (which was often) tended to feel afraid, anxious, and angry. If this sounds familiar, it should. It is the pattern we have found typical of lonely people at every age.

Widowhood. Widowhood in old age is more painful for men than for women; in our studies, elderly widowers were lonelier than widows. Other psychologists have pointed out that men suffer more than women from widowhood because men don't know as much about caring for themselves and their homes, are less likely to move in with a child, and may be less healthy and more socially isolated than widowed women. By now it should be obvious that we believe the sex differences are also due partly to differences in men's and women's learned capacity for intimacy.

Recovery from widowhood may be easier in old age than earlier in life. In an intensive study of bereavement, a British psychiatrist concluded that the age of a widow affects the intensity of her grief, older widows being more psychologically prepared for the death of their spouse. In studying a group of London widows, he found that the older ones were less likely to consult a doctor after their husband's death and less likely to take heavy doses of sedatives.

Other psychologists interviewed widows and widowers, aged sixty to ninety-four, both before and after the deaths of their spouses and found no noticeable effects of widowhood on health, social activity, or other people's judgment of the interviewees' happiness and adjustment. The researchers attribute widows' resilience to the emotional stability they derive from deep religious faith, the fact that they make few drastic life changes after the death, and their reliance on family and friends.

While the death of a spouse late in life certainly makes elderly people feel lonely, by itself it isn't as severe a blow as one might think. Most old people, especially elderly women, expect to have to deal with widowhood and are somewhat prepared for it.

Retirement. A majority of American working men and women retire at sixty-five: only about one of every five men and one of every twelve women are still employed after that age. Remaining at work after sixty-five depends a great deal on occupation; white-collar workers and professionals have more choice in the matter and are more likely to continue working; blue-collar workers are least likely to continue, partly because they often have no choice, but also because they are glad to be rid of boring jobs. Work gives structure and meaning to most people's daily lives, provides them with recognition and companionship, and boosts their self-worth, especially for those in professional and white-collar positions.

We don't know precisely what the impact of retirement on people's feelings is. Some studies suggest that retirement is more devastating than widowhood, others that it is enjoyable. It's our impression that the negative effects of retirement are weaker now than they were several years ago, when most of the existing studies were conducted. More people in the 1980s view leisure as a deserved and gratifying reward for a lifetime of work. Also, in the past few years many books and articles have appeared about how to ease into retirement, cope with its negative features, and learn to enjoy rest and relaxation.

In our studies we found few differences between retirees and the still-employed elderly. The retired were no lonelier, were equally happy, and were just as satisfied with their marriages and sex lives, and they had a similar number of friends. They spent their leisure time actively, and devoted more hours each week than the still-employed to socializing, exercising, and participating in groups, clubs, and civic organizations. Thus, retirement, one of the few psychological strikes against the elderly according to some social scientists, seems to agree with more and more of today's elderly Americans.

Ill Health. Although fewer than 5 percent of the elderly are confined to institutions, a smaller number than most of us imagine, about a third are limited to some extent in their activities each year because of health problems. Certainly the elderly suffer more than the young from chronic and incapacitating diseases. Many studies show, however, that people's *perception* of their health is more important, psychologically, than their actual health (as judged by a doctor). In a large study of the elderly in Denmark, Great Britain, and the United States, people were categorized as "health optimists" (who seemed to ignore or downplay objectively assessed problems), "health pessimists" (who were constantly preoccupied with health problems), and "health realists" (whose assessments agreed with a physician's). The health pessimists were lonelier and less satisfied with life, in part because they underestimated the amount of activity and engagement they were capable of.

Both real and imagined or anticipated health problems can make people feel lonely. To many, illness and other signs of aging imply passivity, dependence, and loss of freedom. Especially among independence-minded Americans, the realization that you can no longer care for yourself is bound to be somewhat frightening, if not humiliating.

Poverty.   While not in the majority, there are some desperately poor elderly people in America. In 1978, 14 percent of the elderly fell below the government-established poverty line. In that year, the median income for men over sixty-five was about $5,500; for women, around $3,100. Yet the finances of old age aren't as bad as most people think. Wealth doesn't decline substantially after retirement, because of pensions, Social Security, savings, and reduced expenses. Almost three quarters of Americans over sixty-five own their own homes, and most of the homes are completely paid for. Many of the elderly exchange services with relatives and neighbors in a kind of barter economy. One older woman we know trades home-baked cookies and hand-knitted sweaters for free lawn mowing in the summer and gratis sidewalk shoveling in the winter.

Still, being old and poor is a sorry situation. One study showed that the elderly were dissatisfied only if their income was below a certain level. In our surveys, too, there was a "poverty line" below which people of every age were lonely. Thus, there seems to be a point dividing those with and those without the resources necessary to maintain an adequate social life.

Both our studies and Louis Harris's indicate that the problem for old people is poverty more than age. Poor adults of all ages are lonelier, lower in self-esteem, and less satisfied with life. Says Harris: "Poverty, not old age, creates very serious problems in people's lives and the poor young suffer just as much as the poor old, if not more."

Personality: Do We Ever Change?

In examining the effects on elderly people of factors such as poverty and illness, we kept noticing how differently people reacted to similar objective situations. Just as there are health optimists, there seem to be poverty optimists. Hazel Andrews, an eighty-seven-year-old woman, claims to live quite comfortably on less than $5,000 a year. With cheerful pride she described some of her thrift secrets: "The only way to beat the high cost of food is to make everything from scratch and walk right past the pastry, deli, and frozen-food counters. I don't know when I've bought a loaf of bread. I make all kinds. It's fun. Anyone can do it. The food value of homemade bread is far higher than the store bought; that's just high-class blotting material."

She protests: "Some folks say they have to eat pet food, their money is so little. Don't they know how many things can be bought for a dime? There's cabbage, carrots, potatoes, soup makings, Jello-O or a banana for dessert, some dumplings in hot applesauce, and many others. . . . There's always a chance to make fresh friends. You can always have some of them in for a game of whist or Scrabble or whatever. Coffee or tea is enough to serve. We all eat too much sweet stuff anyway."

Where does cheerfulness, or its opposite, bitterness, come from? Does it arise spontaneously with age or is it there all along, embedded deep in the personality?

In the Baltimore Longitudinal Study of Aging, psychologists have been studying 1,000 men and women, aged seventeen to ninety-seven, over a twenty-year period. They find that for most people, three major personality traits—*neuroticism, extroversion,* and *openness to experience*—remain the same over the lifespan. People who were anxious, hostile, depressed, impulsive, and vulnerable at twenty are very much the same at forty;

those neurotic at forty are likely still to be so at sixty, and so on. Similarly, those who were gregarious, assertive, excitement-seeking, and who felt good about themselves as young adults, felt the same in middle and old age. Those open to fantasy, artistic feelings, and new actions, ideas, and values remained so until death. In other words, the personality of an elderly person is a natural outgrowth of his or her youthful personal style. This is why, earlier in this book, we stressed the importance of learning intimacy-enhancing, loneliness-avoiding skills early in life. People who master these skills in youth are better equipped for later stages of life.

We believe that biological temperament may play a role in determining personality over the lifespan. As mentioned in Chapter 3, some infants are more sociable than others, for reasons that have nothing to do with experience. Similarly, some have pleasant dispositions while others are, from birth on, irritable and hard to comfort. Some are much more alert and active than others, and so on. Still, temperament obviously does not explain the full range of differences between people. Early experience, especially separation and rejection, plays a part, as do the accumulated ideas, habits, and chance encounters of a lifetime.

We agree with psychologist Bernice Neugarten and her colleagues who have been studying patterns of human aging for several decades: "People, as they grow old, seem to be neither at the mercy of the social environment nor at the mercy of some set of intrinsic processes—in either instance, inexorable changes that they cannot influence. On the contrary, the individual seems to continue to make his own 'impress' upon the wide range of social and biological changes. He continues to exercise choice and to select from the environment in accordance with his own long-established needs. He ages according to a pattern that has a long history and that maintains itself, with adaptation, to the end of life.'' The important thing, then, is to learn to exercise the right choices early in life.

Will We Be Lonely When We Grow Old?

All of the research discussed in this chapter has necessarily focused on a particular group of old people: those who were born around the turn of the century, were involved in World War I, raised children during the Depression and sent them into World War II, reaching retirement during the turbulent sixties. It's hard to imagine that they are typical of all people in this rapidly changing world. They didn't anticipate Social Security and most didn't expect to live as long as they actually have, thanks to improved living standards and health care. During their lifetime, sexual mores, educational standards, family structure, and the level of technology in everyday life have changed drastically. We don't know whether future studies of later birth cohorts—people born during the 1920s, 1930s, and 1940s—will come to the same conclusions about old age. But we can try to make reasonable predictions, partly because—now in our thirties—*we* are the old people of the future.

When over sixty-five, we will probably enjoy old age more than the elderly of today. We are, as a group, less work-oriented than our grandparents and more able to enjoy travel and leisure time—with which we have already had more experience than our grandparents did in a lifetime. We are more willing and able to recognize mental health problems and seek informal and professional help for them. We view receiving welfare and public assistance, when necessary, as more socially acceptable than the elderly of today. Also, our health as old people (forty or fifty years from now) will probably be much improved, as will our economic security (barring a national economic disaster). In our cohort, sexual activity started earlier, intercourse is more frequent outside of marriage, and there is greater openness about sexual diversity. Quite conceivably, when we reach old age we will be more willing to experiment sexually—even if we are widowed—and thus counter any natural tendency toward sexual decline.

We are a large group, part of the postwar baby boom, and will constitute a huge percentage of the population when we reach sixty-five. We cut our political teeth on human rights and antiwar movements. If, in 2020, our rights as old people are threatened, we will organize and fight to protect ourselves. The hippies and protesters of the 1960s will be the Gray Panther activists of the 2020s.

All of this suggests, contrary to doomsday prophecies, that we will be even less lonely than today's elderly, who, as we have shown, are doing quite well in their own right. Pessimists be damned!

What If You Are Old and Lonely?

Every contented old person we interviewed had a similar philosophy: Be active, don't wallow in self-pity, help others. Their punchline was always "Get Involved!" Our favorite older woman, Hazel Andrews, gave us a copy of an article she wrote for *The New York Times* castigating her age-mates for failing to enrich their own lives:

> . . . How come they're so lonely? Did they live 65 years and not make many friends? Relatives may die or move away but there's always a chance to make fresh friends.
>
> I worked on a farm for sixty years and now live in a small apartment in a state-sponsored housing development for the elderly. I truly love it here. Never had it so easy and my life is very full and rich. . . .

For exercise, I can take walks around the sidewalks here and stop to talk with as many folks as I wish. I attend two Bible-study classes a week. I'm secretary of the local garden club, devotions chairman at a church women's group.

I have two girls and two boys living in nearby towns. One girl calls me each morning and we chat for perhaps fifteen minutes. The other calls at night when she gets home from work. I feel very cherished, being checked twice a day.

Hazel has the optimistic, look-at-the-bright-side personal style we discussed earlier. That style is clearly ideal: for the elderly, because optimism improves the quality of life and increases longevity; for the young and middle-aged, because they might be able to incorporate this healthy approach into their personalities before reaching old age. It's an effort that pays off a hundredfold: Every person who meets Hazel Andrews, including us, feels better for it.

For older people looking for creative solutions to the problems of single living there are a host of new approaches. One organization, Housing Alternatives for Seniors (in Los Angeles), for example, helps old people find roommates so that they can live more cheaply and comfortably. As one of the participants in the program remarked: "Getting old isn't easy, but it can be a lot of fun if you have a nice roommate." A New York organization, Foster Grandparents, pairs troublesome teen-agers with paid older companions. The participants, quoted in a newspaper article about the program, said they felt needed and loved in ways that prevented them from feeling lonely. Elderhostel is a growing national program which sponsors the elderly during brief educational stays on college campuses. The program has been a huge success and is growing yearly. The demand from elderly applicants has been overwhelming.

In talking with older people who were reluctant to reach out and get involved, we have sometimes seen them hesitate because they were afraid of being embarrassed or rejected—fears similar to those of socially insecure adolescents. Some older people aren't certain about the acceptability of their wardrobe, the reliability of their dentures, or their need for people to speak up in their presence. In every case, we thought the person looked fine and was well worth speaking louder for. Care in grooming and interest in friendship shows through such minor external flaws.

The elderly have something else in common with adolescents, this time an advantage. They have uncluttered time to experience their perceptions and feelings fully, since they aren't distracted constantly by rush-hour driving, work, or caring for young children. They can come to terms with themselves and their histories, feel their wholeness, experience what Erik Erikson called the *integrity* of old age. At the same time, old age can be intense, like no period since adolescence, because in an absolute sense, time *is* running out.

In a book about the elderly, anthropologist Barbara Myerhoff described the intense determination of Jacob Kovitz, ninety-five, to finish his second autobiography before he died. In it, he wrote: ". . . pick up your pen, don't be lazy, for time runs too swiftly while we humans fall behind. There is a saying in Hebrew, 'The day is short and the work is long.' So, I will begin my work now, and I hope the Angel of Death will allow me to complete my work before he performs his."

7

The Quest for Friendship
and Community

Dear Friend:

   . . . Building one family of man under God is an exciting adventure. . . . Individuals find fresh hope and purpose in life. Families discover new ways to be united in love. And the barriers between races and nationalities disappear as people find true brotherhood in the family of God. . . .—REV. SUN MYUNG MOON, IN A NATIONWIDE PROMOTIONAL CAMPAIGN

Join us in Shady Glen, a friendly, relaxed, secure community where you and your family can recapture the charm of small-town life.—ADVERTISEMENT FOR A SUBURBAN CONDOMINIUM COMPLEX

Honest men esteem and value nothing so much in this world as a real friend. Such a one is as it were another self, to whom we impart our most secret thoughts, who partakes our joy, and comforts us in our affliction; add to this that his company is an everlasting pleasure to us.—BIDIPAI, FOURTH CENTURY B.C.

We all long for and need community; a network of friendships and engaging social activities. Being part of a community is probably harder today than in the past, just as family stability is less certain. But much evidence attests that community is still attainable, so no one need passively accept the loneliness of social isolation.

When most Americans yearn for community they conjure up two images from the past: the extended family and the small town. Both are nostalgic fantasies, not something most of us have ever experienced. Seen through rose-colored glasses, the American family is something like TV's portrait of the Waltons: a large, multigenerational, closely knit rural haven for its members. This is obviously very different from most real families, which comprise only one or two children and perhaps only one parent, living in a small house, condominium, or apartment. In our rose-tinted imagination, the ideal family is always sitting down to enjoy a harmonious, bountiful holiday dinner. They suffer from a few minor conflicts and tensions perhaps—children's mental and physical growing pains, competition for one another's love—but their problems are always resolved—for the better. Every family member, according to the ideal, knows that he or she is loved and valued; everyone has a place.

Having a place and being acknowledged or affirmed is also at the center of our nostalgia for life in a turn-of-the-century small town. We imagine being known and appreciated; strolling past people on Main Street, smiling warmly, greeting each other by name. This is the antithesis of what most of us really experience: being jostled in shopping malls and city streets by strangers who couldn't care less who we are.

Frankly, we are suckers for the nostalgia of small-town life, and advertisers cater to this vulnerability to sell us everything from religion to housing to Country Time Lemonade. We interpret the labels "old-fashioned" and "down home" as synonyms for "good." Clearly, we long for something we think we see in that way of life—not outhouses or rampant childhood disease or crushing conformity—but an essential sense of togetherness and belonging that many of us lack in our own lives.

The advertisements reveal only one side of a basic American conflict. Although we sometimes yearn for life in a mythical small town, we also want immediate access to major airports, fashionable clothes, and live entertainment. We sigh at the thought of friendly, family-owned corner stores, but shop in sprawling discount marts and supermarkets whenever we want good prices, convenience, and a broad selection. Paradoxically, we want peace *and* excitement, community *and* independence, stability *and* change. Every time our society has had an opportunity to move away from interdependence toward individual freedom, large numbers of people have opted for freedom. When the elderly became wealthy enough to live alone instead of with children, for example, many of them chose to live alone. College students and young singles did the same.

In this chapter, rather than take the benefits of interdependence and tightly knit communities for granted, and rather than criticize life in big cities, we want to look carefully at the pluses and minuses of various forms of group life. Most of them offer ingredients essential for intimacy and friendship: a sense of meaning and belonging, a feeling of commitment and closeness, and the knowledge that we will be cared for if needed.

We begin by looking at examples of community to see what they offer to lonely people and what happens to residents when their taken-for-granted life settings are torn apart by natural disasters.

Reverend Moon's Family

The Reverend Sun Myung Moon's Unification Church, a relatively new religious organization, has captured the allegiance of thousands of young Americans. Because this is a neophyte community, deliberately designed to appeal to dissatisfied Americans, its features reveal some of what is missing in our lives.

Moon aims his recruitment pitch at teen-agers and people in their early twenties—the group that our research identified as most lonely. He sends missionaries to places where loners, newcomers, and unattached travelers are most likely to be found: public parks, shopping malls, libraries, bus and train stations, and city streets or streets near university campuses. The missionaries begin with a vague but appealing nonreligious lure: "We're trying to build a community where we can live together in joy, peace, and brotherhood." Often this is followed by an invitation to a free dinner with potential new friends.

Moon defines himself as the "father" of the Unification Church; his followers are to be "a family," repeating a common religious tradition (God the Father, the Pope as "holy father," the priest as father). Why is the family metaphor so alluring? Robert Frost gave the simplest answer when he said home is the place where, when you go there, they have to take you in. It's where, ideally, we receive recognition, unconditional love, and acceptance. It's a familiar, safe place where you can be yourself and feel loved. You can't be voted out of a family, and your right to belong is not based directly on your contribution. The family, in the words of the famous communist slogan, gives to each according to his or her needs, not to each according to ability. The family is based on loyalty and love, not on "What have you done for me lately?" In addition, family members know who you are, they are familiar with your life history, and this reinforces your sense that you actually *are* somebody—a feeling that can easily disappear when dealing with outsiders.

Moon's father image, a natural part of the family metaphor, evokes the comforting thought that someone is in charge, someone cares and knows the answers and can solve every problem. All the better if this "father" claims direct contact or kinship with God, the father of all fathers and the most powerful. The ideal father is wise and firm but loving, offering the perfect reassurance to lone youngsters adrift in a confusing, unsympathetic world.

Besides membership in a family, which appeals to some of a recruit's deepest needs, Moon's promotional literature promises: ". . . a whole new world of friends, in just one day!" "Meet new people who'd like to meet you." Friendship is part of community—having people who share with you, care about you, and include you in their activities. They can put an end to aimlessness, isolation, and confusion. Moon's literature places family and friendship in an irresistible theological framework: "The natural result of experiencing God as a parent is discovering others as true brothers and sisters."

It takes more than images, however, to assuage loneliness. Moonies must offer a totally involving communal experience for new members, one which promises to continue for a lifetime. Sociologists have studied the way Moon handles this. Newcomers are explicitly told to "participate one hundred percent" and that "no one can do anything alone." Recruits are bused to rural retreats where they spend all of their waking hours in group activities. What they sacrifice in individuality and autonomy they gain in feelings of belonging to a group. The novices are "love-bombed" (Moon's own term), forbidden to speak to other newcomers or outsiders, and very soon feel a strong sense of community and solidarity with total strangers whose theology is still a mystery. (The fact that theology comes later indicates that it is secondary to assuaging loneliness and providing a community.) The converts aren't really "brainwashed," in our opinion, although that's what many critics and horrified parents have concluded. They are simply lured by enthusiasm and affection, which to a lonely person is much more appealing than critical, objective thinking. Loneliness can be overcome by a "caring" community, even if the community has an ulterior motive. One Unification Church official said candidly: "If someone's lonely we approach them. And there are a lot of lonely people walking around."

Since loneliness can stem from either social or emotional isolation, Moon's organization, if successful, must provide intimacy as well as friendship. To some extent this is accomplished by the constant talk of "love," to some extent by the genuinely close friendships that gradually evolve between members. Beyond this, we believe that participants can avoid emotional isolation by imaginatively treating Moon and God as loving father figures. Prayer is, after all, an extremely intimate form of conversation. The person who prays, believing that God "sees all," lets down defenses and is honest in ways that are difficult to risk in conversations with real people. Although God doesn't answer directly (we assume), His thoughts on every matter are relayed by the Church, perhaps encouraging the feeling that dialogue has occurred. Also, since God is assumed to be all-wise and all-caring, the believer can interpret any outcome as "for the best."

Not every evangelical Christian group is as life-encompassing as Moon's, but their messages are remarkably similar: God loves you and will cure what ails you. Every time we published our loneliness questionnaire in a newspaper, we received (in addition to thousands of unadorned answer sheets) a pile of letters and an armload of religious tracts and pamphlets from well-meaning evangelical respondents. One Montana resident submitted a typed three-page listing of Biblical quotations and a note that asked: "Now would you like to tell me how anyone could be lonely knowing Christ as a friend and a helper and a rock?" Another Montanan, in answer to our question about how much control she had over her life, wrote: "God has control of my life. I am in control only as I submit to His leading. I receive that leading or guidance through talking with Him (prayer) and reading His Word (The Bible). I talk to God about everything. . . ." Although not sharing her theology, we agree that she has found a real cure for her loneliness.

Commitment to Community

Actually, any community, religious or not, requires faith, sacrifice, and commitment. In describing Reverend Moon's recruitment methods, we have focused on what a ready-made community can offer a lonely person. But studies of communal groups indicate that community membership, if its benefits are to last, must demand a great deal from members in return. In fact, the most important issue turns out to be not what your community can do for you but what you can do for your community. Without strong commitment from members, a community quickly disintegrates, leaving each member alone again.

America has spawned hundreds of utopian communities since 1860—experiments in social relations, so to speak—and it is now possible to draw some general conclusions about them. Sociologist Rosabeth Kanter has studied historical records to see what held these communities together and, when they failed, what caused them to fall apart. One of the most long-lived was Oneida, now known for its silverware production. Founded in the early 1800s, Oneida was based on economic communism, free love, and communal child rearing. Members, all 200 of them, considered themselves one big family.

The adults lived together in a large house that contained spacious and comfortable sitting rooms and very tiny bedrooms, a contrast designed to discourage personal isolation and exclusiveness. Oneidans considered excessive introspection sinful, and members of the commune were criticized if they failed to show "we" (as opposed to "me") spirit. An early Oneida song goes:

> *We have built us a dome*
> *On our beautiful plantation,*
> *And we all have one home,*
> *And one family relation.*

Writing songs was one of many ways in which the community celebrated itself. "Whereas people on the outside are often only vaguely aware of their membership in social communities," noted Kanter, "people who live in a utopian community explicitly know that they do belong, what the community stands for, how it is distinguished from the outside, and who else belongs."

Kanter compared nine "successful" utopian communities, each of which lasted at least thirty-three years (including the Shakers, Oneida, Harmony, and the Amana colonies), with twenty-one unsuccessful communities, all disbanded within a few years. The crucial difference, she decided, was the degree to which the group secured commitment from its members. The successful groups accomplished this through a combination of six devices: *sacrifice, investment, renunciation, communion, mortification,* and *transcendence,* most of which sound vaguely, if not distinctly, unpleasant.

Sacrifice is necessary, says Kanter, to make people feel that group membership is valuable and meaningful. The connection between value and sacrifice has been well established in psychological research: We value what we've sacrificed for. The large majority of successful communes required celibacy and abstinence from alcohol and certain foods. (Moon's converts aren't allowed sexual intercourse for up to six years after joining the Unification Church.) Invariably, the successful communities Kanter studied required a commitment of personal property and savings to the group. (Moon does, too, as do many modern religious sects.) Once in the group, then, there was no way out except through poverty.

Since individual relationships can interfere with group cohesion, couples were often seen as threats to communal groups. Sexual attachments, it was thought, would drain members of their emotional energy and divide their loyalty; even strong nuclear families were seen as harmful to the group as a whole. Many successful communities solved this problem by calling for either free love and group marriage or celibacy. Thus, all group members had similar sexual ties: all or nothing. To further insulate themselves, many groups had special names for people on the inside versus the outside, wore special uniforms, and spoke a foreign language; half of the successful groups separated parents from children at an early age. Needless to say, nonresidents weren't allowed to be members.

The sense of community, a great antidote for loneliness, is central to utopian philosophy. Members of successful communes were called upon to renounce their own attachments and replace them with "collective unity." As Kanter observed: "Connectedness, belonging, participation in a whole, mingling of the self in the group, equal opportunity to contribute and to benefit—are all part of communion." Successful communes required communal work efforts and regular group contact—members rarely had an opportunity for solitude. Persecution of the group by outsiders often contributed to their sense of community; it cut members off from the outside and gave them a feeling of special purpose and solidarity. Every successful commune Kanter studied required group labor without pay, and most excluded members of different religious and ethnic groups. Members of successful groups spent at least twelve hours a day with other members.

To emphasize the importance of the group over the individual, most successful communities resorted to mortification or humiliation. Public confession, mutual criticism, and punishment for deviance were common. On the positive side, group members often experienced a sense of transcendence, a feeling that the community was, rightly, larger and more powerful than they. Kanter noted that successful communes were frequently led by charismatic figures, often addressed as "father." The group's activities, if not directly blessed by God, were felt to be part of a greater, more powerful whole, and group norms provided the individual members with a clear role, a set of daily routines, and a firm system of beliefs.

Comprehensive communities are undoubtedly restrictive and controlling. Yet they have their benefits, as expressed in this comment by a contemporary commune member in Taos, New Mexico: "When I get up in the morning, I'm happy. I know people love me. It's really great waking up and knowing that forty-eight people love you. It gives you all sorts of energy. You're standing alone—but you're standing with forty-eight people."

This is the opposite of what many lonely people feel, as illustrated by comments we received from people who participated in our surveys: "no one needs me," "no one cares about me," "no one knows who I am."

Still, would most Americans be willing to pay the price of membership in a total community? We believe the answer—our own as well as other people's—is no.

Destruction of Community

Focusing on deliberately constructed religious and utopian communities has allowed us to discover what people are looking for in a community and how they proceed to weave a new one from whole cloth. Most people, though, are already woven into a community to some extent, one which existed long before they came into it. Sometimes people don't know what their communities do for them until the communal fabric is ripped apart, and suddenly, members become fully conscious of what they are missing.

Such was the case for the residents of Buffalo Creek, a Pennsylvania mining town devastated by flood in 1972. Most of these people, wrote Kai Erikson, a sociologist who studied the effects of the flood on survivors, had never realized what their community meant to them, how it gave their lives significance and meaning. Steeped in the Appalachian tradition of fellowship, they had been like one big "family"—again the word crops up—"held together by a common occupation, a common sense of the past, a common community, and a common feeling of belonging . . . to a defined place"—precisely the arrangement that prevents loneliness for most people.

Wilbur, a flood survivor, eloquently described his community to Erikson: "We raised our children with our neighbor's children, they was all raised up together, and if your children wasn't at my house on a weekend from Friday to Sunday, mine was at your house with your children . . . we raised them together, more or less like brothers and sisters. The whole community was that way.

"Back before this thing happened [the flood], you never went up the road or down it but what somebody was ahollering at you. I could walk down the road on a Saturday morning or a Sunday morning and people holler out their door at me, and maybe go sit down and have us a cup of coffee or a cigarette or something. And there'd be half a dozen families would just group up and stand there and talk."

Within several hours on an overcast winter day, the coal company dam burst, letting loose a 132-million-gallon "lake of black water.'' "It was not really a flood," said Erikson, "not a straight thrust of water, but a churning maelstrom of liquid and mud and debris, curling around its own center and grinding its way relentlessly into Buffalo Creek. . . . During its seventeen-mile plunge down the hollow, the flood had moved slowly, almost deliberately, but its awesome forces were turning and twisting and seething inside the advance wave so that it pulverized everything caught in its path. The mass had come out of Middle Fork armed with a million tons of solid wastes, but by the time it had passed through places like Saunders and Pardee it had added buildings and railroad ties and vehicles and every conceivable kind of projectile to its arsenal.''

After the flood, every surviving resident of Buffalo Creek suffered some form of anxiety, depression, insomnia, apathy, or a "pervasive feeling of depletion and loneliness." The men and women suffered *individual* trauma—numbness, guilt for having survived, and a loss of confidence in the natural and social order. But they also suffered *collective* trauma; according to Erikson, an almost complete loss of community. They had maintained an illusion of safety by viewing their community as a family, as a secure haven. After the disaster, with their sense of community destroyed, many survivors felt that every minor rainstorm would unleash another killer flood. One man, summing up the feeling, said he lived in a "family of fear.''

With their once-firm community bonds shattered, Buffalo Creek survivors also lost their taken-for-granted sense of reliability and familiarity. They were no longer part of a predictable, loving neighborhood. Randomly shuffled into trailer camps by the federal government, survivors from several nearby communities were robbed of whatever remained of their sense of neighborliness and trust. The crime rate rose and people began to neglect their homes and property. They felt, said Erikson, the "shock of being ripped out of a meaningful community setting." Demoralized and without a sense of connection, the Buffalo Creek "survivors" survived only physically. Psychologically, many were devastated.

Erikson believes that the destruction of the Buffalo Creek community represents, in miniature, the destruction of the social fabric suffered by all Americans in recent decades. All of us have, he claims, lost our sense of safety and security; we are living in a world without "fixed moral landmarks and established orthodoxies." Our anonymous "communities" often seem not to need or even recognize us. We live under constant apprehension, finding it difficult to trust other people, many of whom are strangers to us.

As we intend to show, however, these conditions—if they exist at all—need not spell the end of friendship and community.

Small Towns:
Caring Community or Suffocating Constraint?

As life becomes more complex and less personal and predictable than it once was, many people look back to the "good old days" when townsfolk were presumably unafraid, closely interwoven, and full of the spirit of community. As historian Richard Lingeman puts it: " 'Community' indeed meant small town to many Americans—a link to place, a sense of belonging, a network of personal, primary ties to others, homogeneity, shared values, a collective belief in each individual's worth."

In his social history of small-town America, Lingeman shows that town life wasn't quite as rosy as most of us picture it. In fact, Americans have always been rather ambivalent about their conflicting needs for community and independence. Seventeenth-century New England towns, for example, held to strong communal ideals but, quite like Reverend Moon's sect, strictly controlled their residents via community norms and severe religious values. All town residents were required to live within a half day's carriage ride of the church so that they could attend mandatory Sunday services. People lived for the town more than for themselves, and the church provided surveillance of the morals of its members to ensure that they wouldn't stray from the church's path. Regular meetings evolved so that there would be a "unified, cohesive, harmonious, peaceable town." With that, the Puritans also bequeathed the negative side of "small-townness" to us; they founded American nosiness, gossip, suspicion of outsiders, conformity, and the notion that each person's identity was totally bound up with the town's. The early settlers may not have been lonely, but they didn't have much freedom or privacy either.

According to Lingeman, the close-knit town of the Puritans was short-lived; succeeding generations wanted more independence, individualism, and their own land. When everyone was required to live near the church, towns filled up quickly and younger children (who couldn't inherit land) were forced to move on. Eighteenth-century American pioneers valued independence but were still forced to depend on others for their survival in the wilderness. Simply clearing land and building a cabin required outside help, and communal labor was the main source of socializing on the frontier. "Raisings," writes Lingeman, "eased the curse of loneliness and satisfied the hunger for amusements." A friendly demeanor was required; in the frontier towns of early America, "an eccentric loner might be tolerated, but a man who was not open, who did not proffer the bland, friendly expression of neutrality was considered potentially hostile, or at least suspicious."

As the population grew and immigrants from abroad filtered in, America spread from east to west. Entire towns were born in an afternoon, with cattle or gold the economic incentive.

Still, out of necessity, helping one's neighbor was essential for one's own survival. In the desolate and remote areas of the Great Plains, the farms, few and far between, could be terribly lonely. "The prairie farmers lived lives of lonely toil, unlivened by the social sharing, the mutual help, the common bonds of being in the same boat." The rare small towns, especially for women, were the only "antidote to loneliness." Lingeman notes that many pioneer farmers and their wives were driven to madness or suicide because they couldn't face another lonely day.

By the more sophisticated 1900s, most small towns entered an era of stability; livery stables, barbershops, and saloons provided places for people (mostly men) to congregate, shoot the breeze, and discover everything about everybody in town. For many people, town was not only home, it was the only home they had ever known. Life was sheltered and closed-minded. Bachelors and spinsters were pitied as tragic or grotesque. Says Lingeman, "In small towns, marriage was the sovereign cure for loneliness and the only approved state for men and women." The comforting, lonely-proof town, by today's standards, was intolerant, inflexible, and extremely uncomfortable for anyone who didn't conform.

During the early 1900s, many Americans began leaving the farms for the cities. In 1880, 70 percent of the population lived in rural areas or villages; in 1940 only 40 percent did, and by 1980 only 3 percent did. This movement, and the industrialization of small towns, destroyed whatever community ties existed. The few towns that retained a sense of community were those founded by homogenous settlement groups, such as the Mormons of Salt Lake City, rather than by individuals seeking economic advantages. In a 1924 study of Muncie, Indiana, for example, one out of eight wives of businessmen said they had no close friends; one of every three working men's wives had no such friends. People's sense of belonging shifted from their town to their social class or smaller groups based on background and interests. This phenomenon gradually led sociologists to the conclusion that Americans had lost their sense of community. With this loss, supposedly, came an increasing sense of loneliness and alienation.

Nevertheless, return to small-town life, even if it were possible, is probably not the answer for most of us—especially if we are to believe the small-town residents who wrote to us in connection with our survey in a Montana newspaper. "This town is cliqueish and narrow-minded. It's hard to find a good friend . . . one who shares your background, education, goals, pains, experience. In our small town we only have a movie theater about three or four months of the year. If we want to see a movie, it means driving 60 miles away. So everyone either watches the kids' sports, drinks in the bars, or plays bridge."

Her harsh conclusion: "For those who move to this town and are not on the inside, it is awesome and lonely and defeating."

Another woman, whose nearest neighbor lived nine miles away, complained: "Everybody knows everybody in the community. I hate it. People put you in a box—everybody has a box and everybody knows which one you're supposed to fit into. If you don't fit in, you're headed for gossip and misunderstanding. People cope only with the norm—no big changes, no honesty. Small towns here are big family cliques. Outsiders never make it. Lonely women are all over here—miles separate us—men can go to the bars and socialize. If you don't drink, you rarely socialize. People are lonely here," she claimed, "but they don't even know why."

In these respects, today's small town isn't much different from its stiff-necked seventeenth-century predecessors. Most people who have experienced greater freedom have no serious desire for the restrictions and constant surveillance of small-town life, nor for the tòtal immersion in a modern-day commune or religious cult. We want friendship and community, but not at too high a price.

Today's Temporary Communities

Whether out of choice or necessity, most of us don't live in small towns. Far from having to deal with the constraints and dull sameness of town life, we have to contend with bewildering choices, frequent moves, and never-ending change.

Social critics have repeatedly claimed that a high level of geographic mobility—moving, on the average, fifteen times in a lifetime—destroys Americans' sense of community and leaves them feeling unconnected and remote from others. We are, according to such critics, a nation of strangers. Actually, the truth is more complicated than most of these critics believe.

Americans have always been mobile. In the past, if land and jobs were plentiful, Americans stayed put; if not, they moved. (Prior to 1700, 50 percent of all Boston residents moved each decade, for example.) One sociologist has argued that Americans have always been relatively rootless; now they are simply freer to move when they wish, rather than being forced to do so by economic necessity. People who moved in the past were usually the most disadvantaged, those who had little choice. Now, Americans who move are better educated, on the average, than their more settled peers, and typically move for even better opportunities and advancement. Unlike highly mobile colonial Americans, who usually left friends behind forever when they moved, today's movers can keep in touch by telephone and frequent visits.

According to 1979 Census Bureau figures, about 20 percent of American families move each year, a number that has remained constant for 25 years. All of this moving is not quite as debilitating as we might think. National studies reveal that most people tend to move to places where they already have friends or relatives. Those most likely to move are in their twenties—72 percent of people 25 to 29 moved between 1975 and 1979. Still unconstrained by family ties or home ownership, young adults shift about the country until they are ready to put down roots.

In our loneliness studies, somewhat to our surprise, we found that people who moved often were no lonelier than those who didn't. This was also true for moving during childhood; the number of times a person had moved during childhood was not related to adult loneliness. Only those who had moved in the year prior to our survey were lonelier than average. Another study shows that within one year of moving into a new neighborhood, people have fewer local friends than average. But by the end of the year most have a satisfactory new contingent of friends and acquaintances.

During this difficult transition year, people typically feel lonely. But this is assuaged somewhat by frequent telephone calls to old friends and involvement with local friends and relatives. Perhaps frequent movers are adept at making transitions because they are so familiar with the necessary process of adjustment. (Studies have shown that those who move most often are best able to maintain old friendships and also form new ones.) Like other aspects of social life, moving into a new community requires skills, and these skills can be acquired and sharpened through practice.

It's encouraging to learn that repeated moving doesn't make people lastingly lonely. Still, a not inconsequential 20 percent of the population suffers a one-year adjustment period *each year!* Moreover, most of these people leave behind friends and relatives who will miss them, so the 20 percent figure underestimates the problem. To keep loneliness at a minimum, most of us need to learn how to make social and geographic transitions. Perhaps the most difficult step is acknowledging our social needs, as one southern Florida resident wrote us: "After I moved, I was lonely, sorry for myself. I had little income, I was dependent on my in-laws, and my husband was out on the road. I spent a lot of time and money on the phone, confiding in my old friends who were very far away. Then, with the help of a social worker who didn't realize what she was doing, I was inspired to get involved right here. A drastic change took place that second year. . . . I turned to the church and to the new people I'd met and learned that you can't do things alone without falling flat on your face."

Despite Americans' high mobility, a national study conducted by the Institute for Social Research revealed that most of us know seven out of ten neighbors by name and have visited, on the average, about five of them. Only 5 percent of Americans know none of their neighbors. In addition, 90 percent live near at least one household of relatives and 60 percent of those 90 percent see these relatives at least once a week.

A study in Rochester, New York, showed that residents consciously sought community and were actually more neighborly and had a greater sense of community than they had in the 1950s. They often chatted together, did each other favors, and had picnics. Another recent study revealed the changes in American social life that took place between 1957 and 1976. In 1976, people visited friends and relatives less often and belonged to fewer clubs and organizations than their counterparts in 1957, but they had just as many friends. Moreover, in 1976, many more were talking freely with friends about their problems and they relied less exclusively on their spouses and families than people had in 1957. In other words, while the quantity of social contacts decreased, the quality of the remaining contacts was higher.

The researchers, psychologists at the Institute for Social Research, found that talking out worries has beneficial effects.

People who hash out problems with friends are physically and mentally healthier, happier, less often depressed, and have higher self-esteem. A large number of studies support the idea that having friends and supportive relatives—what social scientists call a "social support network"—helps people cope with stress, illness, and bereavement.

About fifteen years ago, an elderly friend of ours lost her husband. Finding adjustment difficult, she invited a few widows over for brunch one Sunday to talk about their experiences. This small conclave, realizing their potential, invited a few more widowed acquaintances to join what they called "our weekly widows' club." Said our friend: "Some of them had been keeping their husbands' rooms and closets just the way they were before their husbands died, as monuments or shrines or something. We gave them courage to rearrange and redecorate and to look outside for a new life." Together, the women visited art museums, joined a health club, checked out local restaurants, and attended concerts and plays. Once in a while they deliberately chose to do something "crazy," like going to an interpersonal relations workshop or a holistic health conference. Not only did they work through their losses collectively, they established an active mode of living which has sustained them ever since. Today, the group meets less often, because each member has created a unique life of her own; but they still reach out to other widows in their families and neighborhoods, offering them emotional support and valuable advice. Their efforts and thousands like them demonstrate that active, motivated people *can* deliberately construct life- and health-sustaining social networks to meet their special needs.

Having a support network obviously makes people less lonely. In our studies, people with more close friends were less lonely, as were those who: saw their friends more often, knew more of their neighbors, felt they could rely on neighbors to help during an emergency, belonged to more church, social, or civic groups and frequently attended group meetings. When it comes to preventing loneliness, however, *quality counts more than quantity.* Dissatisfaction with friends and social life is a more important cause of loneliness than actual number of friends. Therefore, we should be at least as concerned with what makes for good friends as with things like the number of friends we can count or the prestige of the groups we belong to.

The beauty and tragedy of life in small-town America was that a complete set of friends and relatives—a built-in social network—was provided for, indeed foisted upon, each member of the community. We say "beauty" because little effort or choice was required, "tragedy" because if a person didn't fit into this ready-made network, life could be hell. These days, greater choice is possible, indeed usually demanded, so that friendship is more difficult. But we believe it is also potentially more rewarding.

Special Quirks of Urban Life

Most Americans are currently living in urban areas, not in quaint small towns. Many assume that metropolitan life is qualitatively different from, and worse than, life in smaller towns and that urban centers breed loneliness. What is responsible for this erroneous conclusion?

Certainly not survey data. Our studies, and questionnaire studies by other investigators, fail to find varying degrees of loneliness in small towns and cities of different sizes. There are also no differences in how many friends people have or the number of groups they join.

One possible explanation for the bad reputation of cities is that nonresidents feel uneasy and lonely when they visit. Every first-time tourist in New York, for example, can tell horror stories about intimidating-looking hoodlums, schizophrenic "bag ladies" (who collect remnants from garbage cans and live in the street), drunks and drug addicts, ugly, threatening prostitutes, beggars, muggers, and thousands of gruff, preoccupied citizens. The city appears to be a "zoo," full of strange, frightening, pitiable creatures. (Indeed, if people receive warm treatment in New York they are often shocked enough to document the phenomenon in a letter to the editor of *The New York Times.*) Of course, New York residents are aware of these features of city life, too, but they know what the visitor doesn't—that the "zoo" isn't all there is to city life.

Another reason for the negative misperception of social life in large cities is that outsiders, observing rudeness or total disregard among strangers, assume that such coldness also characterizes the way city dwellers treat their friends. But this is patently untrue. As psychologist Stanley Milgram has pointed out, those of us who live in cities must limit the number of "stimuli" we process mentally. It would be physically and psychologically impossible for us to meet every eye and smile in a friendly way to every stranger we see. City residents severely limit their social contact with strangers in order to retain emotional energy for interactions with friends. They learn to "tune out" the unpleasant aspects of city living. A friend of ours, visiting New York from Indiana, remarked: "How can you live here? There's too much to *look* at!" She hadn't mastered the art of urban tune-out.

Most urban dwellers have their own friends, favorite haunts, admired coworkers, nearby relatives, and intimate relationships—just like people who live anywhere else. As a participant in a recent study of newcomers to New York observed: "We get along very well and I really see no difference between these relationships [in the city] and the ones Nancy and I had with friends in Illinois. The difference is 'out there' in the city, not 'in here' with the people that live in the city. It's peculiar but I haven't met anyone yet who admits to living 'out there'—all say they live 'in here' with us humans. Where are the bastards from?''

The psychologists who conducted this study interviewed newcomers to New York City and a comparable group of people who had moved to a small town of 31,000 in upstate New York. They found that the private world of city friendships is just as satisfying as friendship elsewhere.

After eight months, newcomers to the two areas had the same number of good friends, about five, even though it had taken the fledgling New Yorkers a little longer to find them. The two groups were equally satisfied with their new friendships and seemed equally close. The only difference between the groups was that the New Yorkers found it a bit more difficult to establish these friendships. The reasons will be familiar to anyone who has ever moved to a large city: (1) other people seemed too busy and didn't have enough time and energy for new friends, (2) others were defensive and wary, (3) potential friends lived too far away and were hard to get to. The study showed, however, that, real as these difficulties were, they did not keep the newcomers from making new friends.

The New Yorkers paid a price for adjustment to urban life. They became "more defensive, distrustful, or callous" in dealing with strangers. On the other hand, they also became more broad-minded and more conscious of social injustice: "The whole problem of races becomes exaggerated here." "The slum areas are depressing to me." "People on the street . . . are tense. You can see it in their faces." Most of the New Yorkers also became more cognizant of people with severe problems: "panhandlers, drunks, 'crazies,' addicts, and cripples." At the same time, many enjoyed the diversity and complexity of the city and actually developed a better appreciation of close friendship: "Urban personal relationships may be more intimate, more highly valued, or more emotionally intense than relationships in nonurban settings precisely because they are juxtaposed with so many impersonal contacts.''

Attachment to Place

Most newcomers to New York City will, we suspect, come to love it as we did. The intensity, the difficulty, the contradictions between rich and poor, between barbarity and culture, are unmatched in the United States. Moreover, there is no city with larger or more glittering buildings, more easily accessible shops, good restaurants, or cultural offerings. For the hardcore resident, it's no exaggeration to say, ''I love New York!''

But wherever you live, your social life exists in some environmental context. You and your friends are part of a physical place, which, if it vanished overnight, would cause shock and grief just as the death of a loved one would.

Sociologist Claude Fischer asked people how they felt about the places where they lived. Most people gave *social* answers: they belonged where they were because of ties to work, church, and schools; or ties with particular neighbors; or ties with nearby friends and relatives. But beyond that, people were also fond of the place itself—its buildings, landscapes, and rhythms. The people who were most attached included adults with children, women who weren't working outside the home, home owners, and long-term residents. They were the people with the deepest roots and the greatest reluctance to move.

Laboratory psychological research has shown that people like familiar stimuli much more than unfamiliar ones, when everything else is held constant. For example, laboratory subjects who have been exposed many times to segments of a modern abstract painting later like that painting more than similar but unfamiliar ones. The same thing happens with experimentally familiarized Chinese ideographs, foreign words, and photographs of faces from a previously unfamiliar yearbook. All of us are aware that a new song from our favorite singer sounds a little disappointing at first, then—after repeated playing—begins to sound wonderful. It's possible to reverse this effect temporarily by listening to the song too much, but the "oldie but goodie" phenomenon illustrates the staying power of familiarity. If not heard for a long while, the song can evoke marvelously warm feelings when heard again.

Neighborhoods and cities are like songs in this respect. When unfamiliar they seem foreboding and unpleasant; once familiar, though, they can be as comforting as a cuddly security blanket. Revisited after a long absence or simply reexamined after being taken for granted, their familiarity can be love inspiring. Here is the way writer John Gregory Dunne describes his eventual attachment to Los Angeles, a city that at first seemed to him a very poor substitute for New York:

> When I think of Los Angeles now, after almost a decade and a half of living not only in it but with it, I sometimes feel an astonishment, an attachment that approaches joy. I am attached to the way palm trees float and recede down empty avenues, attached to the deceptive perspectives of the pale subtropical light. I am attached to the drydocks of San Pedro, near where I used to live, and to the refineries of Torrance, which at night resemble an extraterrestrial space station. I am attached to the particular curve of coastline as one leaves the tunnel at the end of the Santa Monica Freeway to drive north on the Pacific Coast Highway. I am attached equally to the glories of the place and to its flaws, its faults, its occasional revelations of psychic and physical slippage, its beauties and its betrayals.
>
> It is the end of the line.
> It is the last stop.
> *Eureka!*
> I love it.

Lonely people often mistakenly assume—falling for what in an earlier chapter we called a rescue fantasy—that "if only" they lived somewhere else, in a friendlier, smaller, prettier town, their lives would be better and they'd feel much happier. Only rarely is this the case. Dissatisfaction with a place usually means dissatisfaction with the people in it, and having difficulty making friends is psychological baggage that we carry wherever we go. Another school, job, or town won't be the remedy for most kinds of loneliness. One man we interviewed in Florida had moved five times in the previous year in search of better friends and a perfect lover. "I finally decided, mostly from exhaustion, that I just couldn't move anymore. I guessed that I would just have to start trying harder than I had been. It's just that nothing ever seemed right and I kept thinking: 'If only I lived back in Kentucky things would be better.' Well, I moved back to Kentucky, and they weren't better, maybe worse, so I finally decided to give it a chance here."

Nevertheless, for reasons of personal taste or background, people can be more or less pleased with a particular place. Some seem literally attached to geography. Many Montanans told us, for example, that they couldn't live any place where the Rockies weren't in sight. Said one man, forty-two years old: "There's something about seeing the mountains every day; it's uplifting somehow—a quickly regenerating experience. You can see such wonders! I wouldn't live anywhere else." A Wyoming man exclaimed: "It's wonderful living here! When I go away, I just can't wait to get back to see the mountains. If you go fifty miles, in any direction, you're right in 'em. Why, I wouldn't trade this part of Wyoming for a dozen South Dakotas." Another man, defending his birthplace, declared bluntly: "I wouldn't be anywhere but Billings, Montana." For many die-hard New Yorkers or Los Angelenos, living in Billings would be just short of receiving a prison sentence. Part of the task each of us faces, then, is to find the right place for our temperament and allow ourselves to feel affection for it.

Community from Afar

In studying the elusive nature of friendship, Claude Fischer asked people how close or intimate they were with friends, how often they got together, how long they had known each other, and how they had met. He found that most intimate friendships had been formed in childhood or were with blood relatives. There are, Fischer said, "friends of convenience," whom we may see often (such as neighbors or coworkers) but toward whom we feel little closeness, and "friends of commitment," with whom we have enduring and intimate ties but whom we rarely see. American Indians defined this difference as that between friends of the road and friends of the heart. College-educated adults tend to have more ties with old friends, whom they periodically call and visit. They also have a greater proportion of nonkin than kin friends; in essence, they have *chosen* more of their friends. Less-educated Americans show the reverse pattern: they have more kin than nonkin ties. They seem more like small-town dwellers of a previous era, since their social networks tend to be assigned rather than freely chosen.

Because much of our ability to express affection is nonverbal (including smiles, eye contact, touching, hugging, gesturing, sharing activities and meals), it's unlikely that long-distance friendships, based only on telephone calls and letters, will ever take the place of face-to-face community. Still, the ability to maintain friendships at a distance is extremely important and may be one reason for our finding that better educated (and wealthier) Americans are, on the average, less lonely than the relatively poor and uneducated even though the educated are also more mobile. They have the resources for keeping in touch with far-away friends.

Creating Community

If you need new friends and a stronger sense of community, you'll have to work for them. Mobility, urbanization, cultural diversity—these forces make establishing a viable community more difficult today than fifty years ago. Nevertheless, mobility need not create lasting loneliness. The average period of social disruption after a major move is only about a year. Similarly, social life in cities is more difficult and requires more initiative than social life in small towns; but for many people it is also richer, more stimulating, and more rewarding in the long run. Wherever you are, there are potential friends available; there is a community you can join or one you can help to create.

The secret of friendship is *caring*. Unfortunately, when lonely we are often desperate to have our *own* needs met, not seeking to meet someone else's. The first step, then, although the most difficult, is to forget your own needs for a while and see what you can do for someone else. In this society, unless you are in an unusual neighborhood or workplace, you will have to *work* at friendship. No one, except groups like the Moonies, will offer you a complete, ready-made community. But wherever you are, there are a host of volunteer groups that would appreciate your involvement. They cannot and should not promise an instant cure for loneliness, but that may well be one of their fringe benefits. Take on their goals as your own, and other benefits will follow automatically.

Having a few intimate friends prevents loneliness better than having many pals or casual acquaintances. Many men, as we've noted, say they have an ample number of friends but seem dissatisfied, unhappy, and lonely. Their so-called friendships tend not to be close, intimate ones. Women may have fewer friends, but their ties are more intimate and ultimately more satisfying. Work on being a good friend, then, rather than collecting a phonebookful of acquaintances. Many of us retain the junior high and high school students' goal of being *popular*. Unless you're running for office, this isn't a very rewarding aim in adulthood. Forget about what "they" want or approve of and focus on the few people you really care about.

American society is no longer organized so that nearness guarantees friendship. Neighbors with different backgrounds and interests may not come to know each other well. More common today are groups with organizing themes—social scientists call them "communities of interest." Such groups include block associations, historical societies, Parents Without Partners, Hispanic-American groups, track or volleyball clubs, and contract bridge organizations. As Americans' interests grow more and more specialized, these groups will become even more prevalent. Figure out what interests you and discover your own local community of interest. If you don't have clear interests (and many of our lonely respondents said they didn't), this is probably a factor contributing to your loneliness—a form of "emptiness" that lowers your chances for friendship. You need to work on interests and a social life simultaneously.

During the 1980s, although most Americans will continue to be independent and self-concerned, they will also come to realize that, like their pioneer ancestors, they need other people to get along. Cooperation and community—the "we" generation—will be a theme of the 1980s. People will begin to realize that a single complaint won't improve garbage collection on the block, but a signed petition from one hundred members of "Neighbors for Neatness" will. If our children don't like their school's cafeteria food, a committee of parents working on the problem will get it solved. And if local muggers attempt to take over the jogger's turf in the park, an organization of determined runners will deter them. This is part of community: a common cause and a sense of togetherness and safety.

Of course, we need not abandon traditional signs of community where these are workable. Many of the people we interviewed had benefited from friendly gestures by new neighbors and coworkers—being invited to dinner or out for drinks, being helped with moving or learning about local stores and customs. Many benefited from the organized community activities of a local church. If you are already a resident of a church or community, reach out to potentially lonely newcomers.

Finally, don't neglect the *place* where you live. Every city and region in the country has fascinating and beautiful features: mountains, storefronts, creeks, distinctive architecture, beaches, ethnic food, museums, cloud patterns, hiking trails, historic landmarks. Get out and examine the special qualities of your local environment. Don't just compare it to other places you have loved; appreciate it for what it is. Gradually, by a process as natural as breathing, you and the place will become first, familiar, and eventually, intimate. One day, like John Gregory Dunne, you'll find yourself exclaiming: "Eureka! I love it."

8

Understanding and Overcoming Loneliness

Our language has wisely sensed the two sides of man's being alone. It has created the word "loneliness" to express the pain of being alone, and it has created the word "solitude" to express the glory of being alone.—PAUL TILLICH

[The effect on loneliness] of just the right sort of relationship with others is absolutely remarkable. Given . . . these relationships, loneliness will vanish abruptly and without a trace, as though it never had existed. There is no gradual recovery, no getting over it bit by bit. When it ends, it ends suddenly; one was lonely, one is not any more.—ROBERT WEISS

Poets often praise solitude, and most relish being alone, especially when they feel creative. In his poem "I Wandered Lonely as a Cloud," William Wordsworth wrote about seeing an endless field of daffodils and bragged that they offered him "a wealth" of company:

> *For oft, when on my couch I lie*
> *In vacant or in pensive mood,*

> *They flash upon that inward eye*
> *Which is the bliss of solitude;*
> *And then my heart with pleasure fills,*
> *And dances with the daffodils.*

In a sense, though, many poets, novelists, and diarists, gifted with ''that inward eye,'' are rarely alone the way most of us are; when they write, they can summon up in imagination a perfect listener or a retinue of devoted followers and readers. Their solitude is protected against loneliness; indeed, it is almost intimate. The eighteenth-century poet William Cowper cunningly admitted:

> *How sweet, how passing sweet, is solitude!*
> *But grant me still a friend in my retreat,*
> *Whom I may whisper—solitude is sweet.*

Ambivalence about aloneness or solitude makes sense. As a cause of loneliness it can be painful, sometimes unbearable, but as an opportunity for creativity, reflection, and renewal, it is indispensable. As one wit put it, solitude is ''a good place to visit, but a poor place to stay.''

Solitude is fully rewarding only for someone who has attained intimacy—with a close friend or lover, an imaginary companion or audience, or with nature itself (a field of daffodils, a vast starry sky). To be healing rather than frightening, solitude requires the same open, trusting willingness to listen that we've associated with intimacy. This is one reason why solitude and intimacy are so closely linked.

In this chapter we consider what lonely people can do to enjoy solitude, achieve intimacy, and overcome loneliness. We will also discuss important differences between people who are and those who aren't vulnerable to loneliness.

We've noticed that advice in popular magazines and self-help books tends to be simple and, in our opinion, simple-minded. Author Martha Lear, writing about how she felt reading such advice after her husband's death, sneered: "Develop the self, eh? Something in its very simplicity, in the overworked sound of the words, offends me. I sit here listening to my loneliness, achingly eager to press whatever button will make it go away, and this is the best that is offered—develop the self? Such two-penny advice is hardly worth the price of admission."

In this chapter we will stay close to research evidence and interviews with lonely and nonlonely people, even if the resulting advice is not two-penny simple. Loneliness doesn't always stem from the same causes, nor is it the same for every person. The paths out of it are therefore diverse and must be selected with particular causes and personal resources in mind. We believe that gaining a deeper understanding of loneliness is the first step along the road to intimacy and community.

Let's begin with the list of reactions to loneliness uncovered in our interviews and surveys. Before saying what lonely people *should* do, let's consider what most of them actually do on their own, without prompting or advice.

What People Do When They Feel Lonely

In our interviews, we asked what people typically do when they feel lonely. Once the list seemed complete—that is, when new people began giving answers we had already heard—we incorporated the list into our newspaper questionnaire. In the newspaper surveys, the largest proportions of people circled one or more of the following reactions to loneliness: watch television, read, listen to music, call a friend. In itself this list isn't very informative, except that it confirms our suspicion that television viewing has become a popular substitute for intimacy and community.

More important is the way these responses to loneliness hang together. Statistical analysis yielded four important "reaction clusters," which, added to the feeling and reason clusters described in Chapter 1, form a fairly complete psychological portrait of loneliness. The reaction factors are: *Active Solitude, Sad Passivity, Social Action,* and *Distraction.* The differences between these four stances provide important clues about how and how not to overcome loneliness.

REACTIONS TO LONELINESS

Active Solitude	Sad Passivity	Social Action
Study or work	Cry	Call a friend
Write	Sleep	Visit someone
Listen to music	Sit and think	
Exercise	Do nothing	**Distraction**
Walk	Overeat	Spend money
Work on a hobby	Take tranquilizers	Go shopping
Read	Watch television	Go for a drive
Play music	Get drunk or stoned	

Active Solitude. For some people, being alone automatically implies loneliness; for them, the word solitude evokes images of isolation, panic, fear, inability to concentrate, numbness, or boredom. For others—poets and artists, for example—solitude carries almost the opposite meaning: bliss, relaxation, personal integration, a feeling of warm connectedness with the world and other people, creativity, and reflection. What are the differences between these people—or between times in the life of a particular person when one rather than another reaction predominates?

The difference is partly one of perspective. Sometimes, because of past or recent experiences, we conceive of aloneness as being cut off, bereft, alienated from others, the way a child feels after being sent to his or her room for punishment. (As the poet Coleridge put it in ''The Rime of the Ancient Mariner'': "Alone, alone, all, all alone, / Alone on a wide wide sea! / And never a saint took pity on / My soul in agony.'') In this state of mind, we feel a keen sense of loss and powerlessness—loss of other people's approval and company, and powerlessness to do anything about it. The loss calls attention to deficiencies in ourselves; we are "bad," unworthy of love, deserving of rejection, vulnerable and helpless. In this state, self-esteem is diminished; we become frightened and defensive. We can't relax or be creative.

In contrast, the orientation we call active solitude emphasizes the positive side of being alone. In solitude, you are together with yourself, physically but not psychologically cut off from other people; free to explore thoughts and feelings without regard for anyone else's immediate reactions. You can hear your own mental voice and react to your own subtle desires and moods. Oddly enough, the result is often a deeper affection for other people. One of our respondents in Billings, Montana, wrote us, for example, that she spends ten days in total solitude each year—causing rumors among her neighbors that her marriage is on the rocks. Leaving husband, children, dog, and three canaries back home, she retreats to a mountain cabin by herself—to think, read, and write. ''I have a ball— no obligations and no distractions. No radio, no TV, no screaming kids or pesky husband. For ten days I have just me. I love being away from it all for those days. Funny thing is though, I appreciate them a whole lot more when I get back— a year's worth of appreciation builds up in just ten days.''

Active solitude recomposes and strengthens the self, making us better suited for friendship. As religious writer Henri Nouwen noted, solitude ''is the gift of a new self, our true identity. That knowledge of who we really are allows us to live and work in community. As long as our life together is based on false or distorted self-understanding, we are bound to become entangled in interpersonal conflict and to lose perspective on our common task.''

Many people find that the first few minutes or hours of solitude are unsettling. While working individually on this book, for example, having set aside time for reflection and writing, we often spent the first half hour (at least) with unnecessary phone calls, irrelevant reading, and distracting, time-wasting trips to the bathroom or refrigerator. The urge to avoid self-confrontation, to escape the feeling of aloneness that solitary thought requires, is powerful indeed. In the first few moments of solitude, many people make a hasty decision to go shopping or turn on the television set, and they immediately lose the opportunity for creativity and self-renewal. If this pattern becomes habitual, their sense of identity and personal strength is eroded and they become chronically afraid of solitude.

The writings of religious hermits throughout history reveal that they too suffered an initial period of doubt, agitation, and panic when they first got out into the wilderness by themselves. Most of them, however, like most of us in our successful attempts at creative solitude, waited out this temporary anxiety and found themselves moved and enriched by the rewards of solitude.

Saint Anthony was the founder and father of Christian monasticism. In about the year A.D. 285, he withdrew to absolute solitude on an Egyptian mountaintop for almost twenty years. He emerged to instruct and organize other Christian hermits and became the standard for all of the Desert Fathers. One of their first tasks, according to Anthony, was to adjust to the naked reality of solitude. The following is a classic Desert Father tale. ''A brother asked one of the Elders saying: What shall I do, Father, for I work none of the works of a monk but here I am in torpor eating and drinking and sleeping and in bad thoughts and in plenty of trouble, going from one struggle to another and from thoughts to thoughts. Then the old man said: Just you stay in your cell and cope with all this as best you can without being disturbed by it. I would like to think that the little you are able to do is nevertheless not unlike the great things that Abba Anthony did on the mountain, and I believe that if you sit in your cell for the Name of God and if you continue to seek the knowledge of Him, you too will find yourself in the place of Abba Anthony.''

If we had added meditation and religious or philosophical contemplation to our list of reactions to loneliness, they would have fallen (statistically) into the active solitude category. Strangely enough, meditation and reflection—although usually solitary activities—are almost the opposite of what we normally think of as self-consciousness or self-preoccupation. When properly pursued, they aren't at all narcissistic. When we are self-conscious in the usual sense (anxious or embarrassed), the self that occupies our attention is, meditation experts say, a figment of our social imagination; it is the self of the adolescent conformist wondering nervously if he is accepted by the group. Surprisingly, when we are alone and allow ourselves to pass through the initial period of agitated discomfort, this social pseudoself eventually evaporates, revealing a more relaxed and substantial self underneath. This genuine self needs no outside approval and is not simply a social creation. People who make contact with this deeper self find that their subsequent social relations are less superficial, less greedy, less tense. They have less need to defend their everyday social selves, their social masks.

Our first piece of advice, then: *When you are alone, give solitude a chance. Don't run away at the first sign of anxiety, and don't imagine yourself abandoned, cut off, or rejected.* Think of yourself as *with yourself*, not *without* someone else. Allow yourself to relax, listen to music that suits your feelings, work on something that you've been neglecting, write to a friend or for yourself in a journal, or just lie back and be at peace. If you are religious, your solitude may take the form of conversations with God or meditation on religious ideas. Whatever the content of your solitude, if you allow the first burst of anxiety to fade, you will open a door to many rewarding hours: of quiet prayer or contemplation; full enjoyment of music, sketching, or painting; total involvement in a novel or book of poetry; recording your own thoughts, feelings, songs, or poems. This solitude is a far cry from loneliness.

If you think about this, you can begin to see why active solitude and intimacy are related. In solitude, we experience our most genuine needs, perceptions, and feelings. We listen to our deepest selves. Intimacy involves the disclosure of this deeper self to trusted friends or lovers, and really listening, in turn, to their needs, thoughts, and feelings. In other words, in solitude we are intimate with ourselves in a way that enhances our intimacy with other people.

If you find that you can't be comfortable with yourself, you are probably a dissatisfying friend and lover as well. Perhaps you fear there is really nothing very interesting about you; your value is assured only when you are with and approved by someone else. This idea was taken to a supernatural extreme by Henry James, in a story called "The Private Life." Lord Mellifont completely vanishes when he is left alone. "He's there from the moment he knows someone else is." Mellifont is "so essentially, so conspicuously and uniformly the public character" that he is simply "all public" and has "no corresponding private life." Discovering this horrible fact, the narrator of the story feels great sympathy for Mellifont. "I had secretly pitied him for the perfection of his performance, had wondered what blank face such a mask had to cover, what was left to him for the immitigable hours in which a man sits down with himself, or, more serious still, with that intenser self his lawful wife."

We know from our research that adults who have suffered painful losses or rejections in the past are more likely to feel this way and to panic when they are alone; we also know that such people tend to have self-esteem problems. But as long as they cling desperately to others rather than confronting and overcoming their fears and feelings of inadequacy, they are unlikely to become confident and independent. For these people, spending time alone is an essential part of overcoming loneliness.

We don't want to oversell solitude. In fact, for some people solitude replaces normal social life, causing them to become self-contained, fussy, and rigid. Psychiatrist George Vaillant described such a man, in his late forties at the time they talked: "During college he had dealt with his very real fear of people by being a solitary drinker. He enjoyed listening to the radio by himself and found math and philosophy his most interesting courses. Although afraid to go out with girls, he was very particular about his appearance. . . . Thirty years later, [he] was less interested in clothes, but had become terribly preoccupied with keeping fit. He admitted that in his life 'things had taken the place of people' and that he loved to retreat into the 'peace and quiet of a weekend alone.' Approaching old age with no family of his own, he daydreamed of leaving his rare book collection to a favorite young cousin; but he had made only a small effort to get to know this cousin personally." Vaillant went on: "Not only had he never married, but he never admitted to being in love. Unduly shy with women in adolescence, at forty-seven [he] was still put off by 'eager women' and still found 'sex distasteful and frightening.' He had gone through life without close friends of any kind, male or female, and . . . still found it difficult to say good-bye to his mother."

How can you tell if solitude is leading you toward or away from other people? In general, if you find yourself soothed and strengthened by solitude, *more aware of your love for other people,* and less frightened or angry in your dealings with them, then solitude is a healthy part of your social balance. If you find, on the other hand, that you use solitude as a chronic escape from other people, and if people generally seem to you to be scary, selfish, cruel, or too messy, then you are retreating into a shell of solitude. We say this not because we wish to impose some superficial standard of sociability on everyone, but because studies like Vaillant's indicate that long-term defensive withdrawal from other people leads to unhappiness, alcohol and drug abuse, underachievement, and vulnerability to illness.

Practice active solitude, then, *but not to the detriment of intimacy, friendship, or community.* Let active solitude be the ground from which your feelings of intimacy and community grow.

Sad Passivity. The second cluster of responses to loneliness is potentially the most self-destructive. Sad passivity includes sleeping, doing nothing, drinking, overeating, taking tranquilizers, watching television, and "getting stoned" alone— none of which is likely to solve personal problems or promote either intimacy or community. People in our studies who responded to loneliness with sad passivity were especially prone to intense, prolonged loneliness, depression, and poor health. Sad passivity reminds us of the psychoanalytic concept of "oral passivity," used to describe people who, like whiny, needy infants, approach life passively and dependently; they whimper, plead, and "suck" (at the breast, bottle, pill box, or television screen), unable or unwilling to help themselves.

When asked how they respond when intensely lonely, some adults say "eat" or "stuff myself," as if food were love and psychological emptiness were the same as an empty stomach. Watching television, while not "oral" in the same literal sense as eating, drinking, and taking drugs, is similar: the viewer passively receives images and stimulation. These images fill the social-psychological void for a time without the viewer engaging in any action. When the set goes off, nothing in the way of intimacy or community has been gained.

According to journalist Marie Winn, author of *The Plug-In Drug,* a book about the harmful effects of television: "Not unlike drugs or alcohol, the television experience allows the participant to blot out the real world and enter into a pleasurable and passive mental state." Such passive uses of solitude are generally associated with continuing loneliness and, as we will show later in this chapter, with symptoms of mental and physical illness. They don't raise self-esteem, build social skills, or encourage intimacy; therefore, they do not alleviate loneliness.

The Downward Spiral. In our studies, Sad Passivity was linked with two clusters of undesirable feelings mentioned in Chapter 1: Self-Blame and Depression. This link, bolstered by interviews with lonely people who were also depressed, suggests that sad passivity is part of a downward spiral leading from emotional and social isolation to depression and illness. (See diagram.)

The first phase of the downward spiral is feeling emotionally or socially isolated (as discussed in Chapter 1), caused by a combination of external and internal factors. External causes include divorce, widowhood, moving, and retirement; internal or psychological causes include poor social skills, destructive mental models, and shyness and low self-esteem. Most people who feel emotionally or socially isolated take steps to satisfy their needs for intimacy and friendship. If they succeed and their feelings of isolation recede, they don't become sad or passive; in fact, their efforts are rewarded and they are more likely to take action in the future. In this way, they escape the downward spiral.

If a person repeatedly tried to escape loneliness and fails,

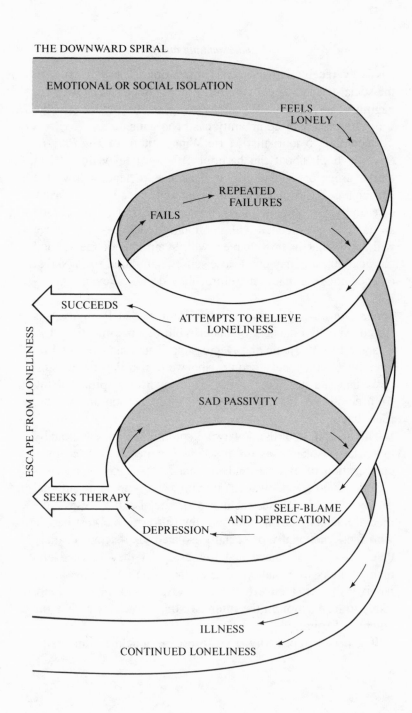

THE DOWNWARD SPIRAL

EMOTIONAL OR SOCIAL ISOLATION

FEELS LONELY

REPEATED FAILURES

FAILS

SUCCEEDS

ATTEMPTS TO RELIEVE LONELINESS

ESCAPE FROM LONELINESS

SAD PASSIVITY

SEEKS THERAPY

SELF-BLAME AND DEPRECATION

DEPRESSION

ILLNESS

CONTINUED LONELINESS

however, he or she becomes prone to self-blame (see Chapter 3): "What's wrong with me? Why can't I do something about these awful feelings?" The consequences of self-blame, help-lessness, and hopelessness are depression and sad passivity. If life is painful and beyond control you might as well admit defeat, right? Why not lie down, prop your head on a pillow, have a few beers, and watch television all night? This is the reasoning of the sadly passive, lonely person. It is also part of the destructive downward spiral.

This leads to our next piece of advice: *Don't allow yourself to descend into sad passivity.* Each of the sad passive re-sponses is acceptable in the short run—crying, sleeping, hav-ing a relaxing drink, getting stoned, watching your favorite reruns. But if relied on for an extended period, they can be not just depressing but deadly. An act of will is required to avoid or escape the downward spiral, but escape *is* possible. You can always short-circuit your descent in ways we will describe in a moment.

Distraction. Watching television is a highly passive and self-defeating form of distraction. Our surveys turned up a cluster of more active distractions—spending money, going shopping, going for a drive—which seem not to affect loneli-ness very much, for better or worse. They take people's minds off problems for a while and have the advantage of being somewhat active, but they aren't usually helpful in the long run.

Martha Lear suggests one way in which such distractions may become part of a cure for loneliness: "Loneliness is not a sensation I sit home nursing and cultivating, like some inner garden of weeds. Nor is it constant. It comes and goes—and when it comes it is intense. But I am capable of distraction and actively seek distraction, and seem to find it most easily by following pursuits that give pleasure—not because they may cure loneliness but simply because they give pleasure." She is referring to active and social distractions, not to television viewing. Playing tennis, shopping for and finding something one really wants, going to an exercise class—these are examples of active, pleasurable pursuits. Aimless driving and shopping are unlikely to help in the same way.

Social Action. We included only two forms of social action in our list of responses to loneliness: "calling a friend" and "visiting someone." After interviewing many of our respondents, we realized that we should also have included "volunteering to help others," "going out and meeting new people," "re-establishing contact with an old friend," and "joining clubs and organizations." These are active strategies used by respondents who are rarely lonely, and in a majority of cases they work. We know from our studies that people who respond to loneliness by taking action aren't lonely for long.

A caution is in order, however. Selfish, self-centered efforts to establish contact probably won't work. A love-hungry, clinging person usually gets rejected, especially in the early stages of a relationship. (With a good friend we can be needy at times and legitimately expect to have our needs satisfied, but strangers and casual acquaintances aren't willing to bear this burden.) So social action means not just reaching out to people, but reaching out with genuine willingness to share and to give—sometimes even to give without receiving.

When Jane Schein answered our questionnaire, she had lived in Worcester, Massachusetts, for almost twenty years. Small and pale, with curly ashen hair oddly tufted all over her head, she limped queerly into the office for our interview. It was clear that something was wrong with forty-four-year-old Schein. But she didn't give us time to feel awkward. Immediately, she admitted: "I had a stroke a few years ago. It left me partially paralyzed on one side." Schein went on to describe the tragedies that ensued in the wake of that rare cerebral hurricane. "My husband left me almost right after it happened. He just wasn't strong enough to deal with a sick wife and three teen-age kids. So he bailed out. At first, I was devastated. 'How could he be so cruel, so miserably unfeeling?' But I realized he was just selfish and weak. He couldn't deal with a wife as a liability and not an asset. So I decided to turn myself into an asset for other handicapped people."

After Jane Schein recovered from her first massive stroke, she had a second, minor one. But she recovered from that one too. Newly divorced and alone, she began to see life not only as a single woman, but as a crippled one. When she tried to run errands downtown, there was often nowhere convenient for her to park. Once, she couldn't find a place to park near City Hall, where she had an important appointment. She lobbied for special handicapped parking spaces near government offices; as a result, she and other handicapped people now have special plates that allow them to park in convenient locations.

When Schein saw how many handicapped people were housebound simply because they couldn't park close enough to their destinations, she decided to organize. She formed the Worcester Stroke Club, inviting others who had had strokes to get together, share their problems and fears, and see what they could do for each other. The local group now has a devoted membership and their ideas have spread to other New England towns. Schein shared her philosophy with us: "The most important thing is to face what is—to accept it and live with it. My faith helped me gain a sense of inner strength. I like to share that with others. I see so many lonely people in the handicapped community who don't have to be lonely. Activity will drive the cobwebs out of your mind. If you keep your hands and mind active, you can't be lonely. I think everyone can take charge of that feeling."

More than most people, Jane Schein would seem to have

had good reason to feel lonely and abandoned. But she chan-
neled her energy and talents into social action. Her goal was
not to go out and find an instant cure for her loneliness—it
was to go out and help people with a problem she had overcome.

Altruism is an effective way out of loneliness. We found, to
our surprise and delight, a large group of active, creative, optimistic older people who felt the same as Jane Schein. "Get
involved; forget your own troubles and help someone else. See
what you can do to improve your community." Their health
and enthusiasm, and the warm feelings they inspired in us,
were proof enough of the wisdom of their advice. We gladly
pass it on: *Forget yourself for a while and attempt to help
others.* Paradoxically, you may solve your own problem in the
process.

As sociologist Margaret Wood noted, "forgetfulness of self
in the service of others" is at the heart of most religious phi-
losophies and was known by the ancient Greeks to be a cure
for loneliness. In a drama by Sophocles, a soldier named Philoctetes was bitten by a poisonous snake when he and his fellow soldiers were on their way to Troy. Philoctetes's wound
festered, and he groaned so miserably that his shipmates abandoned him on an island while he slept. But the Greeks were
told that they couldn't win the war against Troy without the
magic bow that belonged to the wounded Philoctetes. Odys-
seus tried to trick him into returning the bow, figuring that
after such cruel treatment, the suffering and embittered Philoctetes would never give it back. But, as Wood summarized
the outcome, "Philoctetes conquers his deep resentment and
consents to give him the bow, his one talent as it were, to help
his countrymen." As such stories usually turn out, this gesture
heals the wound, and Philoctetes plays a major role in the siege
of Troy.

The ancient advice—forget yourself and help others—isn't

easy to follow. Like Martha Lear's reaction to the suggestion "develop yourself," one of the lonely people to whom we offered this advice retorted, "Bullshit! I've tried helping people, they don't appreciate it." When told about this answer, a woman, sixty-six years old, rejoined: "She's too selfish. She wants too much appreciation too soon. There has to be real caring, real pleasure in service, not a smile masking a greedy heart. The idea is: Do unto others and love thy neighbor, not go in there and grab whatever you can for yourself."

Unfortunately, the person who is lonely and bitter, or desperately afraid of rejection, or so low in self-esteem as to doubt that he or she can make a real contribution to others, will have trouble taking social action. It requires an act of faith that only the lonely person can provide. Everyone has something to offer; think seriously about what you can contribute.

Social Styles of Lonely People

Studies of lonely people reveal that they tend to occupy the extremes of what we call the "clinger-evader" continuum. Clingers are anxious to form secure attachments to others—so anxious and insistent, in fact, that they often force other people to run away in self-defense. Evaders, on the other hand, desire attachments and feel lonely without them but are so concerned with rejection that they have learned to appear detached, aloof, independent, and self-sufficient.

In casual conversations, clingers tend to disclose too much about themselves; they smother or bury others in a barrage of "I this" and "I that." Their message: "I'm hurt, I desperately need help." Unfortunately, few casual acquaintances can commit themselves to meet a clinger's needs. To do so would be like encouraging an acquaintance to borrow money when you know he doesn't have the resources or the desire to pay it back. Clingers make us fear that they will drain us of affection and attention while offering little in return. We can't fully relax with a person who seems nothing but needy.

In talking with evaders, we find that they give an impression that is just the opposite of the clingers'. They appear not to need us, not to be interested. Actually, they are very dissatisfied with their social lives and very needy, but the more lonely they feel the more powerfully they defend against admitting their needs, since openly declared wishes might be openly rejected.

You might think that the solution is for clingers to suppress their needs and for evaders to express theirs. But this is very difficult to do. A more successful, though still difficult strategy for both kinds is this: *Forget your needs and desires for a while and try simply to hear what other people are saying. Empathize with them, think about what they need to feel better.* If you've been lonely, your own painful experiences can contribute to this empathic process. You know what it feels like to be hurt, why not use this knowledge to assist others?

Notice that this advice follows the same principle emphasized in our discussion of Social Action: Forget yourself and serve others. The similarity isn't accidental: every conversation is an opportunity for active involvement, and this always means listening to and caring for others. *You* must take the first step toward intimacy; extend your trust, attentiveness, and caring to other people.

Psychologist Eugene Gendlin's *Focusing* describes a good method of listening. Designed originally for counselors and therapists, it contains ideas applicable to any interchange between sensitive people. A good listener, first of all, listens absolutely. This means not trying to impose your own immediate reactions, judgments, and opinions on the other person. Instead, really listen, your only goal being accurate reception. If you understand the other person, indicate this by nodding or saying "Yes" or "I see." If you don't fully understand, repeat what you did understand and then say, "I didn't quite get what you meant by. . . ." As simple and obvious as this sounds, few people do it well. Most of us jump in with our own judgments, assumptions, and stories. The other person's comments are nothing but springboards for our monologues. Soon, he or she shuts down in disappointment, and another opportunity for intimate communication is lost.

When you offer your own reactions and feelings, be sure you claim them as yours rather than presenting them as an assessment of the other person's evil motives. It's better to say, "I feel a little uncomfortable when you say that," than "You are hostile and manipulative." The first statement conveys your reactions, about which you are the expert. The second statement implies that you are an expert about the other person's character, which most likely you are not. This robs the other person of the freedom to define and explain his own feelings.

You will know that an encounter is going well when the other person becomes more him- or herself, less distracted, more animated and involved. Your conversation moves to a deeper level, and both of you learn something about yourselves and each other. You become closer, even if what you are talking about is sad or unpleasant. You, too, feel less constricted, more "on target," more substantial. You know things are going badly if neither of you learns anything new, the interaction remains tense, formal or superficial, and your need for real contact is left unsatisfied.

George Vaillant, summarizing his interviews with ninety-five middle-aged men, described the difference between those who had achieved intimacy and those who hadn't: "I soon discovered that whether the men liked me or I liked them had far more to do with their lives than with mine. The men who had always found loving easy made me feel warmly toward them, and led me to marvel at both my tact and my skill as an interviewer and at their good fortune to belong to such an enjoyable project. I left the office of one such man feeling ten feet tall; but he had had the same effect on others all his life. In contrast, men who had spent their lives fearful of other people and had gone unloved in return often made me feel incompetent and clumsy. With them I felt like a heartless investigator, vivisecting them for science. During his interview one such man had confessed that he was afraid of dying and leaving nothing of worth to the world. Afterwards I, too, felt drained and depressed, as if I had done all of the work in the interview while he took much and gave nothing.''

We felt the same about our interviews. The least lonely people, while sometimes expressing their unworthiness as interviewees, *gave* all they could—tea, affection, concentration, good humor, and respect. They rewarded us richly for having summoned them to an interview. On the other hand, the most lonely people almost invariably *took*—they wanted advice, help, and approval, support for their opinion of the world as a lousy place. Many agreed to see us only reluctantly, some didn't bother to show up for appointments, others set timers, announcing that they had only fifteen minutes to spare. They tended to be humorless complainers who made us feel tense and defensive. We often came away from such sessions feeling angry or emotionally drained.

The most difficult people to help—and so the hardest to advise—are evaders who don't look like evaders until one gets to know them well. These people appear friendly enough, and may even be successful social organizers and party givers. Their problem is sustaining an intimate relationship; they are likely to be emotionally rather than socially isolated and, underneath it all, terrified of intimacy. Their evasive barriers are close to their psychological centers, well hidden from all but the few who try to love them. Somewhere in the course of relationships with them, others discover a roadblock to intimacy which eventually halts all attempts to be close. If you are such a person—a secret evader—you know it by your lack of truly close friends, your inability to trust anyone with your deepest secrets and feelings, your fear of dependency. The solution is to risk intimacy and reveal yourself to, and care deeply for, someone. If you are a hard-core clinger or evader, someone who has honed that style to a fine edge, professional counseling or psychotherapy may be the best solution. Deeply ingrained social habits are hard to change on your own; outside help will greatly enhance your efforts to change.

Social Skills and Levels of Intimacy

Psychologists generally agree about the qualities necessary for intimate communication—honesty or authenticity, mutual acceptance, and empathy—and on the specific social skills necessary to translate these qualities into action. Robert Bolton, a psychologist who leads communication skills workshops, claims that most of these skills fall into three categories: listening, assertion, and conflict management. All three are important for overcoming loneliness.

Listening, which we've already mentioned, can be thought of as several specific skills—for example, paying attention, maintaining appropriate eye contact, offering "door openers" like "You look troubled, care to talk about it?" and gentle prods like "Tell me more," "Really?" and "Right." The goal of these skills is to hear what your partner has to say and show your willingness to be involved with it. Good listeners are reflective rather than judgmental; they repeat back what other people have said often enough to assure clear communication, reflect the other person's feelings, and offer useful summaries. (For example: "You feel frustrated because he's so inconsistent" or "You seem to be uncertain about whether to tell her the truth.") This might be prefaced by: "Let's see if I have your main point.'' Good listeners pay special attention to body language—facial expressiveness, tone of voice, gestures and posture—because these, perhaps more than what people say, express their feelings; and good listeners, valuing intimacy, listen to feelings. If you are self-preoccupied, unable to trust a particular person, unable to give to another, or just tired or pressured, don't try to carry on an intimate conversation. These are conditions which render absolute listening and sensitive communication impossible.

Assertiveness is another important skill for overcoming loneliness. It is usually contrasted with submissiveness, on the one hand, and aggressiveness, on the other. Submissive people fear that they will be punished or rejected for expressing their needs or opinions. Some are intimacy evaders, who fear that intimacy will lead to hurt feelings. Others are simply shy; they are capable of intimacy but unable to get beyond the initial stages of a relationship.

Aggressiveness is stronger than assertiveness; it is belligerent, intrusive, and selfish. It communicates, intentionally or not, an assumption that the aggressor's needs and values are more important than anyone else's. Aggression is usually associated with anger, but clingers are aggressive too. They are intrusive and disrespectful of others' needs.

Assertiveness is the middle path adopted by people who respect themselves and other people equally. Because they respect themselves, they are willing to express their needs and values openly; because they respect others they do not need to intrude on, abuse, or control them.

It is possible to alternate between submissiveness and aggressiveness. The quiet, self-effacing person accumulates grudges in silence until a particular event breaks the camel's back. Then the person explodes, to the surprise of friends and coworkers, and guiltily returns to quiet submissiveness until accumulated grievances once again become overwhelming. An assertive person, in contrast, generally receives a fair shake and thus rarely needs to feel slighted or resentful. There is no reservoir of past grudges that needs to be let loose.

Assertive people, according to Bolton, usually send a three-part message when they are troubled: (1) a neutral description of the behavior that disturbs them ("When you are late picking me up . . ." instead of "Your perpetual lateness . . ."); (2) a disclosure of their feelings ("When you say that, I tense up . . ."); and (3) a clear description of the concrete effect of the other person's behavior on them (". . . because I lose valuable time while I wait.") Practicing these kinds of statements—based on your own feelings and experiences—and watching out for submissive, clingy, or aggressive ploys will enhance communication, encourage intimacy, and reduce emotional isolation and loneliness.

Learning to manage conflict is also essential in dispelling loneliness. Any two people in a sustained relationship, and all members of ongoing groups, occasionally disagree, hurt each other's feelings, or hold conflicting goals. Thus, anyone who seeks a deep relationship with others has to be prepared to handle conflict.

The most productive conflict management skills are nothing more than combinations of the listening and assertion skills we have already outlined: (1) treat the other person with respect, (2) listen until you are sure you understand—in fact empathize with—the other side, and then (3) assertively (but not aggressively) state your views, needs, and feelings. The feelings on both sides are terribly important—more important, usually, than rational considerations. Says Bolton: "When feelings are strong it is usually a sound strategy to deal with emotional aspects of the conflict first. Substantive issues can be handled more constructively once the emotions have subsided." Therefore, *lis-*

ten for feelings, not just for substantive arguments, and don't put all of your energy into defending yourself.

The term "social skill" we've been using, now widely accepted by behavioral scientists, therapists, and management consultants, is somewhat dangerous. It likens social life to a game or a business. The point is not to manipulate yourself like a puppet, but gradually to incorporate into your "natural" thoughts and actions several patterns crucial for intimacy and friendship. If practiced for a while, the new skills will cease feeling alien or mechanical and will fit comfortably among your other attractive features. The individual skills, while important in their own right, are really less important than the attitude they convey. No one, regardless of "skill training," can listen attentively if he doesn't give a damn for the other person; no one can consistently act assertively if she doesn't respect her goals and motives. Social skills will, however, help you express your genuine interest in other people and discover the rewards of deeper relationships.

The skills needed at different levels of intimacy are somewhat different. Some people have trouble with introductions and casual conversations; others handle the preliminaries beautifully but bog down when deeper self-disclosure or flexible conflict management are required. For most people, relationships with the opposite sex are more difficult than same-sex relationships. And, of course, sex itself is partly a matter of "skill." When you have social difficulties, *try to determine what kinds of skills might be useful, think about these in private, and try them out when you're with the person again. Also, be aware of the kind of relationship you want and of what you might do to move things in that direction.* If the other person doesn't seem to be a rewarding partner, or doesn't seem to agree about the level of intimacy desired, put your energies elsewhere. Loneliness only disappears when relationships meet the social and emotional needs that cause it.

Thinking About the Causes of Loneliness

When lonely, you are likely to ask yourself, consciously or unconsciously, certain kinds of questions about the causes. First: Am I the cause of the problem or is it due to something about my situation? Second: How long is this painful feeling going to last? Is it temporary, permanent, or somewhere in between? Third: Can I control the causes? Can I change things for the better?

Thanks to UCLA psychologist Anne Peplau and her colleagues, who have been studying people's explanations of loneliness, we know a great deal about which answers are helpful and which are harmful. Lonely people, Peplau has found, often ignore the difference between "precipitating" and "maintaining" causes of loneliness. The precipitating causes include moving, traveling, divorce, widowhood, promotion to a new job, and forced retirement. As we all know, such events can trigger loneliness. However, if you still feel terribly lonely a year or more after moving, the cause may no longer be just the precipitating event, but also the way you are reacting to it. If you've withdrawn into sad passivity, believing that solitude is awful and that no social action can be helpful, the maintaining cause is no longer the move itself but your own behavior. (For a list of some of the precipitating and maintaining causes of loneliness, see the list on the next page.)

Most lonely people hold one of four common kinds of beliefs about why they feel lonely and who or what is to blame. The table on page 195 shows the four kinds of beliefs: (1) permanent and in me, (2) permanent and in the situation, (3) temporary and in me, (4) temporary and in the situation. Pe-

---

PRECIPITATING AND MAINTAINING
CAUSES OF LONELINESS

Precipitating Causes:

Death of someone close to you

Breaking up with a friend or lover

Recent move or friend's move

Retirement, being promoted or fired, changing jobs

High school or college graduation

Separation or divorce

Having a debilitating accident or suffering the onset of a
    serious illness

Experiencing a sudden drop in income

Christmas, New Year's, or any holiday season

Sudden change in physical appearance (weight, handicap,
    disfigurement)

Maintaining Causes:

Inability to trust others

Low self-esteem

Behavior and personal style—shyness, awkwardness, lack of
    social skills

Being a clinger or an evader

Self-consciousness

Fear of rejection, fear of intimacy

Unwillingness to take social risks

Tendency to self-blame

Perfectionism (having inhumanly high standards)

Lack of identity or sense of self

Being easily bored, unable to entertain self, having a short
    attention span

Fear of solitude, inability to be alone

Feeling unattractive, ugly

Poverty, lack of transportation, being bedridden or handicapped

---

plau's research tells us that the "permanent–in me" explanation (in the upper left corner) is the most dangerous. To believe that "I am unlovable and will probably always be unlovable" is a sure-fire route to depression and sad passivity (the bottom of the downward spiral).

PERCEIVING THE CAUSES OF LONELINESS

	"In Me"	**"In the Situation"**
Permanent	"I am lonely because I'm unlovable. I'll never really be worth loving. It's depressing, I feel empty. I sit around at night alone, getting stoned, eating, watching TV."	"The people around here are cold and impersonal; none of them share my interests or live up to my expectations. I'm sick of this place and don't intend to stay here much longer."
Temporary	"I'm lonely now, but won't be for long. I'll stop devoting so much time to work and go out and meet some new people. I'll start by calling the man I met at Ken's party."	"My lover and I have split up. That's the way relationships go these days, some work and some don't. Next time, maybe I'll be luckier."

The list of questions below should prove useful in figuring out which of the four kinds of beliefs you hold. For each question, choose one of the following answers:

    1) I'm not the kind of person who handles this well.
    2) I haven't been making enough of an effort.

3) It's not easy to succeed where I live.
4) I've been unlucky lately.

A. Suppose you've had difficulty making friends. What is probably the reason?
B. Suppose you've been having difficulty with your marriage or romantic life. What is probably the reason?
C. Suppose you've had trouble getting along with close friends. What is probably the reason?
D. Suppose you've always had trouble getting close to people. What is probably the reason?
E. Suppose you've been having difficulties or arguments with your lover about sex. What is probably the cause of the problem?

If three or more of your answers fell into a single category (for example, if you used the first answer several times), this is probably the way you think about your social failures. If you used the first answer frequently, you favor "permanent–in me" causes, the ones that lead to sad passivity and depression. If you used the second answer, you are likely to try harder to overcome loneliness, and this is usually successful. If you leaned toward answers three or four, you probably blame loneliness on your circumstances. This is all right in the short run (especially if it's true), but distressing in the long run. You can probably do more than you think to improve or alter your circumstances.

We can derive two valuable lessons from Peplau's research: First, *whenever possible, view the causes of loneliness as changeable and temporary.* Avoid thinking, "I'll *never* fit in." Or: "No one will *ever* love me." These despairing judgments are false and totally debilitating. Don't entertain the idea that you are helpless. You never really are unless you choose to be. Second, *don't blame yourself unless you are sure you're at fault, and even then, recognize that the problem is correctable and therefore temporary.* We've mentioned repeatedly that loneliness is closely tied to low self-esteem, and that low self-esteem increases a person's vulnerability to self-blame after loss or rejection. Don't fall into this trap. If you are doing anything to maintain loneliness, resolve to change constructively. *Don't* accept a view of yourself as helpless or hopeless.

We may sound as if we're encouraging you to ignore the true causes of your loneliness in a rush to find the most upbeat, superficial explanation. Not at all. You should examine the causes as honestly as you can, and where you find yourself at fault (for example, not really caring about another person's feelings), admit it. But do this within a framework that acknowledges the possibility of change, not in a way that finds you guilty for life. Think of yourself as a person who is open to improvement, and when you get an opportunity to improve, take it.

Having dealt with one danger of self-analysis—its tendency to lead you to pessimistic and self-defeating conclusions—we must consider one other. We are, on the one hand, advising you to look carefully at yourself and assess the causes of your loneliness. On the other hand, as we said earlier, too much self-attention can also be self-defeating. How can this contradiction be resolved?

The answer is easy to state in principle, but tricky to apply in practice. The problem is the same as that faced by pianists or dancers who want to alter well-learned but incorrect habits. The pianist makes slow, deliberate, correct hand movements while paying careful attention to them. The dancer does the same with foot position and hand gestures. But once the problems are identified and corrected, and the artists are performing in public, they must forget their problems and attempted solutions and simply perform ''naturally.'' Of course, they hope that what is now natural, thanks to self-analysis and rehearsal, will also be correct and beautiful.

The same principle applies to correcting the way you think and behave socially. You have to run your thought processes by in slow motion and "watch" for the destructive patterns we've discussed in this book: self-blame, distrust of others, pessimism about change. You must then find a constructive substitute and resolve to practice it for a while. Try it out in your imagination. How will the new thought process work in real social situations? Once you have adopted and rehearsed a new thought or behavior pattern, don't worry about it during your next social encounter.

In real social life there is no time for elaborate self-scrutiny, and it's not the proper place for it anyway. Intense self-scrutiny is incompatible with listening and responding to others. Relax, enjoy yourself, be "natural." If "natural" doesn't quite work this time, think about it later. For the moment, pay attention to your partner and forget about yourself.

At a week-long conference a few years ago, psychoanalyst Erik Erikson spoke about his work to two hundred enthusiastic followers. Occasionally the intense lectures and seminars were suspended so that conference participants could ask questions. One young man, the only high school student at the conference and an obvious admirer of Erikson, asked, "Don't you think your work on identity and identity crises should be required reading for people my age?" Erikson hesitated for a moment, not wanting to say that his books were harmful to adolescents, but not wanting to encourage adolescents to worry and be self-conscious either. After a thoughtful pause, he answered: "They should read about it—and then forget it!" The same goes for advice about loneliness and social skills. Of course, Erikson didn't literally mean forget it; he meant be affected by it but don't become obsessed to the point of living your life according to someone else's instructions. Intimacy and love are spontaneous and, fortunately, beyond instruction. You can equip yourself for them, but not manipulate or control them once they appear.

Loneliness and Health

Loneliness is often viewed as a symptom of depression, the nation's number one mental health problem. Many of the most widely used tests of depression include questions about loneliness. But in our opinion, loneliness and depression aren't identical and shouldn't be equated. One psychologist compared a group of people who were lonely *and* depressed with a demographically similar group who were lonely but *not* depressed. (He was able to do this by matching loneliness scores of the two groups while picking people with different depression scores.) Many of the depressed people had suffered *both* social and nonsocial losses or failures; lonely but nondepressed people typically suffered *only* social disappointments and losses. Loneliness can contribute to depression, then, but the two are not the same.

Depression is especially common among certain kinds of people: perfectionists and the overly dependent. Perfectionists set unrealistically high standards for themselves and their acquaintances; everything is supposed to be perfectly beautiful, perfectly interesting, perfectly in line with a set of rules which the perfectionist carries around unconsciously and tries to impose on a world that is too complex, too imperfect for him. One woman we interviewed was miserably lonely after years of short-term relationships with men who "just don't meet my standards." The only men who do meet her high standards are the ones she doesn't yet know very well—most of them married. She constantly criticizes and belittles the people who try to get close to her; after a while, almost everyone gives up. Most of us encounter enough hurdles and examinations in life;

we don't need extra ones from people who supposedly care for us.

Depression is also especially common among people who rely too much on others to confirm their positive view of themselves. The problem is especially severe when one individual fills the role of Master Approver. If the Approver fails to be supportive, or dies or leaves, the overly dependent person is totally bereft. Traditional, submissive housewives are particularly vulnerable to this form of depression. Career women and most men, while subject to other sorts of stress, are less dependent on the approval of just one other person.

Depression is also frequently related to feelings of helplessness and hopelessness. That is why it appears at the end of our downward spiral. If you repeatedly try to escape from loneliness and fail, you are likely to begin blaming yourself and feeling hopeless. Eventually this can lead to serious depression and inactivity. It is very important therefore to: (1) figure out the correct causes of your loneliness, the ones you can attack and change, (2) remain socially active, (3) work toward effective communication, and (4) avoid sad passivity (moping, overeating, drug abuse, excessive television viewing).

Both depression and chronic loneliness are associated with other physical and mental health problems. Like any form of prolonged stress, emotional and social isolation take a physical toll on the body. The table on the next page lists the problems and symptoms we included in our loneliness questionnaires. They are listed in order of importance for loneliness—the first problem, feeling worthless, is most strongly connected with loneliness, and the last, having a disabling accident, is least connected. Still, lonely people were bothered more than the nonlonely by every symptom and problem on the list.

Besides being stressful, loneliness is related to health in other ways. Research indicates that social support from relatives, friends, and intimates acts as a protective buffer against other

PSYCHOSOMATIC PROBLEMS AND SYMPTOMS ASSOCIATED WITH LONELINESS

1. Feelings of worthlessness	12. Trouble breathing
2. Feeling you just can't go on	13. Poor appetite
3. Constant worry and anxiety	14. Headaches
4. Irrational fears	15. Digestive problems
5. Trouble concentrating	16. Loss of interest in sex
6. Feeling irritable and angry	17. Being overweight, feeling
7. Feelings of guilt	fat
8. Crying spells	18. Suffering from a serious
9. Feeling tired	disease
10. Insomnia	19. Having a disabling accident
11. Pains in heart; heart disease	

forms of stress. People who have close, open relationships with others cope better than isolated people do. Close friends and relatives can assist in myriad ways: by helping you formulate and express the problem, by hashing over possible solutions, by absorbing some of the burden for you—either tangibly, by running errands, caring for your children, and lending you money, or emotionally, by doing some of the worrying for you and with you. It also helps to be held, hugged, or touched. Everyone knows that young children are comforted by being held; few realize how important this is for adults.

Most of the difficult stresses in life are due to social loss: divorce; death of a spouse, parent, or child; being fired or promoted; retirement. When part of your social support system is lost in one of these ways, it is particularly important for you to have other people to rely on.

Psychologist James Lynch, author of *The Broken Heart: The Medical Consequences of Loneliness,* carried the connections between loneliness, stress, and poor health to an unhappy but logical conclusion: Loneliness contributes to premature death. There are many dramatic examples of this—for example, the healthy seventeen-year-old boy who died of an aneurism (blood clot) exactly one year after his older brother was killed in an automobile accident, or the man, fifty-two years old, with no known heart disease, who died of a heart attack the day after his young wife's funeral. Lynch called his book *The Broken Heart* because loss of intimacy seemed especially linked with heart problems. As we mentioned in Chapter 5, divorced men die earlier than married men; they have twice the death rate from heart disease that married men have. For women, although the overall rate of heart disease is lower, the divorced are still more likely than the married to die from heart trouble. Even in the sixteenth century, a balladeer seems to have noticed the connection: "Two things doth prolong thy life: A quiet heart and a loving wyfe."

Besides being stressful in itself, loneliness can, according to Lynch, "bring on self-destructive behavior—increased smoking and drinking, for example, or becoming more prone to risk-taking behavior such as reckless driving." Lynch challenges the priorities of joggers and tennis players who exercise to keep their hearts in shape while neglecting to see a "connection between the 'shape' of their marriage, the 'shape' of their general social milieu, and the 'shape' of their hearts!"

Thus, two more suggestions: First, *realize that intimacy and friendship are sources of health; they prolong life.* Second, *don't allow the loss of a relationship to undermine your entire sense of meaning and self-worth.* Mourning is healthy and necessary, but mourning does not necessitate prolonged depression. Rely on friends while you mourn; don't cut yourself off from their healing, life-giving support and intimacy.

Should You Seek Professional Help?

By itself, loneliness doesn't require professional treatment. Everyone is lonely from time to time, and the solutions we've mentioned in this chapter are usually sufficient to overcome it. If you notice, however, that grieving or loneliness has turned into depression—if you have lost your appetite and are dramatically losing weight without trying; if you are suffering from sleep disturbances (having trouble falling or staying asleep), and feel unable to carry out everyday activities—then by all means contact a licensed professional psychiatrist, psychologist, or social worker. Your family doctor is a good source for referral. So is the community mental health center nearest you. If you are a member of a church or synagogue, someone there may also be able to help. Don't allow lack of help to serve as an excuse for sad passivity.

In our opinion, pseudoscientific encounter groups, weekend est sessions, nude marathons—activities for which you are charged a large sum of money to be temporarily jolted, chided, or cuddled—are not particularly effective, although some people seem to like them. As Lynch observed: "It's almost as if we were trapped in some huge marketplace of loneliness, with a thousand hawkers selling different 'scientific' remedies." You can't buy instant love, insight, or acceptance, and attempts to do so usually lead to disappointment. Only genuine friendship and intimacy are truly helpful, and they don't cost money at all. They require only your wholehearted participation.

On the other hand, focused, long-term self-help groups such as Alcoholics Anonymous or Parents Without Partners can be very helpful, as can participation in a wide variety of volunteer activities. Most cities have a central office which steers interested volunteers and self-helpers to appropriate groups. You can find friends and activities there which will cost almost nothing and yet may do you a world of good. Finally, like some of the people we've mentioned, you can start a worthwhile group of your own—for divorced or widowed community members, for example, or for people who share your special interests or problems.

The punchline is this: *If you are lonely*—and not seriously depressed—*you need intimacy, friendship, and a meaningful place in a community. If you are seriously depressed, you need these things in addition to professional help.* Don't accept lesser substitutes.

Life on the New Social Frontier

More than one hundred years ago, when the French aristocrat Alexis de Tocqueville toured the United States to form an impression of the new democracy, he could already foresee some of today's problems: "Not only does democracy make every man forget his ancestors, but it hides his descendants and separates his contemporaries from him; it throws him back forever upon himself alone, and threatens in the end to confine him entirely within the solitude of his own heart." De Tocqueville also observed the "restlessness" of the American, which propelled him to "settle in a place, which he soon afterwards leaves, to carry his changeable longings elsewhere." For a man of noble blood like de Tocqueville, whose family rights and place had been established for centuries, the lonely mobile American seemed a shocking and bizarre creature.

Was he right? Is each of us lonely, each confined entirely within the solitude of his own heart? Throughout this book, while examining loneliness in all its forms, we have avoided becoming pessimistic doomsayers. We found that elderly people are not as lonely as stereotypes would have them; nor are they cut off from family members. A few who are in institutions are lonely, but they do not represent anything like a majority. City dwellers, contrary to the myth of the lonely crowd, prove to have just as many close friends as their counterparts in smaller towns. Yes, moving from place to place leaves a person lonelier than average for about a year, but we could find no evidence that moving has lasting negative effects on children or adults. Yes, some children are lonelier because of divorce, and this is a problem worth working on, but most turn out fine—and that is worth noting, too. As we learn more about easing the stress of divorce for children, the number of emotional casualties should decline.

Certain trends in our society encourage loneliness—loss of community; high divorce, mobility, and crime rates; more young adults and elderly people living alone. These are the prices we have paid for increased longevity and extraordinary freedom—to move, change jobs, marry whomever we please, and enjoy privacy and solitude. There are already signs of countertrends, some freely chosen and some not, which may help reduce loneliness.

Feeling a need for community and a fear of crime, many neighborhoods have organized to repel developers and criminals. People who prefer small-town life, the 1980 census revealed, are causing a slowdown in the growth of urban areas by moving back to the country. Partly for social and partly for economic reasons, more single, divorced, and widowed Americans are joining together as roommates. Moreover, young people who a few years ago would have lived alone find, in this era of inflation, that living at home for a while isn't so bad. Finally, churches, synagogues, and other community organizations, realizing that loneliness is a widespread problem, are reaching out to the elderly, singles, single parents, and newcomers to their neighborhood by holding dances, classes, and social events, and in some cases, financing special housing projects. More colleges and universities are recognizing the plight of lonely students; the federal government is sponsoring research and professional conferences on prevention of loneliness; and hundreds of individual workshops and classes are being held for lonely people of all ages and life circumstances.

Americans are resilient. We are active problem solvers and always have been. We are accustomed to change, and even to redefining what it is that needs changing. At one time the issue was settling a geographical frontier; now we have occupied and tamed the entire country. The frontier that faces us is now social and psychological rather than geographical. We are, in a very real sense, *social pioneers*. This century, especially the past forty years, has witnessed a grand sociological experiment involving mobility, urbanization, increased education, changed relations between the races, rearrangement of sex and family roles, rising crime rates, and adjustment to shortages of essential commodities. Not all of the results of the experiment are in at the moment; our very being—all of our activities, experiences, and beliefs—warrants evaluation as an outcome of this dramatic experiment.

Has the experiment, overall, been good or bad? This is an enormously difficult question to answer. We know that most of us would not choose to live in an oppressive Victorian family, nor in the Moonies' contemporary rendition of it. Most of us would find nineteenth-century small-town life dull and constraining. The people who are moving to small towns today clearly want to bring most of the urban amenities—movies, bookstores, fine restaurants—with them. What we must do, then, is to actively build the kinds of relationships and communities that gratify our needs and make sense to us. Surely this is a challenge worthy of social pioneers.

Psychological research tells us a great deal about the kinds of people who will pioneer successfully. They are, in the words of several psychologists, hardy and stress resistant. They have an identifiable set of attitudes toward life—an openness to change, a feeling of involvement in whatever they are doing (most of which is social), and a sense of control over events despite rapid change. We know from our studies that such people are infrequently lonely and able to overcome loneliness when it does strike. They know how to use solitude creatively and constructively; they are able to commit themselves to close relationships and community projects.

Quite possibly, being able to love others and take part in a community is the most important component of mental and physical health. In George Vaillant's longitudinal study, which we have mentioned, he divided his middle-aged subjects into three groups, the Friendly, the Lonely, and those in between. Friendly meant: getting married without getting divorced, achieving at least ten years of marriage that "neither partner perceived as outright painful," fathering or adopting children, having one or more close friends, and enjoying regular recreation with nonfamily members. Lonely meant meeting only one or two of these criteria. Vaillant concluded: "Of all the ways that I subdivided the ninety-five healthy men [in his study], the dichotomy between the twenty-seven Friendly and the thirteen Lonely proved the most dramatic." It corresponded with vast differences in mental and physical health, for example, and in ability to enjoy life. "Perhaps the biggest difference between the Friendly and the Lonely was that the Lonely were more frightened."

It is frightening indeed to be open to change, committed to uncertain interpersonal relationships and group ventures, asserting control over rapidly shifting events. But these are the requirements of life on the new social frontier, and many have already proved equal to them. The "successful" pioneers aren't free of troubles, of course; all are scarred, as frontiersmen of any kind tend to be. But they are alive, healthy, and eager to carry on.

Without intimacy—emotional openness and closeness—and without friendship and community, their vitality would wither and their lives would become either terrifyingly meaningless or depressingly dull. These pioneers are not loners and do not wish to be.

The price all of us have paid for greater freedom and independence is the *risk* of greater loneliness, not the certainty of it. The gamble can, with effort and wisdom, be won. Intimacy, community, and chronic loneliness are still matters of *choice* for most Americans. To everyone who has energy, creativity, and faith to invest in love and community, the possibilities, the potential projects and partners, are there.

APPENDIX A

The Loneliness Questionnaire

These are the questions asked in our newspaper survey:

1. What is your age? ___ years old

2. What is your sex?
   1. Male   2. Female

3. How would you describe the place where you live?
   1. Metropolis (population of at least a million)
   2. Large city (population of at least 500,000)
   3. Medium sized city (population of at least 100,000)
   4. Small city (population of at least 25,000)
   5. Suburb
   6. Large town (population of at least 10,000)
   7. Small town (population of less than 10,000)
   8. Rural area

4. How long have you been living in your present community? ___ years

5. What is the *total* income of your family?
   1. Less than $5,000
   2. $5,000 to $9,999
   3. $10,000 to $14,999
   4. $15,000 to $19,999
   5. $20,000 to $24,999
   6. $25,000 to $29,999
   7. $30,000 to $39,999
   8. $40,000 to $49,999
   9. $50,000 or more

6. What is the highest level of education you have completed?
   1. Grade school or less
   2. Some high school
   3. Graduated high school

4. Some college
5. Graduated college
6. Some graduate or professional school
7. Received a graduate or professional degree

7. What is your marital status? Please pick the one category which best represents your *current* marital status.
   1. Single
   2. Living with a lover
   3. Married, for the first time
   4. Remarried, once
   5. Remarried, more than once
   6. Separated
   7. Divorced
   8. Widowed

8. If you are currently separated, divorced or widowed, how long has this been true of you? If not applicable, skip to the next question. ___ years

9. Have you ever been separated, divorced or widowed? Circle all that apply.
   1. Separated
   2. Divorced
   3. Widowed
   4. None of the above

10. Who was mainly responsible for your divorce or separation?
    1. I was.
    2. My spouse was.
    3. We were equally responsible.
    4. Not applicable

11. a. How many children (of your own) do you have? ___ children
    b. How many children are living in your home now? ___ children

12. I am:
    1. Pregnant
    2. Caring for one or more preschool children during the day
    3. Both
    4. Neither

13. Which of the following *best* describes your occupation?
    1. Artist, writer, designer, craftsperson
    2. Farming, agriculture
    3. Housewife, homemaker
    4. Managerial, administrative, business
    5. Professional with advanced degree (for example, doctor, lawyer, etc.)
    6. Teacher, counselor, social worker, nurse
    7. Technician, skilled worker
    8. Semiskilled or unskilled worker
    9. Student
    10. White-collar (sales, clerical, secretarial)
    11. Retired
    12. Unemployed
    13. Other (Specify: _____)

14. In how many groups or organizations do you actively participate? ___ groups

15. What is your religion?
    1. Protestant
    2. Catholic
    3. Jewish
    4. Agnostic, atheist
    5. Other (Specify:_____)

16. How religious would you say you are?
    1. Very religious
    2. Moderately religious
    3. Slightly religious
    4. Not at all religious

17. Since you've been an adult, have you ever had the feeling that God (or some supernatural force) was helping you through a particular crisis in your life?
    1. Yes, I'm sure I have.
    2. Yes, I think I have.
    3. No.

18. With which racial/ethnic group (for example: Irish, Italian, Black, Puerto Rican, Jewish, etc.) do you identify most?____

19. Where did you spend most of your childhood (under 18)?
    1. Metropolis (population of at least a million)
    2. Large city (population of at least 500,000)
    3. Medium sized city (population of at least 100,000)
    4. Small city (population of at least 25,000)
    5. Suburb
    6. Large town (population of at least 10,000)

7. Small town (population of less than 10,000)
8. Rural area

20. Which of the following describes your birth order? Were you the oldest, one of the middle children, or the youngest in your family?
    1. Only child
    2. First born
    3. Middle born
    4. Last born

21. While you were growing up, how many children were there in your family? Include yourself and all your brothers and sisters. ___ children

22. During the first 18 years of your life, how many times did you move? ___ times

23. Since the age of 18, how many times have you moved? ___ times

24. Please make a list of the persons close to you who have died. Use words like mother, brother, grandparent, friend, and *not* their names. Give *your* age when each of these people died.

25. If your parents were divorced or permanently separated, how old were you when it happened? If they didn't divorce or separate, skip to the next question. ___ years old

26. Which of the following describes your mother and her relationship with you while you were growing up?
    1. She and I had a warm, loving relationship; we were very close.
    2. She and I had a good relationship; we were fairly close.
    3. She and I had almost no relationship; we were not very close.
    4. She and I had a very conflicted relationship; we argued often.
    5. I didn't live with my mother during most of those years.

27. How much could you rely on your mother for help when you had any kind of problem?
    1. Very much
    2. A fair amount
    3. Some
    4. Not very much
    5. Not at all
    6. Not applicable

28. Which of the following describes your father and his relationship with you while you were growing up?
    1. He and I had a warm, loving relationship; we were very close.
    2. He and I had a good relationship; we were fairly close.
    3. He and I had almost no relationship; we were not very close.
    4. He and I had a very conflicted relationship; we argued often.
    5. I didn't live with my father during most of those years.

29. How much could you rely on your father for help when you had any kind of problem?
    1. Very much
    2. A lot
    3. A fair amount
    4. Not very much
    5. Not at all
    6. Not applicable

30. While you were growing up, how much did you consider your parents to be *trusted* and *secure* bases of support? How much could you really count on them?
    1. Very much
    2. A lot
    3. Some
    4. Not very much
    5. Not at all

31. How much have each of the following problems bothered you during the past year? Use the scale described here.

    0 = Not at all; 1 = A little bit;
    2 = Quite a bit; 3 = A lot
    1. Headaches
    2. Loss of interest in sex
    3. Digestive problems
    4. Pains in heart; heart disease

5. Feeling tired or low in energy
6. Poor appetite
7. Crying spells
8. Feeling irritable or angry
9. Constant worry and anxiety
10. Irrational fears
11. Trouble falling or staying asleep
12. Trouble getting your breath
13. Being overweight, feeling fat
14. Feelings of worthlessness
15. Feelings of guilt
16. Trouble concentrating
17. Feeling you just can't go on
18. Had a disabling accident
19. Suffered from a serious disease (Specify: _____)

32. At present, which best describes your living situation?
   1. Live alone
   2. Single parent with child(ren)
   3. Live with parents
   4. Live with roommate(s)
   5. Live with spouse
   6. Live with spouse and child(ren)
   7. Live with lover
   8. Live with lover and child(ren)
   9. Live with more than two generations of family
   10. Live in an institution
   11. Other (Specify:_____)

33. How satisfied are you with the living situation described in Question 32?

1. Very satisfied
2. Somewhat satisfied
3. Neither satisfied nor dissatisfied
4. Somewhat dissatisfied
5. Very dissatisfied

34. How satisfied are you with the house or apartment in which you live?
   1. Very satisfied
   2. Somewhat satisfied
   3. Neither satisfied nor dissatisfied
   4. Somewhat dissatisfied
   5. Very dissatisfied

35. If you could live anywhere you liked, in what kind of place would that be?
   1. Metropolis (population of at least a million)
   2. Large city (population of at least 500,000)
   3. Medium sized city (population of at least 100,000)
   4. Small city (population of at least 25,000)
   5. Suburb
   6. Large town (population of at least 10,000)
   7. Small town (population of less than 10,000)
   8. Rural area

36. Have you ever lived alone for more than six months?
   1. Yes, and I am now
   2. Yes, but not now
   3. No, never

37. If you are currently living alone, for how long have you lived alone? ___ years

38. At present, about how many pets do you have? ___ pets

39. At present, about how many plants do you have in your home? ___ plants

40. At present, about how many *close* friends would you say you have? ___ friends

41. About how often do you see most of your closest friends?
    1. Every day
    2. Several times a week
    3. Once or twice a week
    4. Less than once a week
    5. Less than once a month
    6. About once a year
    7. Less than once a year
    8. I have no close friends

42. How satisfied are you with the number of close friends you have?
    1. Very satisfied
    2. Somewhat satisfied
    3. Neither satisfied nor dissatisfied
    4. Somewhat dissatisfied
    5. Very dissatisfied

43. How satisfied are you with the quality of friendships that you have?
    1. Very satisfied
    2. Somewhat satisfied
    3. Neither satisfied nor dissatisfied
    4. Somewhat dissatisfied
    5. Very dissatisfied

44. Has your circle of friends recently changed for any of the following reasons? Circle all that apply.
    1. Moved
    2. Changed jobs
    3. Entered or left school
    4. Divorce or separation
    5. Not applicable
    6. Other (Specify:_____)

45. About how many *personal* conversations (with friends, close relatives, intimate acquaintances) do you have every day?
    1. Way too many
    2. A few too many
    3. About the right number
    4. Somewhat fewer than I would like
    5. Many fewer than I would like

46. About how many *casual, nonpersonal* conversations (while at work, shopping, etc.) do you have every day?
    1. Way too many
    2. A few too many
    3. About the right number
    4. Somewhat fewer than I would like
    5. Many fewer than I would like

47. About how many personal phone calls do you *make* and *receive* on an average day? Don't include business calls.

Make ____ calls.
Receive ____ calls.

48. In a typical week, about how many hours do you spend:
    ____ hrs. 48.1 at work?
    ____ hrs. 48.2 by yourself (include time at work, driving, thinking, reading)?
    ____ hrs. 48.3 watching television?
    ____ hrs. 48.4 with the TV on as background? (though not watching closely)
    ____ hrs. 48.5 engaging in competitive sports or exercise?
    ____ hrs. 48.6 socializing with friends? (talking or eating together)
    ____ hrs. 48.7 in prayer or meditation?

49. How often do you eat meals alone?
    1. More than once a day
    2. About once a day
    3. Several times a week
    4. About once a week
    5. Several times a month
    6. Rarely
    7. Never

50. What do you usually do while you are dining alone? Circle all that apply.
    1. Nothing but eat
    2. Read while eating
    3. Work while eating
    4. Listen to the radio while eating

    5. Watch TV while eating
    6. Not applicable
    7. Other (Specify:_____)

51. How well do you know most of your neighbors?
    1. Very well
    2. Fairly well
    3. Somewhat
    4. Not very well
    5. Not at all
    6. I don't have nearby neighbors

52. Besides members of your family, how many people in your neighborhood or community could you rely on to help you in an emergency? (For example, to take you to the hospital, help you when you are sick, etc.)
    ____ people

53. How much pressure do you feel to be successful or to "get ahead" in whatever you do?
    1. Almost none
    2. A small amount of pressure
    3. A moderate amount of pressure
    4. Very much pressure
    5. Constant pressure

54. How often do you participate in each of the following? Use the scale described here.
    0 = Never; 1 = Rarely;
    2 = Sometimes;
    3 = Often
    1. Encounter groups or sensitivity training
    2. Call-in talk shows on the radio

3. Going to bars to meet new
people
4. Singles vacations (arranged
travel to meet people)
5. Social groups or club meetings (of which you are a
member)
6. Church-related activities
7. Going to movies or cultural
events with 1 or more others
8. Civic, community or political organizations

55. How much do you enjoy your
vacations?
1. Very much
2. A fair amount
3. Some
4. Not very much
5. Not at all
6. I rarely take vacations

56. How easy is it for you to reveal
your intimate thoughts and feelings to someone you don't
know well?
1. Very easy
2. Fairly easy
3. Fairly difficult
4. Very difficult

57. Using the 5-point scale shown
below, indicate how often you
feel each of the following *when
you are alone.*
1 = Almost never;   2 =
Occasionally; 3 = About half the
time;   4 = Often;   5 = Most of the
time.
When I am completely alone, I feel:
1. lonely
2. calm, quiet

3. afraid, fearful
4. relaxed, thoughtful
5. anxious, uneasy
6. creative, productive
7. happy, content
8. angry, resentful

58. How often do you feel lonely?
1. All the time, or almost all
the time
2. Most of the time
3. Quite often
4. About half the time
5. Occasionally
6. Rarely
7. Never, or almost never

59. When you feel lonely, do you
usually feel:
1. Extremely lonely
2. Very lonely
3. Fairly lonely
4. Somewhat lonely
5. Slightly lonely
6. I never feel lonely

60. Compared to people your own
age, how lonely do you think
you are?
1. Much lonelier than average
2. Somewhat lonelier than average
3. About average
4. Somewhat less lonely than
average
5. Much less lonely than average

61. At what time of day do you
usually feel most lonely? Specify time and whether it is morning (A.M.) or evening (P.M.).
___o'clock 1: A.M. 2: P.M.

62. At what times of the year
do you feel most lonely?
Circle all that apply.
   1. Summer
   2. Fall
   3. Winter
   4. Spring
   5. Christmas/New Year's
   6. Easter/Passover
   7. Weekends
   8. Birthdays
   9. Vacations
   10. Anniversaries
   11. Other personal dates

63. When you feel lonely, who do
you think is mainly responsible
for your feeling?
   1. I am responsible.
   2. Other people, or the situation is responsible.
   3. I never feel lonely.

64. How do you usually *feel* when
you are lonely? Circle all that
apply.
   1. Down on myself
   2. Sad
   3. Unable to concentrate
   4. Uneasy
   5. Impatient
   6. Sorry for myself
   7. Insecure
   8. Afraid
   9. Melancholy
   10. Bored
   11. Ashamed of being lonely
   12. Without hope
   13. Stupid, incompetent
   14. Depressed

15. Longing to be with one
   special person
16. Vulnerable
17. Empty
18. Alienated, "out of place"
19. Unattractive
20. Isolated, alone
21. Desperate
22. Abandoned
23. Desire to be somewhere
   else
24. Panicked
25. Resigned
26. Helpless
27. Angry, resentful
28. Other (Specify:_____)

65. Listed below are some reasons
that various people have given
for feeling lonely. If you have
been lonely during the past year
or so, circle the *major* reasons.
   1. Having nothing to do, feeling bored
   2. Being alone
   3. Having no close friends; no
   one to talk to
   4. Being far away from
   friends or family
   5. Death of a loved one
   6. Break-up with spouse or
   lover
   7. Having no spouse or lover
   8. Being in a new job or new
   school
   9. No convenient means of
   transportation
   10. No telephone
   11. Not being needed
   12. Coming home to an empty
   house

13. Being hospitalized
14. Being housebound, due to age, illness, or handicap
15. Traveling often
16. Having a loved one who travels often
17. Having no sexual partner
18. Being misunderstood
19. Moving too often
20. Feeling different from everyone else, alienated
21. Other (Specify:_____)

66. How much of the time do you feel bored?
    1. All of the time
    2. Most of the time
    3. Occasionally
    4. Rarely
    5. Never

67. On an average *weekday,* how much of the time are you occupied or busy?
    1. All day
    2. Most of the day
    3. Occasionally
    4. Rarely
    5. Never

68. On an average *weekend,* how much of the time are you occupied or busy?
    1. All day
    2. Most of the day
    3. Occasionally
    4. Rarely
    5. Never

69. Are you currently in love?
    1. Yes, for the first time
    2. Yes, but not for the first time

3. No, but I have been
4. I have never been in love.

70. In many relationships, one person loves more than the other. Who now loves more in your love relationship?
    1. My love is not returned.
    2. I love more than my partner.
    3. We love equally.
    4. My partner loves more.
    5. I don't return my partner's love.
    6. Not applicable.

71. In general, how satisfied are you with your marriage or love relationship?
    1. Very satisfied
    2. Somewhat satisfied
    3. Neither satisfied nor dissatisfied
    4. Somewhat dissatisfied
    5. Very dissatisfied

72. In general, how satisfied are you with your sex life?
    1. Very satisfied
    2. Somewhat satisfied
    3. Neither satisfied nor dissatisfied
    4. Somewhat dissatisfied
    5. Very dissatisfied

73. Over the last few months, about how often have you had sexual intercourse?

    1. More than 6 times a week
    2. 4 to 6 times a week
    3. 2 to 3 times a week
    4. Once a week
    5. Once or twice a month

6. Less than once a month
7. Never

74. In general, how happy or unhappy have you been feeling about your life as a whole during the past several months?
   1. Very happy
   2. Moderately happy
   3. Slightly happy
   4. Neither happy nor unhappy
   5. Slightly unhappy
   6. Moderately unhappy
   7. Very unhappy

75. Have you ever consulted a psychotherapist or counselor?
   1. No
   2. Yes, for 6 months or less and I am now.
   3. Yes, for 6 months or less, but not now.
   4. Yes, for more than 6 months and I am now.
   5. Yes, for more than 6 months, but not now.

76. How attractive are you compared with others of your age?
   1. Much more attractive
   2. Somewhat more attractive
   3. About the same
   4. Somewhat less attractive
   5. Much less attractive

77. How likable are you compared with others of your age?
   1. Much more likable
   2. Somewhat more likable

3. About the same
4. Somewhat less likable
5. Much less likable

78. Which of the following *best* describes your feelings about death?
   1. I am afraid of death.
   2. It troubles me, but I wouldn't say I fear it.
   3. I haven't thought much about it.
   4. I am working toward accepting it.
   5. I have come to accept it.
   6. I am looking forward to it.
   7. Other (Specify:_____)

79. In your opinion, how much control do you have over the things that happen in your life?
   1. Almost total control
   2. Quite a bit of control
   3. A moderate degree of control
   4. A little bit of control
   5. Almost no control

80. Using a 4-point agree-disagree scale, indicate how much you agree with each of the following.

1 = Strongly agree; 2 = Agree;
3 = Disagree; 4 = Strongly disagree
   1. I feel my life has meaning and direction.
   2. I like most people I meet.
   3. I generally take a positive attitude toward myself.
   4. On the whole, I am satisfied with myself.

5. At times, I think I am no good at all.
6. I am introspective, I often examine my thoughts and feelings.
7. I am a shy person.
8. I am an independent person.
9. I am a friendly person.
10. I *am* a lonely person.
11. I always *was* a lonely person.
12. I always *will be* a lonely person.
13. Other people think of me as a lonely person.

81. Using the scale below, state how important each of the following is to you.

0 = Not at all important;   1 = Slightly important;   2 = Moderately important; 3 = Very important

1. to have *many* friends
2. to have *one* close friend
3. to be with people
4. to be alone sometimes
5. to have a romantic or sexual partner
6. to be independent

82. How often do you get drunk or "stoned"?

1. Every day
2. Several times a week
3. About once a week
4. Once or twice a month
5. Rarely
6. Never

83. When you feel lonely, what do you usually do about it? Circle your *most common* reactions.

1. Go for a drive
2. Nothing
3. Take a walk
4. Exercise
5. Sleep
6. Do housework
7. Call a friend
8. Read
9. Go shopping
10. Visit someone
11. Read the Bible or pray
12. Drink or get "stoned"
13. Go to a movie, a play, etc.
14. Sit and think
15. Listen to music
16. Watch TV
17. Work on a hobby
18. Overeat
19. Study or work
20. Cry
21. Write
22. Spend money on myself
23. Play a musical instrument
24. Take tranquilizers
25. Other (Specify:_____)

APPENDIX B

How Lonely Are You?

Calculating Your Loneliness Score

For each question below, circle the most appropriate answer. Then add up the numbers that correspond to the answers you chose. Your total score should fall between 80 (not at all lonely) and 320 (very lonely).

When I am completely alone, I feel lonely:

Almost never	(10)
Occasionally	(16)
About half the time	(24)
Often	(32)
Most of the time	(40)

How often do you feel lonely?

Never, or almost never	(10)
Rarely	(11)
Occasionally	(17)
About half the time	(23)

Quite often	(29)
Most of the time	(34)
All the time, or	(40)
almost all the time	

When you feel lonely, do you usually feel:

I never feel lonely	(10)
Slightly lonely	(13)
Somewhat lonely	(20)
Fairly lonely	(27)
Very lonely	(33)
Extremely lonely	(40)

Compared to people your own age, how lonely do you think you are?

Much less lonely	(10)
Somewhat less lonely	(16)
About average	(24)
Somewhat lonelier	(32)
Much lonelier	(40)

How much do you agree with each of the following?

I am a lonely person.

Strongly disagree	(10)
Disagree	(20)
Agree	(30)
Strongly agree	(40)

I always was a lonely person.

Strongly disagree	(10)
Disagree	(20)
Agree	(30)
Strongly agree	(40)

I always will be a lonely person.

Strongly disagree	(10)
Disagree	(20)
Agree	(30)
Strongly agree	(40)

Other people think of me as a lonely person.

Strongly disagree	(10)
Disagree	(20)
Agree	(30)
Strongly agree	(40)

The average score in all of our newspaper surveys was about 170. If your total score is above 206, you are among the 25 percent most lonely people. If you scored between 170 and 206, you are slightly above average in loneliness. If you scored between 132 and 170 you are slightly less lonely than average. If your score is below 132, you are among the least lonely 25 percent.

LONELINESS SCORES

If your score is:

80 to 132	—you are among the least lonely.
132 to 170	—you are less lonely than average.
170 to 206	—you are more lonely than average.
206 to 320	—you are among the most lonely.

NOTES

The following entries supply references for lengthy quotations and for research mentioned in the text or relevant to a specific point. For complete references, see the Bibliography.

CHAPTER 1

1 For a collection of papers from this conference, see Peplau and Perlman, eds., *Loneliness: A Sourcebook of Current Theory, Research, and Therapy*. See also Rubin, "Seeking a Cure for Loneliness."

2 Defoe, *Robinson Crusoe*. See also the introduction in this edition.

2 Bradburn, *The Structure of Psychological Well-Being*. This book contains one of the few references to the prevalence of loneliness in the United States. A 1978 follow-up of this survey, by the Institute for Social Research, found that 22 percent of Americans reported feeling "lonely or remote from other people" in the weeks prior to the interview.

2 Gunther, *Inside U.S.A.*

4 This research was the basis of a doctoral dissertation at New York University by Rubenstein. Other technical publications on this loneliness research include Rubenstein and Shaver, "The Experience of Loneliness," and Rubenstein and Shaver, "Loneliness in Two Northeastern Cities."

5   The loneliness scale is both reliable and valid, as explained in references in previous note.

9   These categories of feelings were derived by a statistical method called factor analysis. For a more technical description of the method, see Rubenstein and Shaver, as above.

10 Weiss, ed., *Loneliness: The Experience of Emotional and Social Isolation*. See also Mellen, *The Evolution of Love*.

14 Figures on living alone are from U.S. Bureau of the Census, "Population Profile of the United States: 1980."

14 See Tillich, *The Courage To Be*.

15 For provocative discussions of the meaning of *rite de passage,* see Bettelheim, *Symbolic Wounds,* Eliade, *Rites and Symbols of Initiation,* and Van Gennep, *The Rites of Passage.*

15 Suedfeld, *Restricted Environmental Stimulation.*

CHAPTER 2

19 Morris, *Intimate Behaviour.*

19 Erikson, *Everything in Its Path.*

20 See McAdams and Powers, "Themes of Intimacy in Behavior and Thought," McAdams, "Studies in Intimacy Motivation," and Wong, "Typologies of Intimacy."

21 For an analysis of "in-love experience," see McCready, "A Phenomenological Study of Love."

23 For recent research on the differences between men and women in the ability to be intimate, see Bell, "Friendships of Women and of Men," and Fischer and Narus, "Sex Roles and Intimacy in Same Sex and Other Sex Relationships." A classic study on possible origins of this difference is in Douvan and Adelson, *The Adolescent Experience.* Veroff, Douvan, and Kulka, *The Inner American,* documents changes in awareness of the need for intimacy. A summary of masculinity and femininity scoring differences is in Spence and Helmreich, *Masculinity and Femininity.*

24 Personal communication from Harry Reis and Ladd Wheeler on intimacy aptitude among college students.

25 Montagu, *The Natural Superiority of Women.*

26 Quote on social commitment is from Veroff, Douvan, and Kulka, *The Inner American.*

27 For a collection of Harlow's scientific papers, see Harlow and Mears, *The Human Model.*

27   This discussion on infant attachment is based on the extensive writings of British psychiatrist John Bowlby. See *Attachment and Loss*, Volumes I, II, and III.

29   For a seminal work on the way in which familiarity increases liking, see Zajonc, "Attitudinal Effects of Mere Exposure." For a comprehensive discussion of other causes of attachment, see Maccoby, *Social Development*.

30   For a detailed description of individuation theory, see Kaplan, *Oneness and Separateness*, and Mahler, Pine, and Bergman, *The Psychological Birth of the Human Infant*.

33   See Weiss's loneliness book for the earliest discussion of emotional and social isolation.

34   See Harlow and Mears, as above.

34   For up-to-date research on children's friendships, see Asher and Gottman, eds., *The Development of Friendship*.

35   The example of Patty Worth (a pseudonym) is from interviews done by Rubenstein and Gail Sheehy for *Pathfinders*.

CHAPTER 3

38   Scarf, *Unfinished Business*.

39   See Ansbacher and Ansbacher, eds., *The Individual Psychology of Alfred Adler* for discussion of analysis of earliest childhood memories.

39   For a more technical discussion of the parental relationship findings, see Shaver and Rubenstein, "Childhood Attachment Experience and Adult Loneliness." There is even some research indicating that people whose parents divorced are more likely to get divorced themselves; see Pope and Mueller, "The Intergenerational Transmission of Marital Instability."

39   The best discussion of affiliation appears in Schachter, *The Psychology of Affiliation*.

41   Bowlby, *Separation*.

44   Solano, "Loneliness and Self-Disclosure," is a behavioral study of lonely college students.

44   Nietzsche, *The Portable Nietzsche*.

45   From Newson and Newson, *Four Years Old in an Urban Community*, a British study of abandonment threats.

46   For further information on age at parents' divorce, see Rubenstein, Shaver, and Peplau, "Loneliness."

46   See Glick and Norton, "Marrying, Divorcing, and Living Together in

the U.S. Today" for estimates of the number of American children who will live with only one parent.

46 For one of the first studies distinguishing between "unhappy but unbroken" homes and "broken homes," see Nye, "Child Adjustment in Broken and in Unhappy Unbroken Homes."

49 For a recent and comprehensive treatment of the effects of divorce on children, see Longfellow, "Divorce in Context," and Wallerstein and Kelly, *Surviving the Break-Up.*

49 The concept of "mental models" of self is from Bowlby's work.

50 For an overview of research on sibling relationships in adulthood, see Adams, "The Sibling Bond."

50 For further information on birth order effects, see Schachter, *The Psychology of Affiliation,* and Zajonc and Markus, "Birth Order and Intellectual Development."

51 See Ickes, "A Basic Paradigm for the Study of Personality Roles and Social Behavior," for research on birth order and social skills.

51 A summary of research on how close people feel to their parents and siblings appears in Adams, "The Sibling Bond."

52 The study on popular, average, rejected, and neglected boys is by Coie and Kupersmidt, "A Behavioral Analysis of Emerging Social Status in Boys' Groups."

53 Furman, Rahe, and Hartup, "Rehabilitation of Socially-Withdrawn Preschool Children Through Mixed-Age and Same-Age Socialization" documents the efficacy of younger "therapists" in drawing out socially withdrawn children.

53 The quote on social strategies of unpopular children is from Putallaz and Gottman, "Social Skills and Group Acceptance." For other research on children's friendships, see Corsaro, "Friendship in the Nursery School," and Schantz, "Children's Fights."

54 The videotape studies of lonely college students are by Warren Jones; see Jones, Hobbs, and Hockenbury, "Loneliness and Social Skill Deficits," Hansson and Jones, "Loneliness, Cooperation, and Conformity Among American Undergraduates," Jones, "The Social Behavior of Lonely People," and Jones, Freeman, and Goswick, "The Persistence of Loneliness."

55 For additional information on temperament, see Buss and Plomin, *A Temperament Theory of Personality Development,* and Thomas and Chess, *The Dynamics of Psychological Development.*

56 The discussion and quotes about children's friendships are from Rubin, *Children's Friendships.*

CHAPTER 4

62 Twain, *The Adventures of Huckleberry Finn.*
62 Results from the national survey comparing younger and older Americans appears in Campbell, *The Sense of Well-Being in America.*
63 The study of Americans at high school graduation, first marriage, middle age, and preretirement is from Lowenthal, Thurnher, and Chiriboga, *Four Stages of Life.*
63 For research on loneliness among 10- to 18-year-olds, see Brennan, "Loneliness at Adolescence."
63 The part of adolescence that rarely recurs is the dramatically rapid and intense mood changes. Rarely do we feel higher highs or lower lows. See Larson, Csikszentmihalyi, and Graef, "Mood Variability and the Psychosocial Adjustment of Adolescents."
64 For further reading on adolescence as "the second individuation process," see Blos, *The Adolescent Passage.*
64 Quote is from Anna Freud, "Adolescence."
64 Additional information and research on negative dependence can be found in Offer, *The Psychological World of the Teenager.*
65 For a summary of research on the difficulties involved in leaving home, see Goleman, "Leaving Home."
65 For a provocative discussion of adolescence as a relatively new stage of life, see Elder, "Adolescence in the Life Cycle," and Bakan, "Adolescence in America." For a classic work on the modern invention of childhood, see Ariès, *Centuries of Childhood.*
66 Quotes are taken from Scarf, *Unfinished Business.*
67 The research on the effects of puberty are from Clausen, "The Social Meaning of Differential Physical and Sexual Maturation."
67 Additional studies of junior high students include Petersen and Taylor, "The Biological Approach to Adolescence," and Faust, "Developmental Maturity as a Determinant in Prestige of Adolescent Girls."
67 The findings on men in their thirties is also in Clausen, as above.
68 The conclusion that girls do best who develop in synchrony with their peers is from Faust, as above.
68 Simmons, Blyth, Van Cleave, and Bush found that the timing of puberty is more important for boys than for girls; see "Entry Into Early Adolescence."
68 The importance of physical attractiveness for teenagers is discussed in Cavoir and Dokecki, "Physical Attractiveness, Perceived Attitude Similarity, and Academic Achievement as Contributors to Interper-

sonal Attraction Among Adolescents." The best reference on the importance of attractiveness in general is Berscheid and Walster, *Interpersonal Attraction*. See also Dion, Berscheid, and Walster, "What Is Beautiful Is Good."

70 The classic description of the change in adolescent thought processes is in Piaget, *Construction of Reality in the Child*.

70 For a more detailed discussion of adolescent's intense self-consciousness and belief in an "imaginary audience," see Elkind, "Strategic Interactions in Early Adolescence." See also Harter, "Developmental Perspectives on the Self System."

72 James Connell, personal communication concerning ongoing research of children's confusion at moving from sixth to seventh grade.

73 For research on adolescent self-esteem, see Rosenberg, *Society and the Adolescent Self-Image*, Simmons, Rosenberg, and Rosenberg, "Disturbance in the Self-Image at Adolescence," and Bachman, O'Malley, and Johnston, *Youth in Transition*.

74 For information on the effect of low self-esteem on other social problems, see Kahle, Kulka, and Klingel, "Low Adolescent Self-Esteem Leads to Multiple Interpersonal Problems."

75 See Erikson, "Youth: Fidelity and Diversity" and *Identity: Youth and Crisis*.

76 Research on the prevalence of adolescent sexual activity was done by Kantner and Zelnick, "Sexual Activity, Contraceptive Use, and Pregnancy Among Metropolitan-Area Teenagers: 1971–1979." See also Miller and Simon, "The Development of Sexuality in Adolescence."

77 The classic study of teenagers is by Douvan and Adelson, *The Adolescent Experience*.

78 Quote is from Montagu, *The Natural Superiority of Women*.

78 For the most comprehensive study of teenage popularity and cliques, see James Coleman, *The Adolescent Society;* see also John Coleman, *Relationships in Adolescence*.

78 The Illinois study is by James Coleman, *The Adolescent Society*.

79 The finding about identity is taken from surveys we conducted in *Redbook* and *Esquire* and in nationwide volunteer groups for Gail Sheehy's book, *Pathfinders*.

79 For figures on ages at which Americans move, see U.S. Bureau of the Census, "Geographical Mobility."

79 For the University of Pennsylvania study on depression, see Beck and Young, "College Blues."

80 See Cutrona, "Transition to College."

81 The study on members of nine cults is from Levine, "Youth and Religious Cults."

82 Moustakas's thoughts on loneliness have been spelled out in *Loneliness* and *Loneliness and Love*.

83 For a summary of research on adolescent suicide, see Petzel and Cline, "Adolescent Suicide."

83 For a report on psychiatrists who treat adolescents, see Weisberg, "Demographic, Attitudinal, and Practice Patterns of Adolescent Psychiatrists in the United States."

83 From an American Psychological Association press release, "An Adolescent Epidemic: Suicide."

84 The study on adolescent drug use in Illinois is by Levine and Kozak, "Drug and Alcohol Use, Delinquency, and Vandalism Among Upper Middle Class Pre- and Post-Adolescents."

84 The 2–2–2 study is by Blyth, Simmons, and Bush, "The Transition Into Early Adolescence."

85 Quote is from Winn, *The Plug-In Drug*.

85 For his theory on adolescents' need for sensory stimulation, see Blos, *The Adolescent Passage* and *On Adolescence*.

85 The study of television viewers as social failures is from James Coleman, *The Adolescent Society*. The college study is Perloff, Quarles, and Drutz, "Loneliness, Depression, and the Uses of Television Among College Students."

CHAPTER 5

89 Russell, *Marriage and Morals*.

90 Quote is from Degler, *At Odds*.

90 The evidence for the physical and psychological benefits of marriage is voluminous. See, for example, Bloom, Asher, and White, "Marital Disruption as a Stressor," Brown and Harris, *Social Origins of Depression*, Gove, "Sex, Marital Status, and Suicide" and "Sex, Marital Status, and Mortality," Lynch, *The Broken Heart*, Stack, "The Effects of Marital Dissolution on Suicide," and Verbrugge, "Marital Status and Health."

90 Several recent surveys show that married Americans are, on the average, happier than unmarried ones. See Campbell, *The Sense of Well-Being in America*, and Veroff, Douvan, and Kulka, *The Inner American*.

90 A full description of the findings from the Harvard study is in Vaillant, *Adaptation to Life.*

91 The Chicago study is by Pearlin and Johnson, "Marital Status, Life Strains, and Depression."

91 The British study on emotional support is by Brown and Harris, as above.

91 A report on affirmation and intimacy in marriage is in Vanfossen, "Sex Differences in the Mental Health Effects of Spouse Support and Equity."

92 These health differences are emphasized in most research on the benefits of marriage. The top three most stressful life events, most likely to lead to illness, include death of a spouse, divorce, and separation. See Holmes and Rahe, "The Social Readjustment Rating Scale." Also Carter and Glick, *Marriage and Divorce.*

92 See Lynch, *The Broken Heart.*

93 There is even evidence that men fall in love more readily than women, who tend to fall *out* of love more easily than men. See Hill, Rubin, and Peplau, "Breakups Before Marriage."

93 Quotes are from Bernard, *The Future of Marriage.*

94 More wives than husbands file for divorce. See Hunt and Hunt, *The Divorce Experience,* and Spanier and Anderson, "The Impact of the Legal System on Adjustment to Marital Separation."

94 The most recent evidence that women are more critical of marriage than men is in Veroff, Douvan, and Kulka, *The Inner American,* and Douvan, Veroff, and Kulka, "Family Roles in a Twenty-Year Perspective." This was also true in 1957; see Gurin, Veroff, and Feld, *Americans View Their Mental Health.* See also Campbell, "The American Way of Mating."

94 For research on differential adaptation to divorce, see Chiriboga, Roberts, and Stein, "Psychological Well-Being During Marital Separation."

95 That two to five times as many women as men are depressed is accepted by most researchers. See Scarf, *Unfinished Business,* and Weissman and Klerman, "Sex Differences and the Epidemiology of Depression."

96 Results of the Northern California study are summarized in Fischer, *To Dwell Among Friends,* and in Fischer and Phillips, "Who is Alone?"

96 For a historical discussion of American family life, see Hareven, "American Families in Transition."

97 For a discussion of generativity, see Erikson, *Identity: Youth and Crisis* and *Childhood and Society.*

98 The early loss of intimacy in predivorce couples is discussed in Wallerstein and Kelly, *Surviving the Break-Up.* See also Hetherington, Cox, and Cox, "The Aftermath of Divorce."

100 The census figures are from Glick and Norton, as above. One study finds that the likelihood that any married couple will separate during a year is five out of 100. Of couples aged 30 to 34, chances are 23 out of 100 that they will have been separated at some point; see Bloom, et al., "Marital Separation."

100 The quote is from Marris, *Loss and Change.*

100 All the quotes from Seminars for the Separated are from Weiss, *Marital Separation.*

102 Wives usually suffer financially after a divorce more than husbands do. The economic causes and consequences of divorce should not be neglected; see, for example, Cherlin, "Work Life and Marital Dissolution," and Espenshade, "The Economic Consequences of Divorce."

102 The study of divorce trauma is by Chiriboga and Cutler, "Stress Responses Among Divorced Men and Women."

103 Quotes are from Wallerstein and Kelly, as above.

104 Research on the advantage to the divorced provided by social ties is in Chiriboga, Coho, Stein, and Roberts, "Divorce, Stress, and Social Supports." See also Spanier and Casto, "Adjustment to Separation and Divorce."

106 For material on why divorce may be as difficult or even worse than widowhood, see Kitson, Lopata, Holmes, and Meyering, "Divorcees and Widows," Weiss, *Going It Alone* and "The Emotional Impact of Marital Separation."

106 From Marris, *Loss and Change.*

106 The discussion of four stages of mourning is from Bowlby, *Loss.* It is based on nine major studies of people in the United States, Great Britain, and Australia who had lost a spouse.

107 The findings from the Welsh study are from Rees, "The Bereaved and Their Hallucinations."

107 Other studies of hallucinations of the widowed appear in Marris, *Widows and Their Families,* and Yamamoto, Okonogi, Iwasaki, and Yoshimura, "Mourning in Japan."

107 For a detailed discussion of attachment, see Bowlby, *Attachment.*

108 For an overview of studies on widowhood, see Lopata, *Widowhood in An American City*.

108 The British study on depressed women is from Brown and Harris, *Social Origins of Depression*.

109 For a report on the friendship survey, see Parlee, "The Friendship Bond."

109 For the definition of friendship, see Fischer, *To Dwell Among Friends*.

111 Coleridge, "The Friend."

111 The Harvard study is from Vaillant, *Adaptation to Life*.

CHAPTER 6

115 Quote is from Myerhoff, *Number Our Days*.

116 Our study of adult development was done for Gail Sheehy's book, *Pathfinders*. Similar findings are reported in Campbell, *The Sense of Well-Being in America*.

116 "Do Not Go Gentle Into That Good Night," see Thomas, *Collected Poems*.

116 Other recent studies confirming our findings that the elderly are not most lonely include Harris, *The Myth and Reality of Aging in America*, and Shanas, et al., *Old People in Three Industrial Societies*.

117 The international study of the elderly is from Shanas, et al., as above.

118 From Harris, as above.

118 Quotes are from Harris, as above.

119 The study of elderly widows' friendships is from Arling, "The Elderly Widow and Her Family, Neighbors, and Friends."

119 For a comprehensive statistical portrait of elderly Americans, see U.S. Bureau of the Census, "Social and Economic Characteristics of the Older Population: 1978." For a personal account of the situation of older Americans, see Butler, *Why Survive?*

119 The two large-scale studies of the elderly are Harris, as above, and Shanas, "The Family as Social Support System in Old Age."

119 For more information on family relations of the elderly, see Shanas, "Social Myth as Hypothesis" and "Older People and Their Families."

119 The findings on help giving in families are from Harris, as above.

120 The figures on the number of people over 65 with no living relatives are from Shanas, et al., as above. The visiting statistics are from Harris, as above. See also Shanas, "The Family as Social Support System in Old Age."

120   The study of widows is from Arling, as above.

122   The California study of 1,000 married couples is from Gilford and Bengtson, "Measuring Marital Satisfaction in Three Generations."

122   The sex study is from Masters and Johnson, "Human Sexual Response." See also Pfeiffer, Verwoerdt, and Davis, "Sexual Behavior in Middle Life," and Pfeiffer and Davis, "Determinants of Sexual Behavior in Middle and Old Age."

123   The San Francisco study is by Lowenthal and Haven, "Interaction and Adaptation."

123   For research on friendship in old age, see Powers and Bultena, "Sex Differences in Intimate Friendships of Old Age," and Rosow, "Housing and Local Ties of the Aged."

124   The Detroit study is by Gubrium, "Being Single in Old Age."

127   For a more detailed discussion of psychological separation in infancy, see Chapter 3.

128   Jung's discussion of middle age appears in *The Portable Jung.*

128   For recent research on loneliness among the elderly, see Blazer and Williams, "Epidemiology of Dysphoria and Depression in an Elderly Population," Kivett, "Discriminators of Loneliness Among the Rural Elderly," Lowenthal, "Social Isolation and Mental Illness in Old Age," Lowenthal and Robinson, "Social Networks and Isolation," Peplau, Goodchilds, and Bikson, "Old and Alone," Perlman, Gerson, and Spinner, "Loneliness Among Senior Citizens," Revenson and Rubenstein, "Debunking the Myth of Loneliness in Old Age," and Woodward, Gingles, and Woodward, "Loneliness and the Elderly as Related to Housing."

129   Studies on men's and women's differential adaptation to widowhood include: Berardo, "Survivorship and Social Isolation," Cosneck, "Family Patterns of Older Widowed Jewish People," Lowenthal and Weiss, "Intimacy and Crises in Adulthood," and Petrowsky, "Marital Status, Sex, and the Social Networks of the Elderly."

130   The British study of bereavement is by Parkes, *Bereavement.*

130   The study of widows aged 60 to 94 is by Heyman and Gianturco, "Long-Term Adaptation by the Elderly to Bereavement."

130   Figures on retirement are from Harris, as above, and Shanas, et al., as above.

130   An extremely negative view of retirement is taken by Blau in *Old Age in a Changing Society.* More optimistic ones can be found in Birren, et al., *Human Aging,* Palmore, "Advantages of Aging," Palmore and

Luikart, "Health and Social Factors Related to Life Satisfaction," and Rose, "A Current Theoretical Issue in Social Gerontology."

131 Figures on the health of elderly Americans are from Shanas, et al., as above.

131 The health perception research is from Shanas, et al., as above.

132 Poverty and home ownership figures are from U.S. Bureau of the Census, "Social and Economic Characteristics of the Older Population: 1978."

132 The dissatisfaction level of income finding is from Shanas, et al., as above.

132 Quote is from Harris, as above.

133 The Baltimore study findings are from Costa and McCrae, "Influence of Extraversion and Neuroticism on Subjective Well-Being." See also Maas and Kuypers, *From Thirty to Seventy*.

134 The disposition studies are from Buss and Plomin, *A Temperament Theory of Personality Development*.

134 The quote is from Neugarten, Havighurst, and Tobin, "Personality and Patterns of Aging." See also Havighurst, Neugarten, and Tobin, "Disengagement and Patterns of Aging."

135 For discussion of the importance of birth cohort (year of birth) in research and the future of the elderly, see Elder, *Children of the Great Depression*, Horn, "On the Future of Growing Old," Robin, Markle, and Robin, "Toward a Theory of Age Differences," and Siegel, "Prospective Trends in the Size and Structure of the Elderly Population."

136 Quote is from Andrews, "Autumn Tells Summer's News."

138 Erikson's ideas about aging are presented in *Childhood and Society*.

138 The quote from Kovitz is from Myerhoff, as above.

CHAPTER 7

139 Quote is from promotional mailing of Reverend Sun Myung Moon, 1979.

139 Bidipai quote is from Bartlett, *Familiar Quotations*.

140 For information on the sense of community, see Barker and Schoggen, *Qualities of Community Life*, Minar and Greer, eds., *The Concept of Community*, Nisbet, *The Quest for Community*, Sarason, *The Psychological Sense of Community*, Suttles, *The Social Construction of Com-*

munities, and Varenne, *Americans Together*. See also Stack, *All Our Kin*, for an excellent anthropological study of a ghetto community.

141   For a detailed discussion of the history of American mobility, see Fischer, "Comments on the History and Study of 'Community.' "

142   All Moon quotes are from unpublished promotional material.

143   The sociological study of Moon and his organization is from Bromley and Shupe, *Moonies in America*.

145   The study of utopian communities is by Kanter, *Commitment and Community*. Similar studies include Abrams and McCulloch, *Communes, Sociology, and Society*, and Zablocki, *The Joyful Community*.

146   Oneida song and all quotes are from Kanter, as above.

149   See Erikson, *Everything in Its Path*, for the study of Buffalo Creek flood survivors and for these quotes. Another excellent analysis of the destruction of a community is by Lifton, *Death in Life*.

151   The quote is from Lingeman, *Small Town America*, as is the discussion of American towns.

151   Quotes are from Lingeman, as above.

153   Rural dwelling figures are from Lingeman, as above, as is the discussion of the 1924 Muncie study.

155   For a scholarly discussion of the decline of community theory, see Fischer, *Networks and Places*. See also Packard, *A Nation of Strangers*, and Bennis and Slater, *The Temporary Society*.

155   The argument for American rootlessness is emphasized by Packard, as above.

155   The argument that Americans have always been rootless is made by Fischer, *Networks and Places*.

155   See U.S. Bureau of the Census, "Geographic Mobility," for information on the number of families who move.

156   The national studies on reasons for moving include Campbell, *The Sense of Well-Being in America*, and Veroff, Douvan, and Kulka, *The Inner American*.

157   The ISR study on neighborliness is reported in Campbell, as above.

157   The Rochester study is by Hunter, "The Loss of Community."

157   The study revealing changes between 1957 and 1976 is by Veroff, Douvan, and Kulka, as above.

158   Research on the advantage of having a social support network include: Berkman and Syme, "Social Networks, Host Resistance, and Mortality," Cobb, "Social Support as a Moderator of Life Stress," Dean and Lin, "The Stress-Buffering Role of Social Support," and Veroff, Douvan, and Kulka, as above.

159 For research on urban-rural differences (or lack of them), see Campbell, as above, Fischer, *To Dwell Among Friends* and *Networks and Places*, Veroff, Douvan, and Kulka, as above, and Warren, "Helping Networks."

160 See interview with Milgram by Tavris, "The Frozen World of the Familiar Stranger."

160 The New York newcomer study and the quotes are from Franck, "Friends and Strangers."

162 Some sources of information on attachment to place are Proshansky and Kaminoff, "Place Identity," and Stokols and Shumaker, "People in Places."

162 From Fischer, *Networks and Places*.

162 For research on liking familiar stimuli see Zajonc, "Attitudinal Effects of Mere Exposure."

163 Quote is from Dunne, *Quintana and Friends*.

165 For discussions of friends of convenience and friends of commitment, see Fischer, *Networks and Places* and *To Dwell Among Friends*.

167 For a discussion of community groups, see Newman, *Community of Interest*.

CHAPTER 8

169 Quote is from Tillich, *The Courage To Be*.

169 Quote is from Weiss, eds., *Loneliness*.

170 From Wordsworth, "I Wandered Lonely as a Cloud."

170 From Cowper, "Retirement," quoted in Bartlett, *Familiar Quotations*.

170 From Josh Billings, "Comical Lexicon," quoted in Bartlett, *Familiar Quotations*.

170 From Lear, "Loneliness."

173 Coleridge, "The Rime of the Ancient Mariner."

173 Quote is from Nouwen, *Clowning in Rome*.

174 A discussion of the Desert Fathers and this quote appear in Merton, *Contemplation in a World of Action*.

176 Quote is from James, "The Private Life."

177 Quote is from Vaillant, *Adaptation to Life*.

179 Quote is from Winn, *The Plug-In Drug*.

181 Quote is from Lear, "Loneliness."

184 The story of Philoctetes is condensed from Wood, *Paths of Loneliness*.

186 The "Listening Manual" is in Gendlin, *Focusing.*

187 Quote is from Vaillant, as above.

189 The discussion of communication skills and the quotes are from Bolton, *People Skills.*

193 For a technical description of Peplau's research, see Peplau and Caldwell, "Loneliness," Peplau and Perlman, "Blueprint for a Social Psychological Theory of Loneliness," Peplau, Russell, and Heim, "The Experience of Loneliness," and Perlman and Peplau, "Toward a Social Psychology of Loneliness."

193 The structure of the four beliefs is from Weiner, *Achievement Motivation and Attribution Theory.*

198 Shaver attended the Erikson conference.

199 The depression comparison study is by Bragg, "A Comparative Study of Loneliness and Depression."

199 For an in-depth look at the causes of depression, see Arieti and Bemporad, *Severe and Mild Depression.*

200 For a technical description of our health findings, see Shaver and Rubenstein, "Living Alone, Loneliness, and Health."

201 See Lynch, *The Broken Heart.*

202 Quote is from Deloney, "Strange Histories," included in Bartlett, *Familiar Quotations.*

203 Quote is from Lynch, as above.

204 Quote is from de Tocqueville, *Democracy in America.*

207 See Vaillant, as above.

BIBLIOGRAPHY

Abrams, Philip, and McCulloch, Andrew. *Communes, Sociology, and Society.* New York: Cambridge University Press, 1976.

Adams, Virginia. "The Sibling Bond: A Lifelong Love/Hate Dialectic." *Psychology Today,* June 1981.

American Psychological Association, Press Release, "An Adolescent Epidemic: Suicide." February 23, 1981.

Andrews, Hazel. "Autumn Tells Summer's News." *New York Times,* December 10, 1974.

Ansbacher, Heinz, and Ansbacher, Rowena, eds. *The Individual Psychology of Alfred Adler.* New York: Basic Books, 1956.

Ariès, Philippe. *Centuries of Childhood: A Social History of Family Life.* New York: Vintage, 1962.

Arieti, Silvano, and Bemporad, Jules. *Severe and Mild Depression: The Psychotherapeutic Approach.* New York: Basic Books, 1978.

Arling, Greg. "The Elderly Widow and Her Family, Neighbors, and Friends." *Journal of Marriage and the Family,* 1976, *38,* 757–768.

Asher, Steven, and Gottman, John, eds. *The Development of Friendship: Description and Intervention.* New York: Cambridge University Press, 1982.

Bachman, Jerald, O'Malley, Patrick, and Johnston, Jerome. *Youth in Transition: Vol. VI.* Ann Arbor, Michigan: ISR, 1978.

Bakan, David. "Adolescence in America: From Idea to Social Fact." In Jerome Kagan and Robert Coles, eds. *Twelve to Sixteen: Early Adolescence.* New York: Norton, 1972.

Barker, Roger, and Schoggen, Phil. *Qualities of Community Life.* San Francisco: Jossey-Bass, 1973.

Bartlett, John. *Familiar Quotations.* Boston: Little, Brown & Co., 1968.

Beck, Aaron, and Young, Jeffrey. "College Blues." *Psychology Today,* September 1978.

Bell, Robert. "Friendships of Women and of Men." *Psychology of Women Quarterly,* 1981, *5,* 402–417.

Bennis, Warren, and Slater, Philip. *The Temporary Society.* New York: Harper & Row, 1968.

Berardo, Felix. "Survivorship and Social Isolation: The Case of the Aged Widow." *The Family Coordinator,* 1970, *19,* 11–25.

Berkman, Lisa, and Syme, Leonard. "Social Networks, Host Resistance, and Mortality: A Nine-Year Follow-Up Study of Alameda County Residents." *American Journal of Epidemiology,* 1979, *109,* 186–204.

Bernard, Jessie. *The Future of Marriage.* New York: Bantam Books, 1972.

Berscheid, Ellen, and Walster, Elaine. *Interpersonal Attraction.* Reading, Massachusetts: Addison-Wesley, 1969.

Bettelheim, Bruno. *Symbolic Wounds: Puberty Rites and the Envious Male.* New York: Collier Books, 1954.

Birren, James, Butler, Robert, Greenhouse, Samuel, Sokoloff, Louis, and Yarrow, Marian. *Human Aging: A Biological and Behavioral Study.* Washington, D.C.: U.S. Government Printing Office, 1963.

Blau, Zena. *Old Age in a Changing Society.* New York: New Viewpoints, 1973.

Blazer, Dan, and Williams, Candyce. "Epidemiology of Dysphoria and Depression in an Elderly Population." *American Journal of Psychiatry,* 1980, *137,* 439–444.

Bloom, Bernard, Asher, Shirley, and White, Stephen. "Marital Disruption as a Stressor: A Review and Analysis." *Psychological Bulletin,* 1978, *85,* 867–894.

Bloom, B., Hodges, W., Caldwell, R., Systra, L., and Cedrone, A. "Marital Separation: A Community Survey." *Journal of Divorce,* 1978, *1,* 7–19.

Blos, Peter. *On Adolescence: A Psychoanalytic Interpretation.* New York: Free Press, 1962.

Blos, Peter. *The Adolescent Passage.* New York: International Universities Press, 1979.

Blyth, Dale, Simmons, Roberta, and Bush, Diane. "The Transition Into Early Adolescence: A Longitudinal Comparison of Youth in Two Educational Contexts." *Sociology of Education,* 1978, *51,* 149–162.

Bolton, Robert. *People Skills.* New York: Spectrum, 1979.

Bowlby, John. *Attachment and Loss. Vol. I: Attachment.* New York: Basic Books, 1969.

———. *Vol. II: Separation: Anxiety and Anger.* New York: Basic Books, 1973.

———. *Vol. III: Loss: Sadness and Depression.* New York: Basic Books, 1980.

Bradburn, Norman. *The Structure of Psychological Well-Being.* Chicago: Aldine, 1969.

Bragg, Martin. "A Comparative Study of Loneliness and Depression." Unpublished doctoral dissertation, UCLA, 1979.

Brennan, Tim. "Loneliness at Adolescence." In L. Anne Peplau and Daniel Perlman, eds. *Loneliness: A Sourcebook of Current Theory, Research, and Therapy.* New York: Wiley-Interscience, 1982.

Bromley, David, and Shupe, Anson, Jr. *Moonies in America.* Beverly Hills, California: Sage, 1979.

Brown, George, and Harris, Tirril. *Social Origins of Depression: A Study of Psychiatric Disorder in Women.* New York: Free Press, 1978.

Buss, Arnold, and Plomin, Robert. *A Temperament Theory of Personality Development.* New York: Wiley-Interscience, 1975.

Butler, Robert. *Why Survive? Being Old in America.* New York: Harper & Row, 1975.

Campbell, Angus. "The American Way of Mating." *Psychology Today,* May 1975.

Campbell, Angus. *The Sense of Well-Being in America.* New York: McGraw-Hill, 1981.

Carter, Hugh, and Glick, Paul. *Marriage and Divorce: A Social and Economic Study.* Cambridge, Massachusetts: Harvard University Press, 1976.

Cavoir, Norman, and Dokecki, Paul. "Physical Attractiveness, Perceived Attitude Similarity, and Academic Achievement as Contributors to Interpersonal Attraction Among Adolescents." In Robert Grinder, ed. *Studies in Adolescence.* New York: Macmillan, 1975.

Cherlin, Andrew. "Work Life and Marital Dissolution." In George Levinger and Oliver Moles, eds. *Divorce and Separation: Context, Causes, and Consequences.* New York: Basic Books, 1979.

Chiriboga, David, Coho, Ann, Stein, Judith, and Roberts, John. "Divorce,

Stress, and Social Supports: A Study in Help-Seeking Behavior.'' *Journal of Divorce,* 1980, *3,* 121–135.

Chiriboga, David, and Cutler, Loraine. "Stress Responses Among Divorced Men and Women." *Journal of Divorce,* 1978, *1,* 95–106.

Chiriboga, David, Roberts, John, and Stein, Judith. "Psychological Well-Being During Marital Separation." *Journal of Divorce,* 1978, *2,* 21–36.

Clausen, John. "The Social Meaning of Differential Physical and Sexual Maturation." In Sigmund Dragastin and Glen Elder, eds. *Adolescence in the Life Cycle.* Washington, D.C.: Hemisphere Publishing Co., 1975.

Cobb, Sidney. "Social Support as a Moderator of Life Stress." *Psychosomatic Medicine,* 1976, *38,* 300–314.

Coie, John, and Kupersmidt, Janis. "A Behavioral Analysis of Emerging Social Status in Boys' Groups." Presented at the biennial meeting of the Society for Research in Child Development, Boston, April 1981.

Coleman, James. *The Adolescent Society.* New York: Free Press, 1961.

Coleman, John. *Relationships in Adolescence.* Boston: Routledge and Kegan, 1974.

Coleridge, Samuel. "The Rime of the Ancient Mariner." In Arthur Eastman, ed. *Norton Anthology of Poetry.* New York: Norton, 1975.

Coleridge, Samuel. "The Friend." *Collected Works of Samuel Coleridge.* Princeton, New Jersey: Princeton University Press, 1969.

Corsaro, William. "Friendship in the Nursery School: Social Organization in a Peer Environment." in Steven Asher and John Gottman, eds. *The Development of Friendship: Description and Intervention.* New York: Cambridge University Press, 1982.

Cosneck, Bernard. "Family Patterns of Older Widowed Jewish People." *The Family Coordinator,* 1970, *19,* 368–373.

Costa, Paul, Jr., and McCrae, Robert. "Influence of Extraversion and Neuroticism on Subjective Well-Being: Happy and Unhappy People." *Journal of Personality and Social Psychology,* 1980, *38,* 668–678.

Cutrona, Carolyn. "Transition to College." In L. Anne Peplau and Daniel Perlman, eds. *Loneliness: A Sourcebook of Current Theory, Research, and Therapy.* New York: Wiley-Interscience, 1982.

Dean, Alfred, and Lin, Nan. "The Stress-Buffering Role of Social Support." *The Journal of Nervous and Mental Disease,* 1977, *165,* 403–417.

Defoe, Daniel. *Robinson Crusoe.* New York: Signet, 1960.

Degler, Carl. *At Odds: Women and the Family in America from the Revolution to the Present.* New York: Oxford University Press, 1980.

Dion, Karen, Berscheid, Ellen, and Walster, Elaine. "What Is Beautiful Is Good." *Journal of Personality and Social Psychology*, 1972, *24*, 285–290.

Douvan, Elizabeth, and Adelson, Joseph. *The Adolescent Experience*. New York: Wiley, 1966.

Douvan, Elizabeth, Veroff, Joseph, and Kulka, Richard. "Family Roles in a Twenty-Year Perspective." *Economic Outlook U.S.A.*, 1979, *6*, 60–63.

Dunne, John Gregory. *Quintana and Friends*. New York: Dutton, 1979.

Elder, Glen. "Adolescence in the Life Cycle: An Introduction." In Sigmund Dragastin and Glen Elder, eds. *Adolescence in the Life Cycle*. Washington, D.C.: Hemisphere Publishing Co., 1975.

Elder, Glen. *Children of the Great Depression*. Chicago: University of Chicago Press, 1974.

Eliade, Mircea. *Rites and Symbols of Initiation: The Mysteries of Birth and Rebirth*. New York: Harper & Row, 1958.

Elkind, David. "Strategic Interactions in Early Adolescence." In Joseph Adelson, ed. *Handbook of Adolescent Psychology*. New York: Wiley-Interscience, 1980.

Erikson, Erik. *Childhood and Society*. New York: Norton, 1964.

Erikson, Erik. *Identity: Youth and Crisis*. New York: Norton, 1968.

Erikson, Erik. "Youth: Fidelity and Diversity." In Erik Erikson, ed. *The Challenge of Youth*. Garden City, New York: Anchor Books, 1965.

Erikson, Kai T. *Everything in Its Path*. New York: Simon and Schuster, 1976.

Espenshade, Thomas. "The Economic Consequences of Divorce." *Journal of Marriage and the Family*, 1979, *41*, 615–625.

Faust, Margaret. "Developmental Maturity as a Determinant in Prestige of Adolescent Girls." In Dorothy Rogers, ed. *Issues in Adolescent Psychology*. New York: Appleton-Century-Crofts, 1969.

Fischer, Claude. *To Dwell Among Friends: Personal Networks in Town and City*. Chicago: University of Chicago Press, 1982.

Fischer, Claude. *Networks and Places: Social Relations in the Urban Setting*. New York: Free Press, 1977.

Fischer, Claude. "Comments on the History and Study of 'Community.' " *Networks and Places: Social Relations in the Urban Setting*. New York: Free Press, 1977.

Fischer, Claude, and Phillips, Susan. "Who is Alone?" In L. Anne Peplau and Daniel Perlman, eds. *Loneliness: A Sourcebook of Current Theory, Research and Therapy*. New York: Wiley-Interscience, 1982.

Fischer, Judith, and Narus, Leonard. "Sex Roles and Intimacy in Same Sex and Other Sex Relationships." *Psychology of Women Quarterly,* 1981, *5,* 444–455.

Franck, Karen. "Friends and Strangers: The Social Experience of Living in Urban and Nonurban Settings." *Journal of Social Issues,* 1980, *36,* 52–71.

Freud, Anna. "Adolescence." *The Psychoanalytic Study of the Child XIII.* New York: International Universities Press, 1958.

Furman, Wyndol, Rahe, Donald, and Hartup, Willard. "Rehabilitation of Socially-Withdrawn Preschool Children Through Mixed-Age and Same-Age Socialization." *Child Development,* 1979, *50,* 915–922.

Gendlin, Eugene. *Focusing.* New York: Bantam, 1981.

Gilford, Rosalie, and Bengtson, Vern. "Measuring Marital Satisfaction in Three Generations: Positive and Negative Dimensions." *Journal of Marriage and the Family,* 1979, *41,* 387–398.

Glick, Paul, and Norton, Arthur. "Marrying, Divorcing, and Living Together in the U.S. Today," *Population Bulletin,* Vol. 32, No. 5. Washington, D.C.: Population Reference Bureau, 1979.

Goleman, Daniel. "Leaving Home: Is There a Right Time to Go?" *Psychology Today,* August 1980.

Gove, W. "Sex, Marital Status, and Mortality." *American Journal of Sociology,* 1973, *79,* 45–67.

Gove, W. "Sex, Marital Status, and Suicide." *Journal of Health and Social Behavior,* 1972, *13,* 204–213.

Gubrium, Jaber. "Being Single in Old Age." *International Journal of Aging and Human Development,* 1975, *6,* 29–41.

Gunther, John. *Inside U.S.A.* New York: Harper & Brothers, 1947.

Gurin, Gerald, Veroff, Joseph, and Feld, Sheila. *Americans View Their Mental Health.* New York: Basic Books, 1960.

Hansson, Robert, and Jones, Warren. "Loneliness, Cooperation, and Conformity Among American Undergraduates." Unpublished manuscript, University of Tulsa, 1981.

Hareven, Tamara. "American Families in Transition: Historical Perspectives On Change." Paper presented at the White House Conference on Families, April 9, 1980.

Harlow, Harry F., and Mears, Clara. *The Human Model: Primate Perspectives.* New York: Halsted Press, 1979.

Harris, Louis, and Associates. *The Myth and Reality of Aging in America.* Report prepared for the National Council on the Aging, Inc., 1975.

Harter, Susan. "Developmental Perspectives on the Self System." In Paul Mussen, ed. *Carmichael's Manual of Child Psychology.* New York: Wiley-Interscience, in press.

Havighurst, Robert, Neugarten, Bernice, and Tobin, Sheldon. "Disengagement and Patterns of Aging." In Bernice Neugarten, ed. *Middle Age and Aging.* Chicago: University of Chicago Press, 1968.

Hetherington, E. Mavis, Cox, Martha, and Cox, Roger. "The Aftermath of Divorce." In J. Stevens, Jr., and M. Mathews, eds. *Mother-Child, Father-Child Relations.* Washington, D.C.: National Association for the Education of Young Children, 1977.

Heyman, Dorothy, and Gianturco, Daniel. "Long-Term Adaptation by the Elderly to Bereavement." *Journal of Gerontology,* 1973, *28,* 359–362.

Hill, Charles, Rubin, Zick, and Peplau, L. Anne. "Breakups Before Marriage: The End of 103 Affairs." *Journal of Social Issues,* 1976, *32,* 147–168.

Holmes, Thomas, and Rahe, Richard. "The Social Readjustment Rating Scale." *Psychosomatic Research,* 1967, *11,* 213–218.

Horn, John. "On the Future of Growing Old." Unpublished manuscript, University of Denver, 1980.

Hunt, Morton, and Hunt, Bernice. *The Divorce Experience.* New York: McGraw-Hill, 1977.

Hunter, Albert. "The Loss of Community: An Empirical Test Through Replication." *American Sociological Review,* 1975, *40,* 537–552.

Ickes, William. "A Basic Paradigm for the Study of Personality Roles and Social Behavior." In W. Ickes and E. S. Knowles, eds. *Personality, Roles, and Social Behavior.* New York: Springer-Verlag, 1982.

James, Henry. "The Private Life." In Leon Edel, ed. *Stories of the Supernatural.* New York: Taplinger Publishing Co., 1970.

Jones, Warren. "The Social Behavior of Lonely People." in L. Anne Peplau and Daniel Perlman, eds. *Loneliness: A Sourcebook of Current Theory, Research, and Therapy.* New York: Wiley-Interscience, 1982.

Jones, Warren, Freeman, J. E., and Goswick, Ruth. "The Persistence of Loneliness: Self and Other Determinants." *Journal of Personality,* 1981, *49,* 27–48.

Jones, Warren, Hobbs, Steven, and Hockenbury, Don. "Loneliness and Social Skill Deficits." Unpublished manuscript, University of Tulsa, 1980.

Jung, Carl. *The Portable Jung.* Joseph Campbell, ed. New York: Viking Press, 1971.

Kahle, Lynn, Kulka, Richard, and Klingel, David. "Low Adolescent Self-

Esteem Leads to Multiple Interpersonal Problems: A Test of Social Adaptation Theory.'' *Journal of Personality and Social Psychology,* 1980, *39,* 496–502.

Kanter, Rosabeth Moss. *Commitment and Community.* Cambridge, Massachusetts: Harvard University Press, 1972.

Kantner, John, and Zelnick, Melvin. ''Sexual Activity, Contraceptive Use, and Pregnancy Among Metropolitan-Area Teenagers: 1971–1979.'' *Family Planning Perspectives,* September/October 1980.

Kaplan, Louise. *Oneness and Separateness.* New York: Simon and Schuster, 1978.

Kitson, Gay, Lopata, Helen, Holmes, William, and Meyering, Suzanne. ''Divorcees and Widows: Similarities and Differences.'' *American Journal of Orthopsychiatry,* 1980, *50,* 291–301.

Kivett, Vira. ''Discriminators of Loneliness Among the Rural Elderly: Implications for Intervention.'' *The Gerontologist,* 1979, *19,* 108–115.

Larson, Reed, Csikszentmihalyi, Mihaly, and Graef, Ronald. ''Mood Variability and the Psychosocial Adjustment of Adolescents.'' *Journal of Youth and Adolescence,* 1980, *9,* 469–490.

Lear, Martha. ''Loneliness: More Common Than the Common Cold.'' *Redbook,* November 1980.

Levine, Edward, and Kozak, Conrad. ''Drug and Alcohol Use, Delinquency, and Vandalism Among Upper Middle Class Pre- and Post-Adolescents.'' *Journal of Youth and Adolescence,* 1979, *8,* 91–101.

Levine, Saul. ''Youth and Religious Cults: A Societal and Clinical Dilemma.'' In Sherman Feinstein and Peter Giovacchini, eds. *Adolescent Psychiatry: Vol. VI.* Chicago: University of Chicago Press, 1978.

Lifton, Robert Jay. *Death in Life: Survivors of Hiroshima.* New York: Random House, 1967.

Lingeman, Richard. *Small Town America.* New York: G. P. Putnam, 1980.

Longfellow, Cynthia. ''Divorce in Context: Its Impact on Children.'' In George Levinger and Oliver Moles, eds. *Divorce and Separation: Context, Causes, and Consequences.* New York: Basic Books, 1979.

Lopata, Helen. *Widowhood in An American City.* Cambridge, Massachusetts: Schenkman, 1973.

Lowenthal, Marjorie. ''Social Isolation and Mental Illness in Old Age.'' *American Sociological Review,* 1964, *29,* 54–70.

Lowenthal, Marjorie, and Haven, Clayton. ''Interaction and Adaptation: Intimacy as a Critical Variable.'' *American Sociological Review,* 1968, *33,* 20–30.

Lowenthal, Marjorie, and Robinson, Betsy. ''Social Networks and Isolation.'' In Robert Binstock and Ethel Shanas, eds. *Handbook of Aging and the Social Sciences*. New York: Van Nostrand Reinhold, 1976.

Lowenthal, Marjorie, Thurnher, M., and Chiriboga, David. *Four Stages of Life*. San Francisco: Jossey-Bass, 1976.

Lowenthal, Marjorie, and Weiss, Lawrence. ''Intimacy and Crises in Adulthood.'' *The Counseling Psychologist*, 1976, *6*, 10–15.

Lynch, James. *The Broken Heart: The Medical Consequences of Loneliness*. New York: Basic Books, 1977.

Maas, Henry, and Kuypers, Joseph. *From Thirty to Seventy*. San Francisco: Jossey-Bass, 1975.

Maccoby, Eleanor. *Social Development*. New York: Harcourt Brace Jovanovich, 1980.

Mahler, Margaret, Pine, Fred, and Bergman, Anni. *The Psychological Birth of the Human Infant*. New York: Basic Books, 1975.

Marris, Peter. *Loss and Change*. New York: Pantheon, 1974.

Marris, Peter. *Widows and Their Families*. London: Routledge and Kegan Paul Ltd., 1958.

Masters, William, and Johnson, Virginia. ''Human Sexual Response: The Aging Female and The Aging Male.'' In Bernice Neugarten, ed. *Middle Age and Aging*. Chicago: University of Chicago Press, 1960.

McAdams, Dan. ''Studies in Intimacy Motivation.'' In Abigail Stewart, ed. *Motivation and Society*. San Francisco: Jossey-Bass, 1982.

McAdams, Dan, and Powers, Joseph. ''Themes of Intimacy in Behavior and Thought.'' *Journal of Personality and Social Psychology*, 1981, *40*, 573–587.

McCready, Larry. ''A Phenomenological Study of Love.'' Unpublished doctoral dissertation, New York University, 1981.

Mellen, Sidney. *The Evolution of Love*. San Francisco: W. H. Freeman, 1981.

Merton, Thomas. *Contemplation in a World of Action*. Garden City, New York: Image Books, 1973.

Miller, Patricia, and Simon, William. ''The Development of Sexuality in Adolescence.'' In Joseph Adelson, ed. *Handbook of Adolescent Psychology*. New York: Wiley-Interscience, 1980.

Minar, David, and Greer, Scott, eds. *The Concept of Community*. Chicago: Aldine, 1969.

Montagu, Ashley. *The Natural Superiority of Women*. New York: Macmillan, 1974.

Morris, Desmond. *Intimate Behaviour*. New York: Random House, 1972.

Moustakas, Clark. *Loneliness*. New York: Prentice–Hall, 1961.

Moustakas, Clark. *Loneliness and Love.* New York: Prentice–Hall, 1972.

Myerhoff, Barbara. *Number Our Days.* New York: Simon and Schuster, 1980.

Neugarten, Bernice, Havighurst, Robert, and Tobin, Sheldon. "Personality and Patterns of Aging." In Bernice Neugarten, ed. *Middle Age and Aging.* Chicago: University of Chicago Press, 1968.

Newman, Oscar. *Community of Interest.* New York: Anchor Press, 1980.

Newson, John, and Newson, Elizabeth. *Four Years Old in an Urban Community.* Chicago: AVC, 1968.

Nietzsche, Friedrich. *The Portable Nietzsche.* Walter Kaufman, ed. New York: Viking, 1977.

Nisbet, Robert. *The Quest for Community.* New York: Oxford University Press, 1953.

Nouwen, Henri. *Clowning in Rome: Reflections on Solitude, Celibacy, Prayer, and Contemplation.* New York: Doubleday, 1979.

Nye, Ivan. "Child Adjustment in Broken and in Unhappy Unbroken Homes." *Marriage and Family Living,* 1957, *19,* 356–360.

Offer, Daniel. *The Psychological World of the Teenager.* New York: Basic Books, 1969.

Packard, Vance. *A Nation of Strangers.* New York: McKay, 1972.

Palmore, Erdman. "Advantages of Aging." *The Gerontologist,* 1979, *19,* 220–223.

Palmore, Erdman, and Luikart, Clark. "Health and Social Factors Related to Life Satisfaction." In Erdman Palmore, ed. *Normal Aging II.* Durham, North Carolina: Duke University Press, 1974.

Parkes, Colin Murray. *Bereavement: Studies of Grief in Adult Life.* New York: International Universities Press, 1972.

Parlee, Mary. "The Friendship Bond." *Psychology Today,* October 1979.

Pearlin, Leonard, and Johnson, Joyce. "Marital Status, Life Strains, and Depression." *American Sociological Review,* 1977, *42,* 704–715.

Peplau, L. Anne, and Caldwell, Mayta. "Loneliness: A Cognitive Analysis." *Essence,* 1978, *2,* 207–220.

Peplau, L. Anne, Goodchilds, Jacqueline, and Bikson, Tora. "Old and Alone." In L. Anne Peplau and Daniel Perlman, eds. *Loneliness: A Sourcebook of Current Theory, Research, and Therapy.* New York: Wiley-Interscience, 1982.

Peplau, L. Anne, and Perlman, Daniel, eds. *Loneliness: A Sourcebook of Current Theory, Research, and Therapy.* New York: Wiley-Interscience, 1982.

Peplau, L. Anne, and Perlman, Daniel. "Blueprint for a Social Psychological Theory of Loneliness.'' In M. Cook and G. Wilson, eds. *Love and Attraction*. Oxford, England: Pergamon, 1979.

Peplau, L. Anne, Russell, Dan, and Heim, M. ''The Experience of Loneliness.'' In Irene Frieze, Daniel Bar-Tal, and John Carroll, eds. *New Approaches to Social Problems: Applications of Attribution Theory*. San Francisco: Jossey-Bass, 1979.

Perlman, Daniel, Gerson, Ann, and Spinner, Barry. ''Loneliness Among Senior Citizens: An Empirical Report.'' Paper presented at the 87th annual convention of the American Psychological Association, New York City, September 1979.

Perlman, Daniel, and Peplau, L. Anne. ''Toward a Social Psychology of Loneliness.'' In Robin Gilmour and Steve Duck, eds. *Personal Relationships in Disorder*. London, England: Academic Press, 1981.

Perloff, Richard, Quarles, Rebecca, and Drutz, Marla. ''Loneliness, Depression, and the Uses of Television Among College Students.'' Unpublished manuscript, Cleveland State University.

Petersen, Anne, and Taylor, Brandon. ''The Biological Approach to Adolescence: Biological Change and Psychological Adaptation.'' In Joseph Adelson, ed. *Handbook of Adolescent Psychology*. New York: Wiley-Interscience, 1980.

Petrowsky, Marc. ''Marital Status, Sex, and the Social Networks of the Elderly.'' *Journal of Marriage and the Family*, 1976, *38*, 749–756.

Petzel, Sue, and Cline, David. ''Adolescent Suicide: Epidemiological and Biological Aspects.'' In Sherman Feinstein and Peter Giovacchini, eds. *Adolescent Psychiatry: Vol. VI*. Chicago: University of Chicago Press, 1978.

Pfeiffer, Eric, and Davis, Glenn. ''Determinants of Sexual Behavior in Middle and Old Age.'' In Erdman Palmore, ed. *Normal Aging II*. Durham, North Carolina: Duke University Press, 1974.

Pfeiffer, Eric, Verwoerdt, Adriaan, and Davis, Glenn. ''Sexual Behavior in Middle Life.'' In Erdman Palmore, ed. *Normal Aging II*. Durham, North Carolina: Duke University Press, 1974.

Piaget, Jean. *Construction of Reality in the Child*. New York: Basic Books, 1954.

Pope, Hallowell, and Mueller, Charles. ''The Intergenerational Transmission of Marital Instability: Comparisons by Race and Sex.'' *Journal of Social Issues*, 1976, *32*, 49–66.

Powers, Edward, and Bultena, Gordon. ''Sex Differences in Intimate Friendships of Old Age.'' *Journal of Marriage and the Family*, 1976, *38*, 739–749.

Proshansky, Harold, and Kaminoff, Robert. "Place Identity: The Physical Socialization of the Self." Unpublished manuscript, City University of New York, 1981.

Putallaz, Martha, and Gottman, John. "Social Skills and Group Acceptance." In Steven Asher and John Gottman, eds. *The Development of Friendship: Description and Intervention.* New York: Cambridge University Press, 1982.

Rees, W. Dewi. "The Bereaved and Their Hallucinations." In B. Schoenberg, B. Gerber, A. Wiener, A. Kutscher, D. Peretz, and A. Carr, eds. *Bereavement: Its Psychosocial Aspects.* New York: Columbia University Press, 1975.

Revenson, Tracey, and Rubenstein, Carin. "Debunking the Myth of Loneliness in Old Age." Paper presented at the annual meeting of the Gerontological Society, San Diego, California, November 1980.

Robin, Ellen, Markle, Gerald, and Robin, Stanley. "Toward a Theory of Age Differences: Cohorts, Master Cohorts, and Social Generations." Paper presented at the annual meeting of the Gerontological Society, Washington, D.C., November 1979.

Rose, Arnold. "A Current Theoretical Issue in Social Gerontology." In Bernice Neugarten, ed. *Middle Age and Aging.* Chicago: University of Chicago Press, 1968.

Rosenberg, Morris. *Society and the Adolescent Self-Image.* Princeton, New Jersey: Princeton University Press, 1965.

Rosow, Irving. "Housing and Local Ties of the Aged." In Bernice Neugarten, ed. *Middle Age and Aging.* Chicago: University of Chicago Press, 1968.

Rubenstein, Carin. "A Questionnaire Study of Adult Loneliness in Three U.S. Cities." Unpublished doctoral dissertation, New York University, 1979.

Rubenstein, Carin, and Shaver, Phillip. "Loneliness in Two Northeastern Cities." In Joseph Hartog, J. Ralph Audy, and Yehudi Cohen, eds. *The Anatomy of Loneliness.* New York: International Universities Press, 1980.

Rubenstein, Carin, and Shaver, Phillip. "The Experience of Loneliness." In L. Anne Peplau and Daniel Perlman, eds. *Loneliness: A Sourcebook of Current Theory, Research, and Therapy.* New York: Wiley-Interscience, 1982.

Rubenstein, Carin, Shaver, Phillip, and Peplau, L. Anne. "Loneliness." *Human Nature,* 1979, *2,* 59–65.

Rubin, Zick. *Children's Friendships*. Cambridge, Massachusetts: Harvard University Press, 1980.

Rubin, Zick. "Seeking a Cure for Loneliness." *Psychology Today*, October 1979.

Russell, Bertrand. *Marriage and Morals*. New York: Liveright, 1929.

Sarason, Seymour. *The Psychological Sense of Community*. San Francisco: Jossey-Bass, 1974.

Scarf, Maggie. *Unfinished Business: Pressure Points in the Lives of Women*. New York: Doubleday, 1980.

Schachter, Stanley. *The Psychology of Affiliation*. Stanford, California: Stanford University Press, 1959.

Schantz, David. "Children's Fights: The Relationship Between Winning, the Use of Aggression, and Whether One Is Invading or Defending." Presented at the biennial meeting of the Society for Research in Child Development, Boston, April 1981.

Shanas, Ethel. "The Family as Social Support System in Old Age." *The Gerontologist*, 1979, *19*, 169–174.

Shanas, Ethel. "Older People and Their Families: The New Pioneers." *Journal of Marriage and the Family*, 1980, *42*, 9–15.

Shanas, Ethel. "Social Myth as Hypothesis: The Case of the Family Relations of Old People." *The Gerontologist*, 1979, *19*, 3–10.

Shanas, Ethel, Townsend, Peter, Wedderburn, Dorothy, Friis, Henning, Milhøj, Paul, and Stehouwer, Jan. *Old People in Three Industrial Societies*. New York: Atherton Press, 1968.

Shaver, Phillip, and Rubenstein, Carin. "Childhood Attachment Experience and Adult Loneliness." In Ladd Wheeler, ed. *Review of Personality and Social Psychology: Vol. I*. Beverly Hills, California: Sage, 1980.

Shaver, Phillip, and Rubenstein, Carin. "Living Alone, Loneliness, and Health." Paper presented at the 87th Annual Convention of the American Psychological Association, New York, September 1979.

Sheehy, Gail. *Pathfinders*. New York: Morrow, 1981.

Siegel, Jacob. "Prospective Trends in the Size and Structure of the Elderly Population, Impact of Mortality Trends, and Some Implications." Washington, D.C.: U.S. Department of Commerce, Bureau of the Census, *Current Population Reports*, Series P–23, No. 78, 1979.

Simmons, Roberta, Blyth, Dale, Van Cleave, Edward, and Bush, Diane. "Entry Into Early Adolescence: The Impact of School Structure, Puberty, and Early Dating on Self-Esteem." *American Sociological Review*, 1979, *44*, 948–967.

Simmons, Roberta, Rosenberg, Florence, and Rosenberg, Morris. "Disturbance in the Self-Image at Adolescence." In Robert Grinder, ed. *Studies in Adolescence.* New York: Macmillan, 1975.

Solano, Celia. "Loneliness and Self-Disclosure." Presented to the 87th Annual Convention of the American Psychological Association, New York City, September 1979.

Spanier, Graham, and Anderson, Elaine. "The Impact of the Legal System on Adjustment to Marital Separation." *Journal of Marriage and the Family,* 1979, *41,* 605–613.

Spanier, Graham, and Casto, Robert. "Adjustment to Separation and Divorce: A Qualitative Analysis." In George Levinger and Oliver Moles, eds. *Divorce and Separation: Context, Causes, and Consequences.* New York: Basic Books, 1979.

Spence, Janet, and Helmreich, Robert. *Masculinity and Femininity.* Austin, Texas: University of Texas Press, 1978.

Stack, Carol. *All Our Kin: Strategies for Survival in a Black Community.* New York: Harper & Row, 1974.

Stack, Stephen. "The Effects of Marital Dissolution on Suicide." *Journal of Marriage and the Family,* 1980, *42,* 83–92.

Stokols, Daniel, and Shumaker, Ann. "People in Places: A Transactional View of Settings." In John Harvey, ed. *Cognition, Social Behavior, and the Environment.* Hillsdale, New Jersey: Lawrence Erlbaum, 1980.

Suedfeld, Peter. *Restricted Environmental Stimulation: Research and Clinical Application.* New York: Wiley-Interscience, 1980.

Suttles, Gerald. *The Social Construction of Communities.* Chicago: University of Chicago Press, 1972.

Tavris, Carol. "The Frozen World of the Familiar Stranger." *Psychology Today,* June 1974.

Thomas, Alexander, and Chess, Stella. *The Dynamics of Psychological Development.* New York: Brunner/Mazel, 1980.

Thomas, Dylan. *Collected Poems.* New York: New Directions, 1971.

Tillich, Paul. *The Courage To Be.* New Haven, Connecticut: Yale University Press, 1952.

Tocqueville, Alexis de. *Democracy in America.* New York: Washington Square Press, 1976.

Twain, Mark. *The Adventures of Huckleberry Finn.* New York: Signet, 1969.

U.S. Bureau of the Census, U.S. Department of Commerce. *Current Population Reports,* Series P–20, No. 331, "Geographical Mobility: March 1975 to March 1978." Washington, D.C.: U.S. Government Printing Office, 1978.

U.S. Bureau of the Census, U.S. Department of Commerce. *Current Population Reports,* Series P–20, No. 363, "Population Profile of the United States: 1980." Washington, D.C.: U.S. Government Printing Office, 1981.

U.S. Bureau of the Census, U.S. Department of Commerce. *Current Population Reports,* Series P–23, No. 85, "Social and Economic Characteristics of the Older Population: 1978." Washington, D.C.: U.S. Government Printing Office, 1981.

Vaillant, George. *Adaptation to Life.* Boston: Little, Brown & Co., 1977.

Vanfossen, Beth. "Sex Differences in the Mental Health Effects of Spouse Support and Equity." *Journal of Health and Social Behavior,* 1981, *22,* 130–143.

Van Gennep, Arnold. *The Rites of Passage.* Chicago: University of Chicago Press, 1960.

Varenne, Herve. *Americans Together.* New York: Teachers College Press, 1977.

Verbrugge, Lois. "Marital Status and Health." *Journal of Marriage and the Family,* 1979, *41,* 267–285.

Veroff, Joseph, Douvan, Elizabeth, and Kulka, Richard. *The Inner American: A Self-Portrait from 1957 to 1976.* New York: Basic Books, 1981.

Wallerstein, Judith, and Kelly, Joan. *Surviving the Break-Up: How Children Actually Cope with Divorce.* New York: Basic Books, 1980.

Warren, Donald. "Helping Networks: Key Social Bonds of Urbanites." Unpublished manuscript, Oakland University, 1979.

Weiner, Bernard. *Achievement Motivation and Attribution Theory.* Morristown, New Jersey: General Learning Press, 1974.

Weisberg, Paul. "Demographic, Attitudinal, and Practice Patterns of Adolescent Psychiatrists in the United States." In Sherman Feinstein and Peter Giovacchini, eds. *Adolescent Psychiatry: Vol. VI.* Chicago: University of Chicago Press, 1978.

Weiss, Robert, ed. *Loneliness: The Experience of Emotional and Social Isolation.* Cambridge: M.I.T. Press, 1973.

Weiss, Robert. "The Emotional Impact of Marital Separation." *Journal of Social Issues,* 1976, *32,* 135–145.

Weiss, Robert. *Going It Alone: The Family Life and Situation of Single Parents.* New York: Basic Books, 1979.

Weiss, Robert. *Marital Separation.* New York: Basic Books, 1975.

Weissman, Myrna, and Klerman, Gerald. "Sex Differences and the Epidemiology of Depression." *Archives of General Psychiatry,* 1977, *34,* 98–111.

Winn, Marie. *The Plug-In Drug*. New York: Viking Press, 1977.

Wong, Herbert. "Typologies of Intimacy." *Psychology of Women Quarterly,* 1981, *5,* 435–443.

Wood, Margaret. *Paths of Loneliness.* New York: Columbia University Press, 1953.

Woodward, Harriette, Gingles, Ruby, and Woodward, John. "Loneliness and the Elderly as Related to Housing." *The Gerontologist,* 1974, *14,* 349–351.

Wordsworth, William. "I Wandered Lonely as a Cloud." *Norton Anthology of Poetry.* New York: Norton, 1975.

Yamamoto, J., Okonogi, K., Iwasaki, T., and Yoshimura, S. "Mourning in Japan." *American Journal of Psychiatry,* 1969, *125,* 1660–1665.

Zablocki, Benjamin. *The Joyful Community.* Baltimore: Penguin, 1971.

Zajonc, Robert. "Attitudinal Effects of Mere Exposure." *Journal of Personality and Social Psychology Monograph Supplement,* 1968, *9,* 2–27.

Zajonc, Robert, and Markus, Hazel. "Birth Order and Intellectual Development." *Psychological Review,* 1975, *82,* 74–88.

INDEX